Rethinking Teacher Education

Edited by
David Hopkins and Ken Reid

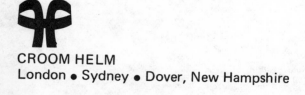

CROOM HELM
London • Sydney • Dover, New Hampshire

© 1985 David Hopkins and Ken Reid
Croom Helm Ltd, Provident House, Burrell Row,
Beckenham, Kent BR3 1AT
Croom Helm Australia Pty Ltd, First Floor,
139 King Street, Sydney, NSW 2001, Australia

British Library Cataloguing in Publication Data

Rethinking teacher education.
    1. Teachers, Training of—England 2. Teachers,
Training of—Canada
I. Hopkins, David II. Reid, Ken
370'.7'10942   LB1725.G7

ISBN 0-7099-3705-9

Croom Helm, 51 Washington Street, Dover,
New Hampshire 03820, USA

Library of Congress Cataloging in Publication Data
Main entry under title:

Rethinking teacher education.

    1. Teachers — Training of — Addresses, essays, lectures.
2. Teachers — Training of — England — Addresses, essays,
lectures, 3. Teachers — Training of — Wales — Addresses,
essays, lectures. 4. Teachers — Training of — Canada —
Addresses, essays, lectures. I. Hopkins, David.
II. Reid, Ken.
LB1715.R44 1985 370'.7'1 84-28555
ISBN 0-7099-3705-9

Printed and bound in Great Britain
by Billing & Sons Limited, Worcester.

CONTENTS

Acknowledgements

Translating an idea into a book is an enterprise fraught with difficulty. On this particular occasion our task has been made much easier by the collaboration and help of our colleagues.

Our contributors responded to the idea of the book with enthusiasm, encouraged us to pursue it and more importantly, sent us their chapters on time. We would never have completed the book without the help of our secretarial and editorial team of Janet Davies, Beverly Morris and Community Psychology (West Glamorgan) and, also, the help of Tony Brindley, Manager of the Computer Unit at West Glamorgan Institute of Higher Education, Swansea for enabling use of word-processing facilities. Peter Sowden was a patient editor at Croom Helm. Our profound thanks to them all.

Although the editors participated in much of the research quoted in this book, they do not accept responsibility for the conclusions drawn by other contributors.

Finally, we are grateful to Charles Belanger of the Canadian Journal of Higher Education, John Pratt of the Higher Education Review and Marian Lagrange of Harper and Row for allowing us to reprint material.

David Hopkins
Ken Reid
Swansea

Chapter One

INTRODUCTION - RETHINKING TEACHER EDUCATION

David Hopkins and Ken Reid

The last decade or so may have seen the best and worst of
times for teacher education. On both sides of the Atlantic
teacher training institutions have undergone radical
transformation (and for many transformation has meant
extinction), procedures for the training and certification of
prospective teachers have changed dramatically, and the
quality of teachers and teaching has become a matter of public
debate. The best of times was the rapid expansion in the
1960s, and the optimism with which innovative change was
initiated in the early 1970s. The worst of times has been the
hiatus and dislocation created by the recession, a downward
turn in demographic projections, and the general contraction
in the educational system that is occurring while these
changes are being worked through. Consequently, aspirations
have not been fulfilled, plans that were predicated on a small
but continuing growth in budgets have been shelved, and
blueprints have been adjusted to fit futures very different
from those for which they were intended. Although we cannot be
sure that the worst times are over, it is certain that the
best of times are gone for good. The heady and sanguine days
of the late 1960s and early 1970s were a flourish based on an
ephemeral economic and social resurgence that foundered
emphatically in the face of the oil crisis and a general
return by Western countries to a conservative political and
social ethic. The future, although uncertain, will inevitably
be constrained by fiscal restraints and a cautious approach to
problem solving.
    What has happened to teacher education during this
period, and in particular the changes that have occurred, has
taken place within the context of increased public awareness
and concern about the quality of education. In England and
Wales, for example, the closing of large numbers of teacher
training institutions, the 'Great Debate' on education, the
contraction of the teaching force, the arguments surrounding
the recent Government White Paper on 'Teaching Quality', and
the proposed increase of parental involvement in school

1

governance, have all been worked through within the public arena.

The popularisation of the education debate would perhaps be no bad thing if it were not for the fact that the debate is so often rhetorical, and based on prejudice and intuition rather than on understanding. That this is so is partly a function of the lack of a research tradition in education and partly the public nature of the debate – everyone nowadays is an expert on education!

In this regard teacher education is in a particularly disadvantaged position. As a relatively small and discrete educational sub-system, teacher education is far more vunerable to external influence than are the schools. This vunerability is compounded by internal features of teacher training institutions (TTIs) that predispose them towards organisational insecurity and thereby allow external forces to exert too great an influence. This concern with the organisational and programmatic nature of teacher education and with the way TTIs respond in periods of change and contraction provide the focus for this book.

Four themes are explored in some detail. First is an analysis of the contemporary context of teacher education, the various influences currently operating on it, and the likely ways these influences will affect its future. Second is the organisational nature of teacher education, its internal features, and ecological context. Third is an analysis of the programmatic nature of teacher education – the way in which it provides a training for student teachers. Fourth is a review of some of the major issues currently facing teacher education – in particular the teaching practice or practicum components of courses and the integration of theory and practice.

Taken together, the substance of these themes provides a fairly gloomy picture of teacher education. They suggest that teacher education is vunerable to the whims of politicians and bureaucrats and that departments of education within the academic community are generally regarded as second rate. TTIs do not respond well to change and are largely ineffective at managing it. Courses tend to be didactic in form and capricious in content. Teacher education lacks credibility as an academic discipline and lecturers, being in the main practitioner-oriented, do not have the intellectual stature of their university colleagues. Consequently, teacher education has failed to carve out a unique and distinctive role for itself.

Fortunately, the picture painted of teacher education is not all gloom and despair. There are indications of good practice and signposts for positive development. Two of the four themes previously identified (the context and organisational nature of teacher education) are not readily amenable to change. It is not too fanciful, however, to suggest that by concentrating on the two other themes (programmes and issues) progress will concurrently be made towards amending the other, more structural, problems. What is important is that these themes lie within the control of teacher educators. Consequently, the most crucial change that needs to be accomplished in teacher education lies within teacher educators themselves.

In chapter eleven, Fullan draws the distinction between surface and deep structure; most of the contributors identify this as the most critical area for change. We contend that if teacher educators adopt a deep structure perspective to teacher education, then many of the problems and issues raised in this book would begin to be resolved. A deep structure approach to teacher education would result in programmes that are more school based, contain a systematic and rigorous teaching practice component, mesh with the probationary year, and thus be a precursor to induction and further professional development. Consequently, teacher education will become more credible, will establish itself as a coherent and discrete entity, and be able to more effectively integrate theory and practice. When this is achieved, teacher education will stand more chance of being taken seriously.

The book is divided into six sections. Section one discusses the origins and context of teacher education in England and Wales. In their chapter on the historical context, Bernbaum, Patrick, Jackson and Reid survey the forces of continuity and change in postgraduate teacher education in England and Wales over the past 100 years, and stress the evolutionary nature of its development. Reid's chapter on recent developments begins where the historical survey ends and provides a comprehensive review of the complex situation in which teacher education in England and Wales currently finds itself.

Section two is specifically concerned with initial postgraduate teacher education in England and Wales. Chapters four and five present and discuss data drawn from the Structure and Process of Initial Teacher Education (SPITE) research project. In chapter four Bernbaum, Patrick and Reid discuss the findings that relate to the teacher training courses. In chapter five Reid reviews some of the data on the probationary year.

Section three contains a Canadian perspective. In chapter six Wideen draws on data gathered from two recent research projects, one Canadian the other international, and uses this data to present an analysis of the organisational characteristics and internal features of faculties of education. The major theme of Wideen's chapter is that TTIs are relatively ineffective at managing change. In chapter seven Hopkins elaborates on this theme by making an ecological analysis of Canadian teacher education. From this he develops a grounded theory of change in teacher education characterised as 'drift'.

Section four focuses on perhaps the most important feature of teacher education - the school practice known as internship, teaching practice, or the extended practicum. In chapter eight Hopkins surveys much of the recent North American research literature on the extended practicum. He argues that the form of the teaching practice (i.e. the elements under the control of individual tutors, teachers and students) is critical to the effective preparation of student teachers. This point is further emphasised in chapter nine where Rudduck and Sigsworth report on a small scale research study they undertook on 'partnership supervision' - a collaborative form of monitoring and supporting student teacher progress during teaching practice based on the clinical supervision model.

Section five is devoted to current issues in teacher education. In chapter ten Eggleston enters the debate between training courses that emphasise subject centered approaches and courses that emphasise school centered approaches. In chapter eleven Fullan focuses on another perennial problem - that of integrating theory and practice in teacher education programmes. In chapter twelve Thomas illustrates the difficulties involved in preparing teachers for a specialised area of teaching (in this case special needs) in the context of a nine month postgraduate certificate of education (PGCE) training course. These chapters are not attempts to solve these ongoing problems, but serve to illustrate three of the most characteristic and overiding issues facing teacher trainers as they prepare and deliver their programmes.

Section six focuses on the future of teacher education. In chapter thirteen Taylor sets a range of predictable and important issues in teacher education against projections for demographic and economic trends until the end of the century. From this analysis he suggests some possibilities and scenarios for teacher education in the next few decades.

The book is the result of a happy coincidence. By chance the editors took posts in the same institution soon after they had been involved in similar major research projects on teacher education in Canada (Hopkins) and England and Wales (Reid). These research projects (the Social Science and Humanities Research Council of Canada's project, 'The Management of Change in Teacher Education', and the SPITE project funded by the Department of Education and Science) were unique in so far as they were the first national research projects to gather information on the practice of teacher education. It was this background of experience, a continuing interest in teacher education, and the ease of collaboration that encouraged us to work on the book.

Our collaboration has had three important implications for the style of the book. First, because much of the book reports on research and is an attempt to inform a debate, most of the chapters are empirical in the sense that they reflect data gathered during a research process, or are reviews of research. They are grounded in the actuality of teacher education (albeit distanced by the research process) rather than being speculative or argumentative. Their utility therefore lies in the fact that collectively they represent as accurate a picture of teacher education in the early/mid 1980s as is posssible at the present time. Second, because much of the research reported in these pages is recent, most of it has not been published (except in reports and conferences) elsewhere. Third, we and the contributors have attempted to provide as broad a perspective on teacher education and scholarship as our combined experience will allow.

Despite the national rather than international or local perspective of individual chapters, an implicit assumption of the book is that teacher education in most Western countries is broadly similar and facing predictable and common problems. Similarly, although a majority of the chapters take as their main context PGCE courses in England and Wales, there are a number of chapters that adopt a Canadian or international perspective and consequently broaden the analysis. Because of this we would suggest (albeit a little tentatively) that the conclusions drawn and generalisations made are applicable across national boundaries to teacher education in general. It is the research orientation of the contributions, their originality, and the broad scope of the book in general that gives it its distinct flavour.

It is against this background that we use the term Rethinking in the title of the book. The book is an attempt to inform the current debate on teacher education in the hope that this debate will become more informed and disciplined. The book is not an attempt at re-conceptualising teacher education. The knowledge base is too fractured and insecure for that at present, and any consensus would likely prove to be a chimera. Instead, the book presents a series of analyses and perceptions based on long work in the field from many who have devoted their careers to understanding teacher education. Such efforts, we believe, are a precondition to rethinking teacher education.

SECTION ONE - BACKGROUND

Chapter Two

A HISTORY OF POSTGRADUATE INITIAL TEACHER EDUCATION IN ENGLAND AND WALES, 1880-1980

Gerald Bernbaum, Helen Patrick, Sheila Jackson and Ken Reid

Initial postgraduate teacher education in England and Wales is currently the subject of much speculation and apparent innovation and change. This was also the case in the 1880s, where the origins of the present system of training graduate teachers are to be found.

Throughout the middle years of the 19th century there had been a gradual and uncertain extension of elementary education and equally faltering attempts to provide the teachers necessary for those schools. It remained the case, nevertheless, that teaching in elementary schools was a low paid, low status activity carried out mostly by teachers who had themselves originated in the working class and who now devoted their expertise to teaching that class. Such teachers, if trained at all, were products of teacher training colleges which were dominated by the churches and whose students were not expected to attain either high status or intellectual achievement. Indeed, teacher training in the colleges was narrow, mechanical in its attitude to teaching and learning, and fostered an approach to learning which restricted intellectual development and the desire for knowledge.

From the 1850s onwards there had been complaints about the lack of intellectual merit and liberal breadth in teacher training courses. The establishment of the Cross Commission in 1886 to consider the working of the 1870 Education Act provided an opportunity for consideration of the provision of the supply of teachers. As the work of the Commission proceeded and the need for change became more evident, the idea of involving the universities in teacher education gained ground. Such proposals were not, in fact, novel. As early as 1858 J.D. Morrell H.M.I. had suggested that Owens College in Manchester should offer courses of training for intending teachers in public elementary schools, and that students should read for London University external degrees as well as attending professional courses at the college. Nothing formal came of the proposal, nor of others in the 1870s from the National Union of Elementary Teachers and the Educational

Reform League that universities and university colleges should be given grants to train teachers.

Nevertheless, by the 1880s some universities had established tentative and informal associations with the world of teacher education and the schools. Owen College and the Yorkshire College, Leeds had, for example, started to provide courses for practising teachers in subjects like classics and mathematics. University College, Nottingham, had been even bolder and in 1885 had started evening classes on the science of teaching and school management. In addition, following the founding of the Teachers University Association under the presidency of S.A. Barnett, Oxford University had, from 1885, organised vacation courses for London elementary schoolteachers. Reporting on the success of this venture Sir William Markby of Balliol noted that:

> The schoolmasters expressed a strong sense of the benefit they had derived from their stay in Oxford. They showed a keen appreciation of the lectures given to them as something different in both kind and degree from the instruction they had previously received. They had also plainly conceived a warm attachment for the University, and had gained an entirely new insight into the services which the University is capable of rendering to the general education of the country (Tomlinson, 1968).

When the Cross Commission reported in 1888 there was, therefore, a context of university association, albeit tentative, upon which it could build if it chose to do so. In a cautious series of recommendations the Commissioners proposed an experimental scheme of day training colleges attached to universities or university colleges. Although the specific recommendations did not command the support of all members they did produce, in 1890, changes in the elementary school code which enabled the establishment of non-resident day training colleges with the condition that they must be 'attached to some university or college of university rank'.

The day training colleges which were established as a result of the changes in regulations provided universities with the first official encouragement to become engaged with teacher education. It was from this beginning that the present schools and university departments of education originated, and hence that the universities evolved, over a number of years, a training system for postgraduates.

Several universities responded to the opportunities offered by the new regulations. Within twelve years of the opening of the first day training college the number had grown to twenty, with provision for 1355 students, at a time when the more established residential colleges offered about 3500 places. There is little doubt that the establishment of the day training colleges gave teacher education a place in the

universities, and it has been suggested that their students
and grants 'saved the younger universities from remaining
glorified technical colleges' (Armytage, 1954).
It must be emphasised, however, that the new courses in
the universities were not, with one small exception,
postgraduate. Students enrolled for teacher training
programmes and some attempted to study for degrees in the
ordinary way alongside their teacher training work. Much of
the teacher training programme remained firmly under the
control of the central Department of Education in London.
Postgraduate teacher training barely existed even though
changes in the regulations in 1891 made some modest provision
for it. The numbers were small, for the very good reason that
teacher training for graduates to work in the secondary
schools was not considered necessary by those who were
actively involved in secondary schooling. Many of their
anxieties related to status and, particularly, to the
generally low regard in which they held teacher training in
the residential colleges. There were, furthermore, marked
differences in social origins between the elementary school
teachers and their counterparts in the secondary schools. The
involvement, however, of the universities in teacher
education, served to weaken secondary school teachers'
hostility to teacher education in the period up to 1914. Also,
the success of the arrangements made in the late 19th century
for the secondary training of women gave further support to
the arguments for a wider form of teacher training for
secondary teachers.
By the time of the Bryce Commission in 1895 there were
three separate training colleges and three secondary training
departments for women, supplying over 100 teachers each year.
The commission reported in favour of special professional
education for intending secondary teachers and commented that
'the case of professional preparation was urged with
impressive force by many witnesses who had paid considerable
attention to the subject' (Bryce Report, 1895).
Interest in the training of secondary teachers was given
further impetus by curriculum changes which were occurring in
secondary schools. Also, the 'registration' of teachers
(intended to bring the occupation into line with other major
19th century professions) had obvious relevance to the issue
of training, and was central to the idea of an autonomous and
self-regulating profession (Searby, 1982).
It was in this context that, in the summer of 1896, a
Training Committee was appointed by the Incorporated
Association of Headmasters to look into elementary training
and its relation to secondary education, to make a survey of
existing facilities for secondary training, and to study and
report on secondary training in other countries. The Committee
became a Joint Committee on the Training of Teachers and
included representatives from the Association of Headmasters,

the Association of Headmistresses, the College of Preceptors, the Teachers' Guild, the Assistant Masters' Association, the Assistant Mistresses' Association and the Preparatory School Association. Its first meeting was held in 1897. The Report which it issued is significant in that it closely foreshadowed the future pattern of secondary training. It recommended, for example, that candidates should not be admitted before 19 years of age and should possess a general education equal to that demanded by other professions. The student should first take a B.A. which was not to include the study of education, and then take a diploma course which should include the theoretical study of education, psychology, methods of teaching, hygiene, school organisation and administration and the history of education. The course of training should last for a minimum of one year and should be carried out at an institution (associated with a university) which would assume responsibility for both the theoretical and practical parts of the course. It was recommended that secondary training should not be undertaken at training colleges for elementary teachers, as the overall aims and attainments of the two groups were very different. The staff of the institution should be lecturers of university standing, preferably with experience of teaching in secondary school. Before obtaining a diploma the student should satisfy his lecturers, public examiners and the heads of the schools where teaching practice had been carried out of his overall competence, (Jones, 1924).

The definite and precise nature of these recommendations should not disguise the piecemeal and informal progress that had been made in the decade either side of the turn of the century. Once established, the day training departments began to make some kind of provision for secondary teachers. Professor Laurie, in his inaugural address at the Day Training College at Liverpool in 1890, had said that although the day training colleges were primarily concerned with the preparation of elementary teachers, before long their main role would be the supply of teachers for higher grade elementary schools and secondary schools. The signs were already there. In 1883 the University of London instituted a Diploma in Education which was open only to graduates. Others followed, and at Durham the Certificate for Teachers in Secondary Schools (like the Diploma in the Theory and Practice of Teaching) was instituted in 1895. In the same year Owens College, Manchester began to prepare students for the Teachers Diploma of the Federal University, while at Oxford an examination in the theory, history and practice of education, leading to an Education Diploma, was established in 1895.

It was, however, the Education Act of 1902 which acted as a significant stimulus for secondary teacher training. It did so by providing a framework in which secondary schooling could develop. It thus provided not only opportunities for the employment of secondary teachers, but also a supply of trained young men and women students suitable to be admitted to read for degrees.

The first Board of Education regulations for the training of teachers for secondary schools were issued in 1908. The Board stipulated that secondary training was to be strictly postgraduate and that applicants were required to hold either a degree or its equivalent. Courses were to be purely professional and include instruction in the theory and practice of education. 60 days contact with school work was required, of which not less than two thirds was to be spent in secondary schools. Colleges and university departments could delegate the practical training to an approved secondary school, but when they opted to undertake the work themselves, the principal and not less than half the staff had to have had reasonable experience on the teaching staff of a secondary school. By July 1914, 21 institutions were recognised by the Board for secondary training. Of these, 14 were eligible to receive grants - nine being departments of universities and university colleges.

It is important to note that, despite these moves, the number of secondary trained students, and of secondary trained teachers, remained very small. The number of students completing courses of secondary training rose from 174 in 1910 to 205 in 1914, while in 1913 out of a total of 5246 male teachers in grant aided secondary schools, only 180 had been trained for secondary school work and a further 970 had been trained for elementary teaching (Gosden, 1972).

In the light of much present day discussion of the nature of postgraduate certificate of education (PGCE) courses, it is interesting to consider Lance Jones' account of two pre First World War syllabuses for secondary training courses, the Cambridge Teachers Certificate and the Manchester University Diploma (Gosden, 1972).

The Cambridge Certificate was open to external candidates and consisted of two parts - one theoretical and one practical. The theoretical part involved four papers - two on the principles of education, one on the history of education and one on educational practice with reference to the teaching of special subjects. The study of the principles of education involved a consideration of educational aims and of the bearing of psychology on education. Also included was a study of the functions of the school, general principles of method and instruction and the hygiene of school life. In the history of education section all students were required to study a specific period (in 1922/23 this was the 19th century) with emphasis on the relation of educational development to general social and intellectual movements. Those who wished to obtain more than a pass had also to study the works of selected educational writers, such as John Locke and Thomas Arnold. The fourth paper on the teaching of special subjects included questions dealing with practically all the main subjects represented in the curriculum of the secondary school, but was arranged so that candidates might concentrate on their specialist subject if they wished to obtain an endorsement of their certificate as a specialist teacher. On the practical side, students required either a report from the college staff or a report from the head teacher of an approved secondary school where they had taught for a year. In addition, notes of lessons had to be submitted and, finally, a lesson given in the presence of an examiner.

The Diploma in Education at Manchester University was confined to internal candidates only and covered a wider field including, in addition to the Cambridge syllabus, a course of five lectures in the administration of education and a course in the psychology of adolescence and experimental psychology given by the university professor of psychology. Optional courses included social economics and social and economic history – both taught by university professors. At the end of the course, examination papers were set on the compulsory parts of the syllabus (principles of education, methods of teaching, educational psychology, the physical life of school children and school hygiene), but students were permitted, under certain conditions, to prepare an essay or essays in lieu of any one of these papers. As with the Cambridge students, teaching ability was assessed by reports on their work during the year, written records kept by the students and one or more lessons given before examiners.

While most of the secondary training departments followed courses of a similar broad pattern, then as now there was also a considerable degree of diversity. At Bristol, for example, there were no final examinations and the Diploma was granted on the strength of the written and practical work undertaken throughout the year. A similar arrangement existed at Oxford for practical work, but students were additionally required to prepare notes of lessons for submission to examiners. At Birmingham and Liverpool it was also possible to present theses. There were differences too in the relationships which existed between the elementary and secondary departments. Although all the day training colleges were originally established for the training of elementary teachers, at Cambridge (under the guidance of Oscar Browning) no formal distinction was ever made between elementary and secondary training. A similar situation prevailed at the London Day Training College. From its foundation in 1902 its purpose was twofold – the professional training of elementary teachers who were reading for a B.A. or B.Sc. at the University of London, and a postgraduate course leading to the London University Teachers Diploma. From the outset there was a minimum division between the two groups and they shared the same teaching staff and attended common lectures. At other universities, however, the pattern was different. The elementary and secondary departments were established at different times and were

organised as separate units, eventually joining together at
varying stages of their development. Sometimes the marriage
was a forced one. This was the case at Bristol, where the
vice-chancellor spent nearly ten years trying to persuade the
respective heads of the Women's College, the Men's College and
the Secondary Training Department that economies of time and
of staff could be achieved if they were to co-ordinate their
activities.

It must be emphasised that in the period before the First
World War the university departments were teaching mainly two
year certificate students, who were studying the theory and
practice of education alongside the specialised lectures they
attented in conventional academic subjects. Indeed, the
liberalising idea of mixing potential schoolteachers with the
normal undergraduate population had been one of the main
arguments for involving the universities in teacher education.

Nevertheless, the arrangements were not without their
problems and some of these early difficulties established a
pattern of institutional and status relationships which
university departments have found it difficult to unravel even
after 70 years.

One of the early problems was that the students entering
the university to prepare for teaching were less qualified
than the normal undergraduate. Hence, the regular university
lectures, part of a three year degree course, were frequently
unsuitable for the weaker students. As a result the education
students did not do well according to conventional university
criteria. Not surprisingly, the failure rate was high and the
number of students who managed to gain degrees was small. As
the first decade of the century progressed, and the scope and
nature of secondary education improved, so the quality of
entrants to teacher training courses also improved and, as a
result, the day training colleges could become somewhat more
selective in their admission policies. Consequently, the
colleges and departments tried to recruit either those who
were already graduates or those who clearly intended to read
for a degree. Some were more successful than others in
pursuing such policies. From as early as 1901 colleges in
Wales and the Victoria University in Manchester had decided to
admit only students of degree calibre. Nevertheless, it was
not until as late as the 1930s that the two year students
effectively disappeared from the universities.

Nor were the problems of initial teacher education in the
universities confined to the issue of low standards. Students
reading for degrees were at the same time required to cover
the professional syllabus laid down by the Board of Education,
which had now been extended to include hygiene and physical
education. Education students, therefore, had much heavier
loads than the normal undergraduates and were left no time for
recreation or for engagement with the wide social life of the
university. Failure rates remained high. Thus, in 1911, new

regulations were introduced which, under certain conditions, allowed training departments attached to university institutions to provide a four year course of training - the first three years to be devoted wholly to degree work and the fourth to professional training 'in preparation for the work of teaching in a public elementary school'. The new regulations were published as part of the normal teacher training regulations in 1913. From then on the four year course gradually replaced the three year one which was eventually discontinued in 1926.

Academic matters were not the only source of tension between the host universities and the new teacher training departments. The early students in the day training colleges were almost exclusively working class in origin, having previously been pupil teachers. In this respect, therefore, they differed from the great majority of ordinary undergraduates who came from the middle class and who had experienced secondary education. The education students were, as a result, closely supervised and strict residential conditions were imposed upon those who lived away from home lest they were corrupted by the liberal atmosphere of the university! The students lacked private means, the grants were low and, as a result, the quality of residential accommodation was a persistent problem and one to which academic staff were forced to devote much time. One, unsatisfactory, solution was for the students to continue to live at home and travel daily. Return journeys of more than 100 miles were not unknown. Even after 1904 when the Board of Education dropped its formal distinction between 'day' and 'residential' students, the situation was not resolved. Indeed, it probably facilitated the further separation of the education students as many departments established special hostels for them and thus reinforced their isolation from the rest of the university.

Overall, therefore, the early education students came from a lower social class than their fellow university students, they were academically inferior, those that studied for degrees had a burden of work far beyond that of the normal undergraduate and, in addition, they were frequently kept together in separate (often inadequate) accommodation. Little wonder that full acceptance by, and integration with, the wider university life did not occur. 'Even at Leeds', wrote one student mournfully of the early 1930s, 'the Department of Education was a bit outside the pale' (Heppenstall, 1956).

Nor was the relationship between the university departments of education and other elements in the university always as close and equitable as had been hoped. In many ways, departments of education were the 'Cinderellas' of the universities - frequently situated, in Boris Ford's graphic phrase, 'down the road'; with relatively impoverished facilities; with fewer resources than elsewhere in the university; and with students who were certainly less prestigious and probably less able (Bernbaum, 1976). There was, moreover, the additional problem of the practical and vocational nature of much of the work undertaken in departments of education. Such work, strongly controlled by the Board of Education, gave rise to further difficulties over the status accorded to staff and students of education in the scholarly, liberal regimes that characterised universities (at least at a rhetorical level!).

The war of 1914–18 disrupted the flow of recruits to the teaching profession. After the war there was, inevitably, a marked shortage of secondary school teachers and, by various devices, university departments were encouraged to increase the numbers in their secondary sections. One consequence of the changes that occurred in response to these expansionary initiatives was that the secondary and elementary sections in university departments were amalgamated to form one united department. The most significant post-war development, however, was the establishment (in 1922) of a committee of enquiry into teacher training under the chairmanship of Lord Burnham.

Various opinions existed as to the ways in which teacher education might be improved. The arguments of the early 1920s have a significant ring for the 1980s. The Permanent Secretary at the Board of Education (Selby-Brigge) was, for example, anxious 'to rely for the academic training of teachers much more on the schools and much less than on the colleges' (Niblett, 1975). Other interested parties, however, favoured extending the universities' role in teacher education. These groups were, nevertheless, divided. Some favoured placing more students for training in universities with the long-term aim of establishing an all graduate teaching profession; some aimed only at a more general association of the teacher training colleges with their local universities.

In the event, the Committee did not recommend that all teachers should hold degrees, nor was it very specific about closer links between universities and colleges, though it generally approved of such closer links. As far as universities were concerned the Committee acknowledged the part they played directly in training (by 1924 nearly a quarter of all teacher training students were in universities), and hoped that the numbers in universities might increase over time. In fact, in the period up to 1939 the universities continued to provide just under 25% of all new entrants to the teaching profession. The students were of two types. One group were four year students studying for a degree which included a professional year of training. Such students had to commit themselves to teaching in order to secure financial support. The second group were graduates voluntarily undertaking one year of training, though it remained the case that many graduates took up secondary school teaching without any training.

Once again, however, war provided an opportunity for educational change. The plans to reform schooling which developed from 1942, and which were enacted in the legislation of 1944, had clear consequences for teacher education, which was itself subjected to further enquiry by the Board of Education committee established in 1941 under the chairmanship of Sir Arnold McNair. Once again the relationship between the teacher training colleges and the universities was central to the debate that occurred.

The universities' initial impetus to become involved in teacher training had been pragmatic and they had gradually come to concentrate upon the more prestigious secondary school sector and to ignore the low status elementary schools. Moreover, even by the early 1940s the relationships between the wider universities and their education departments remained uncertain and tense. It was not surprising, therefore, that the vice-chancellors were wary of extending their relationship with teacher training colleges which would, seemingly, only bring to the universities poor students of low status and a range of inadequate facilities. They felt:

> that the disadvantage which the training colleges suffer from segregation cannot be cured by the universities ... Our reply to the specific question of Dr. McNair's Committee must be that the universities are not adequately staffed for closer relationships with the training colleges (McNair Report, 1956).

Though the present discussion is not centrally about the relationships between universities and teacher training colleges, reference to the debate does provide an insight into the ambivalence felt in universities about teacher training generally and, hence, helps an understanding of the problems facing the universities' own departments of education with respect to status and credibility.

The years after the Second World War did, in fact, bring about some closer association between the universities and the colleges. This came as a result of diverse discussions and negotiations following the publication of the McNair Report. Universities established Area Training Organisations during the early 1950s which embraced their local colleges and which gave the universities some general oversight of the work of colleges without involving them directly in it. As far as the university departments of education were concerned student numbers rose sharply in the immediate post-war period. In 1945/46 there were 898, but in 1946/47 the number had increased to just over 2000. By 1951/52 the figure was 3113 and it remained around 3000 until the expansion of the 1960s.

The most important post-war change was the demise of the four year 'pledged' student. The scheme had long been criticised for providing a form of indentured labour and was made anachronistic by the widespread availability of grants for university courses after 1945. Students could go more easily to university to study any subject and, after graduation, could choose to teach with, or without, receiving training. As a result the four year grant system or 'pledge' was abolished in 1951.

In these ways, therefore, the pattern of the modern postgraduate training of teachers was established - university based, but with relatively low status because of its association with schools and its narrow vocational base. Gradually the university departments of education struggled to overcome some of their disadvantages by concentrating upon training teachers for the secondary grammar schools which were more prestigious than the elementary schools. This enabled the departments to specialise in a relatively narrow range of academic school subjects which were readily recognisable in a university context. The situation changed, however, during the 1960s and early 1970s.

Several factors combined to produce certain changes with respect to the universities' engagement with the field of education. Firstly, there was a rapid expansion of teacher training both inside and outside the universities. The number of postgraduates training in universities rose to nearly 5000 in the late 1970s, with a similar number pursuing the postgraduate certificate in non-university institutions. Secondly, the schools were changing rapidly to provide a form of comprehensive education. As a result, the secondary grammar school tradition was forced to accommodate the elementary school tradition which had been maintained in the secondary modern schools since 1945. Thirdly, following the Robbins Report of 1963 and the development of newer forms of higher education, degrees became more readily available in a wide range of non-university institutions. These new degrees included the Bachelor of Education which was taught in non-university institutions but frequently validated by universities, and carried their name. In this way the universities were brought into closer association with that part of teacher education from which they had progressively withdrawn since the beginning of the century - a development which took place at the same time as their own students were seeking jobs in comprehensive schools and when the comfortable links between university teacher education and the secondary grammar schools were being broken.

As a result of these changes, the period from the mid 1960s to the mid 1970s was characterised by much change within university PGCE courses. There was a general expansion which enabled more staff and students to be recruited. Most of the staff, as before, were ex-schoolteachers - mainly from grammar schools. As a consequence, they were more likely to have the academic qualifications which would satisfy university appointment committees. The central specialised subject work of university departments of education was, therefore, maintained and students continued to be recruited on the basis of their degree subjects. New features were, though, added to the courses. In particular, there was a revision of what had previously been taught as the theory of education. This work now became more specialised and was broken into component parts which emphasised sociology, psychology, philosophy and history of education. At the same time, a variety of new courses were added to the PGCE in order to accommodate the fact that students, now aiming at comprehensive schools, would be likely to face a range of experiences not previously encountered by those who had been trained in universities. Thus, courses were mounted on topics such as mixed ability teaching, counselling and multi-cultural education. At the same time an effort was made to broaden the teaching practice experience of students. Overall, therefore, PGCE courses became 'overcrowded' and it became common for students to be presented with the opportunity to choose, from a range of options, the courses that they would pursue. For students, therefore, within and between departments, the experience of the PGCE varied greatly. A core of subject-related method work, however, remained common and, as before, the nature of that work and the student response to it was greatly affected by the personality, energy and professionalism of the individual method tutor.

It was against this background that the Department of Education and Science funded, in the late 1970s, an enquiry into the operation of the PGCE in the universities of England and Wales. A presentation and discussion of the results of that study forms the substance of chapters four and five. The material reported therein is largely derived from the study and full details are presented in the final report of the research team, The Structure and Process of Initial Teacher Education within Universities in England and Wales (Bernbaum, Patrick and Reid, 1982).

REFERENCES

Armytage, W.H.G. (1954) The Role of the Education Department in a Modern University, Inaugural Lecture, University of Sheffield.

Bernbaum, G. (1976) Education: the Desert Mind, Inaugural Lecture, University of Leicester.

Bernbaum, G., Patrick, H. and Reid, K. (1982) The Structure and Process of Initial Teacher Education in England and Wales, University of Leicester, School of Education.

Bryce Report (1895) Royal Commission on Secondary Education.

Gosden, P.H.J.H. (1972) The Evolution of a Profession, Oxford: Basil Blackwell.

Heppenstall, R. (1956) 'Redbrick University - Leeds 1929-34'

Chapter Three

RECENT RESEARCH AND DEVELOPMENTS IN TEACHER EDUCATION
IN ENGLAND AND WALES

Ken Reid

THE SITUATION IN MAY 1984

The teacher training system – reeling after a decade of
closures, amalgamations and change – is now facing an
unprecedented round of accreditation procedures for all its
courses. Recent events have moved quickly since the
publication of the Government White Paper Teaching Quality
(CMND 8836, 1983). This was followed by the Report of the
Advisory Council on the Supply and Education of Teachers
(ACSET, 1983) which endorsed such White Paper proposals as the
establishment of a council to accredit initial teacher
education courses, and issued a set of specific criteria by
which such courses should be judged.
      College, polytechnic and university departments of
education are currently digesting, evaluating and responding
to aspects of the new policies which were first confirmed in a
Department of Education and Science (DES) Circular Initial
Teacher Training: Approval of Courses in December 1983 and
largely reiterated in Circular 3/84 in April 1984. Like other
new 'quangos', the council will be appointed by the Secretary
of State and will report directly to him. Its power will be
vested in its right to comment on the professional status of
courses and make recommendations to the Secretary of State.
Scrutiny by the Teacher Accreditation Council will be
additional to the academic validation of courses carried out
by the Council for National Academic Awards (CNAA) and some
universities. One proposal is that courses will not be able to
seek accreditation or validation unless they are first
approved by local committees which include representatives of
teachers, trainers and employers – which may further
complicate an already complicated system. In some quarters
there is a very real fear that such committees will add an
unwarranted tier of bureaucracy and well-meaning interference
into a notoriously disparate system.
      Certain points clearly stand out from the events of 1983
and 1984. First, current policy on teacher training is,

according to taste, variously regarded as dangerous centralisation or bold innovation. Second, quality and accountability have become the watchwords of the 1980s in much the same way as quantity and expansion dominated the halycon era of the 1960s. Third, there is a widespread feeling amongst many teacher educators that instead of concentrating on initial teacher training – the products of which have improved in standard remarkably over the last few years – the Government would be better advised to spend money on more in-service training for the ageing majority of staff who were the products of the 1950s, 1960s and 1970s. By common consent, these people had a different and less than adequate training in the first place. Fourth, within a remarkably short space of time, the most far reaching and fundamental changes in initial teacher training since the War have been and are taking place without any real evidence of their short or long-term consequences. Certainly, popular feedback (O'Connor, 1984) suggests, for example, that the operation of the local committees may be just as capricious as those who run existing B.Ed. and postgraduate certificate of education (PGCE) courses. Fifth, the changes are happening during a period of constraint in higher education which means that many college and university departments – with their own experienced but increasingly ageing staff – will be unable to satisfactorily meet some of the new criteria (such as recent teaching experience) without contriving their own local solutions. Sixth, the resource implications of the proposed changes are, at the time of writing, a matter of particular concern for both sectors of higher education. Moreover, the administrative repercussions of the proposed course changes, including selection and school experience programmes, have too rarely been contemplated. In fact, local departments and authorities are being left to devise their own solutions to this complex matter. Seventh, no official research or monitoring scheme has been devised to evaluate the scale, scope and effects of the changes which are being contemplated and introduced, or the operation of the Teacher Accreditation Council. Seventh, while the aim of some of the proposed changes may be to centralise the system, in practice the outcome could lead to widespread local variations, at least over matters of detail. Furthermore, rather than helping local universities and colleges to 'pull together' for the sake of the system and common sense, the opposite may occur, especially if, as seems likely, survival and vested interests are brought into the debate. This is not a hollow issue. Given the substantial contraction of the 18 year old population which is forecast until the mid 1990s, it appears that the Government is embarked on a policy towards higher education which is determined by financial considerations rather than by need. When one institution receives a larger 'slice of the cake', another must get less. The present National Advisory Body

RECENT DEVELOPMENTS

(NAB) and Welsh Advisory Body (WAB) allocation of programme
areas to specific institutions is but one manifestation of the
consequences of Government policy impinging on all aspects of
higher education, including teacher education. The long-term
significance for teacher education, however, is especially
stark, as too many teachers are currently being trained for
existing population forecasts. Unless changes in course length
or direction are implemented soon, further 'cuts' are
inevitable - which in effect means that colleges, polytechnics
and universities will increasingly have difficult decisions to
make on their own and, often, at one another's expense. The
announcement (May 1984) of a preliminary list of twelve
colleges which are facing either closure or enforced
amalgamation is but further proof - as if any was needed - of
these trends, especially as size rather than quality appears
to have influenced the latest 'hit list'. The fact that the
choices were made ahead of the main accreditation exercise,
and against advice from at least certain sections of NAB, is
further worrying evidence of the influence of central control.

RESEARCH IN EDUCATION: POLICY CHANGES

These major alterations in teacher education have coincided
with new policies for the central funding of educational
research. The DES has recently changed its own rules for
funding research in education. The Department now normally
only awards grants to research projects which have the
capacity to inform policy rather than funding proposals which
have the sole potential of making contributions to specialised
fields of study. This means that a project must be likely to
help a policy decision to be made; or to help with the
implementation of a policy decision; or to help to evaluate
outcomes of policy; or to be likely to improve the quality of
education in an area of policy concern.
        This revision of former practice may well have certain
beneficial as well as detrimental effects upon research into
teacher education. First, proportionally more research into
teacher education may be centrally funded than has previously
been the case, despite overall cutbacks. Second, research may
become increasingly used as a vehicle and justification for
change. Third, the new policy will enable the DES to influence
and exert greater control on the kind of research activity
which takes place - especially when research funds are set
aside for specific purposes and 'bids' invited. Fourth, the
implementation of DES policy will ensure that the monitoring
of, and control exerted on, the research activity will be
greater than ever before. Consequently, quality and
accountability will become 'the name of the game' in research
into teacher education as well as in the everyday practice of
teacher training itself.

Only time will tell whether the long-term advantages of this change of policy towards educational research will outweigh the disadvantages. Clearly, however, there are a number of 'hidden' dangers when research outcomes are deemed to be of greater significance for policy than is the resultant knowledge. Illustratively, future historians may judge Hirst's Cambridge Study into school focused initial teacher education courses (Hirst, 1979) to have been more influential in changing the direction of existing PGCE and B.Ed. courses in line with current DES and his own thinking, than in contributing anything new to our knowledge of the process of initial teacher education.

The change of policy may also lead to some mistakes being made about the funding of research projects for reasons of expedience, lack of resources or political considerations. The original proposed extension of the SPITE Project, for example, was withdrawn and substituted by a grant towards an evaluation of the National Scholarship Scheme (Patrick and Bernbaum, 1983). Hence, a unique opportunity for using the longitudinal potential of the SPITE cohort was lost, when the career information which these data would have provided might have solved many unanswered questions regarding promotion, male and female and regional differences, and the scientific match between initial and in-service training (Reid, 1984a). The uncertainty of the funding system is one of the many reasons which contribute to the low standing, insecurity and nebulous outcomes of project staff and their research enterprises alike – but that is part of another story (Whitfield, 1981; Reid, 1983, 1984b).

Of course, research into teacher education is often funded by numerous other bodies apart from the DES and Welsh Office. The evidence to date, however, suggests that many of these agencies prefer to fund specialised fields rather than teacher education projects. Moreover, a great deal of local research into aspects of teacher training and education is never published, possibly because of the potential ramifications of the findings. Previously unpublished data from the SPITE enquiry, for example, showed that a considerable proportion of postgraduate students did not follow courses on certain topics (such as the training of pupils for public examinations; discipline and control in the classroom; and the special educational needs of children with handicaps) despite widespread acknowledgement that beginning teachers need this kind of information (Reid, Bernbaum and Patrick, 1981). There is little doubt that like data obtained from B.Ed. courses would reveal similar deficiencies. The fact remains that both PGCE and B.Ed. courses suffer from inherent structural weaknesses like shortages of time and constraints imposed by validating bodies. In Wales, for instance, following the James Report, the Diploma of Higher Education structure in the first two years of B.Ed. courses formerly proved a major obstacle to implementing change and introducing school focused approaches. The academic needs of students were then considered paramount - even at the expense of practical proficiency.

THE LACK OF RESEARCH INTO TEACHER EDUCATION

Without question, there is (and has been for many years) a dearth of research into teacher education. This is especially disappointing when it is considered that there are approximately 1200 staff in university departments of education alone who, to a greater or lesser extent, contribute to the training of teachers at a variety of levels. At least the lack of research activity in teacher education is partially explainable when a number of diffuse but far reaching factors are taken into sufficient account. First, teacher education per se is not widely regarded as a discipline in its own right (Reid, forthcoming). Second, most staff in colleges and university departments of education are appointed on the basis of their practical and pedagogical skills and research potential, rather than on their contributions to research. Appointments of people with a background of research in teacher education are rare. Staff appointments in departments of education are generally first made from people who are somewhat older than their contemporaries in arts, social science and science faculties, owing to the requirement of substantial proven teaching experience generally being applied as a pre-condition. Third, unlike the United States and Canada, it remains unusual for postgraduate students to follow research programmes in the field of teacher education - a situation which surely needs rectifying. Hence, following their appointments, most staff in university or college departments of education continue to specialise and generate research activity in those areas in which they are particularly interested such as psychology, sociology, reading and Piagetian theory. Indeed, it is noteworthy en passant that many influential figures and decision makers in the teacher education world have never themselves contributed anything to the discipline of teacher education. They continue to engage in research activity into specialised areas of their own volition, or operate as full-time administrators, often taking up their positions as a consequence of their contributions to other professional activities. This leads to an unusual, but not unique, problem in teacher education. Ironically, like the general public on matters of schooling, some figures in the teacher training world think they understand all the issues involved in teacher education 'politics' and supply and demand situations when, in reality, all they are doing is responding to local trends which have been apparent for years (Sharples and Wicksteed,

1981; Taylor, 1981; Wragg, 1981). Consequently, and by way of example, some teacher education courses are only now responding to the conditions laid out in the ACSET criteria. Not surprisingly, therefore, despite the proliferation of various pressure groups, the real decision making in teacher education (outside the DES and Welsh Office) lies with a few astute thinkers whose power and influence behind the scenes is so much greater than many realise - not least because they are very often the only people to fully comprehend the implications of all the issues involved in particular edicts or ploys. Undoubtedly, this is one of the reasons why initial teacher education within universities has expanded so rapidly in the last decade, especially as university departments of education have had the foresight and good sense to remain united whatever the issues, while at the same time allowing their non-university rivals to fight amongst themselves - a perennial problem.

An examination of recent reviews (Hoyle and Megarry, 1980; Cortis, 1981; Blackstone and Crispin, 1982; Alexander, Craft and Lynch, 1984; McNamara,1984) suggests that, traditionally, there are three particular areas that have provoked much of the debate and research in the field of teacher education. These are the place of theory in teacher education; the form and function of teaching practice; and the nature of pedagogical skill training (Reid, Patrick and Bernbaum, 1981). To these can now be added: the details of course structure, content, teaching methods, staff characteristics and student types (Taylor, 1969; Grainge, 1974; Lacey, 1977); and the recent research into the PGCE (Dow, 1980; Patrick, Bernbaum and Reid, 1982), pre-service B.Ed. courses (McNamara and Ross, 1982), in-service B.Ed. courses (Evans 1980) and teacher induction and probationary year programmes (Bolam, Baker and McMahon, 1979; Reid, 1984a; Patrick, Bernbaum and Reid, forthcoming). Despite this new work, none of these aspects has been fully explored and many critical areas of teacher education remain unexamined. Moreover, studies into teacher effectiveness are in their infancy, as is the debate on the potential contribution of research to quality in teacher education (McIntyre, 1980). The present lack of research activity in teacher education needs rectifying if research is seriously to be used to illuminate policy and if decisions are to be made on the basis of fact rather than informed speculation.

ISSUES AND PROBLEMS

While many of the ACSET proposals and the Government's response make good sense in this day and age, not everything in the document should be allowed to pass without comment. In fact, there is little hard evidence to support some of the

proposals. The following pages will consider, therefore, some
of the implications of impending changes upon selection
procedures; links between training institutions and schools;
subject studies; educational and professional studies; and
quality advice.

Selection Procedures

1. There is no research whatsoever which shows that appointing
experienced teachers onto the interviewing panels of
candidates for initial teacher training courses will
automatically lead to an improvement in the quality of intake.
In recent years, for example, at the PGCE level (where there
is a vast surplus demand for admission to courses) some
university departments of education found there was little
quality difference between interviewed and non-interviewed
candidates. Prior to the publication of the ACSET criteria,
therefore, some university departments had ceased to interview
PGCE candidates because they believed it was a waste of time
and energy. Presumably, these departments will now have to
reverse their decision.

2. There is little evidence which shows that appointing
experienced teachers onto interviewing panels of candidates
for initial teacher training courses will lead to greater
equality of intake between subjects on PGCE courses. Clear
evidence from SPITE (Bernbaum, Patrick and Reid, 1982)
indicates that arts and modern language postgraduate students
tend to be much better qualified than their social science and
science peers at the point of entry. Similarly, females tend
to be better qualified than males and students in England
better qualified than those in Wales. Surely these variations
are as much to do with supply, demand and teachers' pay as
inherent subject differences?

3. There is no evidence that appointing experienced teachers
onto interviewing panels of candidates for B.Ed. courses will
raise the quality of the course or the degree and usefulness
of the interaction which takes place between students, their
tutors and the schools. As many B.Ed. courses have been only
too pleased to fill their allocation of quota places in the
past, in many institutions quality control arguments have
tended to simmer beneath the surface. Given the recent upsurge
in demand, quality control measures are being re-applied.
Clearly, put in a position of strength and choice, colleges
will endeavour to select the best suited as well as the best
qualified candidates for teaching.

4. Finally, it is a fallacy to argue that the presence of
teachers on initial teacher training selection panels will
automatically lead to an improvement in the charismatic and

personality qualities of student teachers embarking on initial training courses. What personality characteristics are ACSET talking about? After all, personality is not a stable commodity (Fontana, 1977). In any event, how are teachers supposed to identify these qualities at the interviewing stage? By magic? Surely teacher educators who have developed considerable professional acumen over many years are in a better position to know what they are looking for than are some teachers? Anyone who has supervised students on teaching practice is aware that many teachers are inherently more sympathetic to students than are college and university staff. On a related matter, evidence from SPITE indicates that the procedures used by university and school staff to inform students of their progress on teaching practice are identical, as are the kinds of criticisms and feedback system used, (see chapters 4 and 5). If anything, school staff are more reluctant to criticise students than are lecturers. Similar traits are found in The New Teacher in School (HMI, 1982). What evidence exists, therefore, to justify the financial and time commitments to selection schemes which authorities will have to make in an era of restraint? Furthermore, how will any positive traits which emerge be measured?

Apart from these criticisms, the general requirements for entry to undergraduate courses mostly make sense. Nevertheless, in an era of high demand for postgraduate teacher training places, it might have made better sense to be tighter on the special entry requirements in paragraph 16 of Initial Teacher Training: Approval of Courses for B.Ed. courses. The statement that 'at least 75% of the students entering any one course should possess the normal qualifications for entry to a first degree course' is a considerable and, in an age of supposed quality, surprising loophole.

Links between training institutions and schools

The general move towards establishing closer links between schools and training institutions and involving more teachers in the training process is a welcome step in the right direction. Once again, however, there are snags:

1. Any increase in time in schools is likely, to a greater or lessor extent, to be at the expense of subject work and pedagogy. For B.Ed. students, the loss in time spent on education courses is likely to be outweighed by the benefits which accrue from additional school experience. The same cannot be said for PGCE courses. Even after PGCE courses have been extended to 36 weeks, the amount of time likely to be spent on theoretical courses is so short as to disadvantage potentially gifted teachers.

2. By contrast, most PGCE courses are already heavily school focused, if not school based – students on PGCE courses spent approximately 40% of their time in schools in 1979/80. This raises another definitional issue: how long do people need to spend in schools before a course is defined as being school focused and/or school based? In point of fact, a considerable number of PGCE students spent more time in schools on one year courses in 1979/80 than some of their three and four year B.Ed. counterparts. Consequently, many undergraduate courses will need to change their emphases in this direction far more than will some of their postgraduate equivalents.

3. Many PGCE courses have long established and close school department links through a variety of elaborate designated tutor schemes. Indeed, the requirement that 'experienced teachers from schools should assume joint responsibility with the training institutions for the planning and supervision of students' school experience and teaching practice, and should take a major role in the assessment of students' practical performance' is already being met in some parts of the country. Cambridge School of Education, for example, emphasises the assessment of their student teachers by staff in the teaching practice schools. Less is known about B.Ed. courses on this matter because no equivalent to SPITE took place in the public sector. It is not fully appreciated, therefore, that some existing B.Ed. courses currently incorporate a substantial number of school focused dimensions. At the West Glamorgan Institute of Higher Education, for example, some staff voluntarily spend one day a week in schools in addition to their normal teaching and departmental duties, as do some individuals in many other departments and schools of education.

4. Likewise, many B.Ed. and PGCE courses already include elements of schoolteacher and training staff collaborating on parts of the training programme. Leicester, Bristol and Cardiff schools and departments of education, for instance, have long established school experience schemes, in addition to teaching practice, for at least some of their students.

5. The proposals mean that PGCE students have only to experience school focused courses for the one year of their training. Conversely, B.Ed. courses need to provide for four years continuity in their teaching practice and school experience schemes. Developing these courses should give college and polytechnic staff a considerable challenge and provide rich opportunities for the development of B.Ed. courses which will provide student teachers with the best possible forms of subject, pedagogical and school experience. It may also provide the opportunity for B.Ed. courses to get rid of some of their strait-jackets. Many B.Ed. students, for

example, are 'overtaught' within their institutions — 18 or 21
hours a week of class contact time is not unusual compared
with, say, ten hours a week within university departments of
education on PGCE courses. Ironically, however, many B.Ed.
tutors readily admit that on existing time allocations it is
extremely difficult to 'cram' all the requisite subject matter
into four years. Moreover, many colleges are understandably
sensitive about the non-academic labels given to some of their
B.Ed. graduates and are further constrained by the limitations
imposed on them by validating bodies as well as staff
conditions of service. Historically, for example, tutors on
B.Ed. courses in colleges enjoy far less 'autonomy' than their
university equivalents and many have less time for research.

6. As previously mentioned, the extra time spent in schools on
PGCE courses is likely to be at the expense of subject and
pedagogical work. This is, to say the least, a worrying
situation. Clearly, postgraduate students require as much
subject and pedagogical preparation as anyone else — yet
existing PGCE courses are already far too short, especially on
some aspects and phases of training such as primary education.
If the Government is serious about quality in teacher
training, then the time will soon come when it acknowledges
that 36 week PGCE courses are far too short — irrespective of
the financial implications involved in lengthening courses. In
the meantime, some PGCE routes — such as primary education —
should initially be extended to two years (always assuming
PGCE courses are to be allowed a long-term stake in the
training of primary specialists). Ideally, all PGCE courses
should last for a minimum of two years and consist of a two or
(preferably) three year sandwich structure which would include
the probationary year. This would be not only the most logical
step but a scheme which would command widespread support from
all involved in teacher education. As a consequence, the
status of teaching as a profession would be enhanced in the
eyes of the general public — something which is long overdue.

7. A very high proportion of staff in colleges, polytechnics
and colleges do not have recent teaching experience. Some
institutions are particularly disadvantaged in this respect,
especially as new appointments can be so difficult to make. If
this requirement is enforced rigidly, then some departments
will soon be sending a lot of their staff out on secondments
or schemes for tutor/schoolteacher exchanges — with all the
administrative and training consequences implied by these
arrangements.

8. Another source of concern is that a number of so-called
primary 'specialists' are secondary trained and have no
substantial primary school teaching experience. Nevertheless,
most of these staff have important subject knowledge and have

developed their teacher training skills over a considerable period of time. How valid is their experience in the light of recent policy? It should be remembered that some of these staff find themselves in their present invidious positions because of former teacher training re-organisations.

9. The requirement that 'initial teacher training courses should be so planned as to allow for a substantial element of school experience and teaching practice which, taken together, should be not less than 15 weeks in a postgraduate course, a three year B.Ed. or concurrent undergraduate course, and not less than 20 weeks in a four year B.Ed. does not seem a massive step forward in making teacher training courses either more school focused or school based. A considerable number of institutions already comply with these regulations, while others require little change to also comply. Being cynical, one is tempted to ask what all the fuss is about in the move towards more varied and longer school experience programmes if these are the major time requirements. Is a B.Ed. which sends students out to school for, say, 20 weeks teaching practice over four years, backed up by a certain amount of other forms of school experience, really school focused? Surely philosophical commitments to the notion of school based training are as important as any structural changes which occur as a result of new regulations?

10. The statement that 'institutions should seek to identify students who are satisfactory academically but unsuited to teaching early in the course, to allow for the possibility of transfer to another course' is an interesting one. In reality, there are few alternatives to B.Ed. courses, and to PGCE's there are none. It could well be that the time has come to revive a version of the B.A. (Education) notion of the James (Para 6.13) era. Ways need to be found of enabling tutors to be more liberal about failing students·on teaching practice for poor practical performance. Decisions of this kind are made easier if tutors know they have a fall-back situation. Not surprisingly, some tutors on both B.Ed. and PGCE courses are reluctant to fail students who would then receive nothing after three or four years honest, if unsuccessful, endeavour. Once again, if the quality exercise is to be taken seriously, perhaps departments should be encouraged to accept a higher proportion of students than their quotas each year - say 10% - and then weed out those students whose performances are weak either academically and/or practically. Such policies should be conveyed to the students at the time of their selection interviews. Sir Keith Joseph and his successors might well find this the best quality safeguard of the lot. Certainly, it would mean that only highly motivated students would embark on courses and there would be little time for 'slacking'.

Subject studies

A number of issues and problems need to be resolved about the
directives on subject studies. Part of the philosophy behind
the new guidelines appears to be that subjects studied in
school and as components of a degree course should be directly
linked to subjects taught in schools. Sir Keith has, for
example, virtually banned graduates in sociology from taking
postgraduate teacher training courses, and is urging employers
to look carefully at 'A' level and degree subjects when making
appointments.

These edicts suggest five problems.

First, primary teachers are, and must be, generalists in
an age of small schools. Moreover, there is no necessary
connection between the academic study of 19th century english
literature and, say, the teaching of reading and writing to
young children. ACSET appear to have accepted this point to
some extent by modifying the proposals in Teaching Quality on
the content of primary training courses, but they have
continued to suggest that courses should equip primary
teachers to make 'a strong contribution to at least one part
of the curriculum', and that maths and language should 'devote
a substantial amount of their time to the study of teaching
language and mathematics and the understanding of their
significance across the curiculum' (the Bullock and Cockroft
Reports recommended about 100 taught hours on each). The
apparent contradictions in the statements on primary education
(which suggest that some eminent educationalists have not
enjoyed recent primary experience!) have led to an escalation
of the generalist/specialist debate about the nature of
primary training. Furthermore, the new criteria are
particularly difficult to meet through the PGCE route which
the Government has actually been strengthening as a
preparation for primary teachers. In fact, there is already
widespread concern about the content of some PGCE primary
courses, especially as primary method work sometimes appears
merely to have been tacked on to the framework of many
existing secondary orientated schemes. The notion that primary
specialists need a different kind of training altogether from
secondary students does not appear to have occurred to some
PGCE course planners.

Second, it is wholly indefensible to suggest that
undergraduates who study 'non-appropriate' degree subjects
(e.g. sociology, law, social anthropology) should be debarred
from training as teachers. What nonsense! What has suddenly
happened to the idea that a purpose of higher education is to
broaden the intellectual and experimental horizons of
undergraduate students. What has happened to the democratic
notion of free choice? Does the Government seriously believe
that all sixth form students are capable of rationally
deciding at 18 years of age whether they wish to take a degree
in geography rather than sociology or philosophy because it

will enable them to train as teachers? Such obvious limitations on student choice may lead to a number of unhappy students at polytechnics and universities. What will happen, for example, to students who change their mind about entering teaching during their second year of undergraduate study? Will they be allowed to change their degree courses if they so wish? Again, the SPITE Project clearly showed that many student teachers do not make their career decisions until they have reached the university stage and beyond. Similarly, as more females than males decide to enter teaching at a younger age, the sex imbalance in some subjects may well be increased by the new measures. Already, the shortage of men in certain fields (e.g. special education, modern languages) is a cause for concern.

Third, a subject based course even for secondary teachers may not necessarily fit easily with some of the changes taking place in the secondary curriculum - often with the encouragement of the Government. A challenging secondary curriculum which is more flexible, more practical, and capable of innovation in the interests of slow learners, underachievers and potential disrupters may not be strictly based on traditional subjects at all. Once again, this aim appears to be at odds with the decline in B.Ed. secondary courses in favour of the short PGCE route, and is yet another strong argument in favour of lengthening the PGCE to a minimum of two years.

Allied closely to these issues is the fact that the manpower planning exercise which is being done makes no allowance for such factors as improvement in pupil-teacher ratios; supply teachers being increasingly used to allow time for in-service training and the extra demands imposed by the ACSET proposals; the extra staff needed to integrate special needs children into ordinary schools; the protection of the secondary school curriculum in an era of falling rolls; and emerging studies such as microelectronics and computing across the curriculum.

Fourth, as the secondary B.Ed. route declines, and as few PGCE's currently offer specific training for work with less able, underachieving and difficult pupils, the implications for pupil care are not good.

Fifth, if a regulation was implemented (in keeping with the prevailing spirit) which stated that only qualified maths and english subject specialists could teach these subjects in secondary schools, then the teaching of these subjects in some parts of Britain would collapse overnight. Thus, if rules on mismatch were strictly applied, some subjects would immediately be placed in a shortage situation once again. What would happen to quality then? Finally, no apparent steps are planned to halt the sad decline of such subjects as religious education and certain foreign languages.

Educational and Professional studies

The major problem with the proposals on educational and professional studies is simply stated. There is insufficient time on PGCE courses to cover the breadth of topics referred to in Initial Teacher Training: Approval of Courses in enough detail to provide students with the adequate conceptual basis which they will need as teachers in schools. With increasing moves towards school based and school focused courses, the conflict between meeting practical and pedagogical demands is so obvious, and potentially so serious, as to make a mockery of the whole notion of quality. Postgraduate subject specialists need a basis in educational understanding as much as anyone else. As things now stand, there is enough tension between education and subject studies in three and four year B.Ed. courses, not to mention the shorter PGCE route, without adding to the problem.

Quality Advice

The Teacher Accreditation local and national panels may soon be making frequent demands for information. What will they be looking for? The CNAA have already identified seven areas upon which the quality of a department of education is to be judged, and these can be used as a rough guide.

1. Academic Staff - scholarly and professional activity; general subject and intellectual authority.
2. Research and consultancy - research and subject strength; research income and contribution to professional development through consultancy and short courses.
3. Courses - structure, content and coherence; the level of intellectual demands on students and its success in meeting its stated aims.
4. Students - quality of student intake and their academic performance as measured by examinations, course work and projects and as monitored by external examiners.
5. Resource provision - level of academic, technical and non-academic support staff; facilities for the course, including accommodation.
6. Evaluation - the ability of an institution to monitor and evaluate their courses and maintain academic standards.
7. Development - quality of course leadership and management; potential for future development.

To these can probably be added the relevance of school experience; the quality of teaching practice; the relationship between practical and pedagogical work; students' views of courses; recreational facilities; local authority and regional support and employment opportunities; the crucial opinions of HMI and the local accreditation committees; recent staff experience of teaching; the match between staff qualifications and the phase for which they are training students; and the link between initial and in-service courses and between initial and postgraduate degree courses.

Regretfully, there will be major problems in accurately evaluating courses and, in particular, making quality judgements between institutions. When looking at PGCE courses, the most significant SPITE finding was the disparity between and within PGCE courses on almost every aspect investigated. The simple truth is that every PGCE course, like every B.Ed., is efficient and deficient to a greater or lesser extent depending upon such unmeasurable factors as staff enthusiasm, interests and abilities. Hence, even measures like taking samples of students' views, have their limitations.

Given, therefore, the state of present knowledge, the lack of fool-proof evaluative machinery and the dearth of research into effectiveness, any attempt to devise accurate means of making objective assessments between courses should be a matter for serious concern to all those engaged in the teacher education process. After all, evaluation is no respector of reputation - deserved or otherwise.

In any event, if the length and focus of existing courses were changed to accommodate altering societal and teaching demands for better in-service and initial training, then all the remaining teacher education establishments will, for the foreseeable future, be needed to cope with the work. If the aim is to alter the present balance between the university and non-university sector or the total number of institutions involved in teacher education courses, then this is another matter entirely.

Despite these serious reservations, the general moves towards accountability and quality control make good sense. After all, a desire to improve courses to their maximum potential should be the common concern of all those involved in further and higher education - not only those involved in teacher education courses. Nevertheless, effective, fair, apposite and efficient ways of monitoring and evaluating courses need to be found if institutions are to avoid being the urchins of homologous and scagliolic exercises which result in hollow decision making aimed solely at avoiding unjustified membranous expansions and implementing policies aimed at restraint and cut-backs.

CONCLUSIONS AND PROSPECTIVE OUTLOOK

And so to the crux of the matter. The Government remains undecided about whether it really should strengthen the postgraduate route at the expense of the concurrent. In some

quarters there appears to be a profound belief that there is a
correlation between degree classification and teaching ability
- and that B.Ed. degrees are inferior. The implication is,
therefore, that people with upper seconds in history make
better teachers than those with B.Ed. upper seconds. There is,
however, virtually no evidence that the best qualified
teachers make the best classroom teachers, once again
highlighting the absence of controlled experiments in teacher
education. Certainly, there is a case for arguing that
postgraduates should undertake most sixth form teaching, but
there is no evidence to show that PGCE trained teachers are
better than B.Ed. trained teachers in primary schools or who
teach in the first three years of secondary education.
Paradoxically, therefore, it is equally feasible to argue that
postgraduate primary teachers are over qualified and less well
prepared for teaching than their B.Ed. peers - a point made
earlier in the chapter.

Much more thought needs to be given to the links between
initial teacher education, induction and in-service training.
In the twelve years since the James Report, and despite much
rhetoric and some enlightened initiatives and research, too
little progress has been made on improving the interface
between initial and subsequent training. Consequently, teacher
training and lifelong teacher education remain largely
unscientific processes. Although, for example, much 'lip-
service' is often paid to the notion of sandwich training
systems, no experimentation along these lines has ever taken
place. Surely it is not beyond the bounds of possibility that
a controlled experiment could be organised whereby matched
groups of postgraduate and undergraduate trainees follow an
innovative sandwich route and are then compared with matched
samples of traditionally trained student teachers,
probationers and serving teachers? Likewise, there is no
reason why more and similar experimentation on the length of
PGCE courses should not take place. After all, why should all
teachers require the same length and type of training
irrespective of subject, phase or ability? Could, for
instance, the present concern about the standard of
mathematics teaching in schools be related to the preparation
of mathematics teachers as much as to conditions in schools,
quality of mathematics entrants and subject related matters?

In the interest of teacher education and the future well-
being of the teaching profession, a great deal more research
activity is needed into the evaluation and monitoring of
impending accreditation processes. This will help allay the
present suspicion that present policies are ultimately to be
used to introduce regional teacher training based on financial
(cost-effective) and economic needs rather than human and
educational factors.

Undoubtedly, in the next ten years the role played by HMI
in the evaluation and monitoring of teacher education courses

will increase - which may see the doubling of their numbers. Explicitly, HMI may follow the progress of some B.Ed. and PGCE students from their acceptance to the completion of their courses. This means that HMI will require ready access to university as well as non-university departments of education.

Initial teacher education is entering a new, exacting but exciting era. Given a more enlightened attitude towards teacher training and the needs of the teaching profession, present policies of accountability and quality may not necessarily lead to further closures but to major structural changes taking place in existing B.Ed. and PGCE courses.

The evaluation and monitoring of initial teacher education courses could also lead to more in-service programmes; longer PGCE courses; better B.Ed. courses; improved links between industry, schools and teacher training institutions; a happier interface between the public and private sectors; and the growth and development of new and traditional subject areas. Where there is a will, there is a way.

REFERENCES

Alexander, R.J., Craft, M. and Lynch, J. (eds) (1984) Change in Teacher Education: Context and Provision since Robbins, London and New York: Holt, Rinehart and Winston.

ASCET (1983) Criteria and Mechanisms for the approval of initial teacher training courses: Advice to the Secretaries of State, London: Advisory Council on the Supply and Education of Teachers.

Bernbaum, G. Patrick, H. and Reid, K. (1982) The Structure and Process of Initial Teacher Education within Universities in England and Wales, Leicester: University of Leicester School of Education.

Blackstone, T. and Crispin, A. (1982) How Many Teachers?, Bedford Way Papers, London: University of London Institute of Education.

Bolam, R., Baker, K. and McMahon, A. (1979) The Teacher Induction Pilot Schemes National Evaluation Report, Bristol: School of Education.

CMND 8836 (1983) Teaching Quality, London: Her Majesty's Stationery Office.

Cortis, G. (ed) (1981) 'Teacher Education for the 1990's', Special Edition 13, Educational Review, 33 (2), 151-156.

DES Circular 3/84 (1984) Initial Teacher Training: Approval of Courses, London: Department of Education and Science.

Dow, G. (1980) Learning to Teach: Teaching to Learn, London: Routledge Kegan & Paul.

Evans, N. (1980) The In-Service B.Ed: Six Case Studies, Cambridge: Cambridge Institute of Education.

Fontana, D. (1977) Personality and Education, London: Open

Books.

Grainge, P. (ed) (1974) Guidelines, Chichester: ATCDE
Education Section.

Hirst, P. (1979) 'Professional Studies in initial teacher
education: some conceptual issues', in Alexander, R.J.
and Wormald, E. (eds) Professional Studies for Teaching,
Guildford: Society for Research into Higher Education.

HMI (1982) The New Teacher In School, London: Her
Majesty's Stationery Office.

Hoyle, E. and Megarry, J. (1980) 'Professional Development
of Teachers', World Yearbook of Education, London: Kogan
Page.

Lacey, C. (1977) The Socialisation of Teachers, London:
Methuen.

McIntyre, D. (1980) 'The contribution of research to quality
in teacher education', in Hoyle, E. and Megarry, J. (eds)
'Professional Development of Teachers', World Yearbook of
Education, London: Kogan Page.

McNamara, D.R. and Ross, A.M. (1982) The B.Ed. Degree and
its Future, Lancaster: University of Lancaster.

McNamara, D.R. (1984) 'Research in Teacher Education: The
Past Decade and Future Trends', in Alexander, R., Craft,
M. and Lynch, J. (eds) Change in Teacher Education:
Context and provision since Robbins, London and New York:
Holt Rinehart and Winston.

O'Connor, M. (1984) article published in Education Guardian.

Patrick, H. Bernbaum, G. and Reid, K. (1981) 'The Way we
were: the staff of University Departments of Education',
UCET Conference Paper (mimeo), London: Universities
Council for the Education of Teachers.

Patrick, H. and Bernbaum, G. (1983) The National
Scholarships for Priority Teachers Scheme, Leicester:
University of Leicester School of Education.

Patrick, H., Bernbaum, G. and Reid, K. (forthcoming) 'The
PGCE and the Probationary Year', British Journal of In-
Service Education.

Reid, K. (1983) 'Educational Research: The Way Forward –
Issues and Solutions', Journal of Further and Higher
Education, 7 (2), 67-79.

Reid, K. (1984a) 'The Probationary Year: Facts, Fallacies,
Research and the Practical Implications', CORE:
forthcoming.

Reid, K. (1984b) 'The Anatomy of a Research Project',
Durham and Newcastle Review, X (52), 137-141.

Reid, K. (forthcoming) 'Teacher Education is a Discipline',
Times Educational Supplement.

Reid, K., Bernbaum, G. and Patrick, H. (1981) 'On Course:
Students and the PGCE', UCET Conference Paper (mimeo),
London: Universities Council for the Education of
Teachers.

Reid, K., Patrick, H. and Bernbaum, G. (1981) 'Future

Research Issues in Teacher Education', Educational
Review, 33 (2), 143-150.
Sharples, D. and Wicksteed, D. (1981) 'Public Sector Teacher
Education in the 1990's: diagnosis, prognosis and
prescription', Educational Review, 33 (2), 115-122.
Taylor, W. (1969) Society and the Education of Teachers,
London: Faber.
Taylor, W. (1981) 'Professional Development or Personal
Development', in Hoyle, E. and Megarry, J. (eds)
'Professional Development of Teacher', World Yearbook of
Education, London: Kogan Page.
Whitfield, R. (1981) Survey of Educational Researchers in
Britain, Aston: University of Aston in Birmingham.
Wragg, E.C. (1981) 'Teacher Education in the Universities in
the 1990's', Educational Review, 33 (2), 105-114.

SECTION TWO – POSTGRADUATE TEACHER EDUCATION IN ENGLAND
         AND WALES

Chapter Four

POSTGRADUATE INITIAL TEACHER EDUCATION
IN ENGLAND AND WALES: PERSPECTIVES FROM THE SPITE PROJECT

Gerald Bernbaum, Helen Patrick and Ken Reid

The material reported in this chapter is largely derived from
a research study on initial teacher education, undertaken
between 1979 and 1982, commonly known as the SPITE Project
(The Structure and Process of Initial Teacher Education within
Universities in England and Wales, Bernbaum, Patrick and Reid,
1982).
      The study dealt with postgraduate certificate of
education (PGCE) students in universities who began their
course in 1979. In that year 4947 students entered PGCE
courses in universities in England and Wales. These students
were asked to complete one questionnaire at the beginning of
their course in October 1979 and a second towards the end of
their course in the summer of 1980. 4350 students (88%)
completed our first questionnaire and 3350 (68%) our second.
In addition, a sub-sample of students was selected for closer
study. They were chosen to provide more detail and
illustration than could be gained from the main sample. They
were in seven selected departments of education, chosen
deliberately to represent, though not in a strict sense, the
broad range of types of department. Within these seven
departments, the sub-sample students were studying seven
subjects: english, modern languages, history, biology,
physics, mathematics and physical education.
      The study showed clearly that old traditions die hard.
The staff of university departments of education expressed
anxieties of a kind clearly recognisable in the context of the
historical development of university teacher education. The
staff were anxious about their career prospects. Promotion
opportunities in education departments were fewer than
elsewhere in the universities, and the staff were very
sensitive to the fact that much of the practical activity with
which they were inevitably concerned apparently counted for
little in the general culture of the university. Moreover, the
changes of the last 20 years, which have resulted in more
specialist staff being appointed to departments to teach the
academic disciplines relating to education, have introduced a

further problem as these newer categories of staff frequently
define themselves as being closer to the university than to
the practical and pragmatic world of the schools. In many
departments there is now a tension between those who relate
their work primarily in scholarly terms, emphasising research,
publications and advanced teaching, and those who relate their
work closely to that of the schools and emphasise the value of
experience in inducting young graduates into the world of the
teaching profession.

There is a very real sense, therefore, in which many of
the contemporary university departments of education remain
locked into problems which have their origins in an earlier
period. Our research indicated, however, that there was one
important area where there was a dramatic change when the late
1970s were compared with the early years of teacher education
in the universities.

SOCIAL AND EDUCATIONAL BACKGROUNDS OF STUDENT-TEACHERS

Overall, the students undertaking the PGCE course in 1979–80
were well qualified. Though they had proportionately fewer
first class degrees than the total graduating population (3.7%
compared with 6.5%); they had also been awarded
proportionately fewer poor degrees. In general, both divisions
of the second class degree are over-represented in comparison
with the total recently graduating population. (Upper second
class degrees: PGCE students 31.3%, graduating population
28.4%. Lower second class degrees: PGCE students 45.9%,
graduating population 37.4%.) It was also interesting to note
that of the 4350 students who replied to our questionnaire on
entry to their courses, almost a quarter (23.7%) were aged
between 23–25 years, and, of this group, most had had some
kind of work experience. A further 18% were aged 26 or over,
and most of these had previously worked in industy, commerce
or some kind of public service occupation. The oft-criticised
pattern of 'school/university/teaching' is perhaps not quite
so common as is frequently suggested.

There were also interesting differences in the sex ratios
of the entrants to the PGCE courses. The majority (57%) of the
entrants to PGCE courses in universities in 1979 were female.
This represents a significant change over more than a decade.
At the time of the Robbins enquiry in the early 1960s only
about 40% of PGCE students were women, but by the mid 1970s
figures from the Graduate Teacher Training Registry showed
that about half of the students entering PGCE courses were
female and more recent evidence suggests a continuation of
that trend. Indeed, the planned expansion of primary level
PGCE courses in universities during the second half of the
1980s will tend to an increasing 'feminisation' of those
courses. Moreover, our evidence highlighted the disparity

between the sexes when analysed by subject. For example, whereas approaching 80% of modern language students were female, a majority of mathematicians and physics entrants continued to be male - which may tell us something about trends in secondary education.

Finally, in considering the social origins of PGCE students, it is worth examining their social class backgrounds as measured by their fathers' (or guardians') major lifetime occupation.

Table 1

SOCIAL CLASS OF STUDENTS

	Number	%
Professional I	719	17.4
Intermediate II	1918	46.4
Skilled Non Manual IIINM	450	10.9
Skilled Manual IIIM	757	18.3
Partly Skilled IV	220	5.3
Unskilled V	71	1.7
Total	4135	100.0

Missing cases - 215

Given that all the students already had experience of higher education and that nearly 90% had graduated in British universities, it is not surprising to find the over-representation of the children of middle class and professional families. More than 60% of our students had fathers in social class I and social class II, although less than a quarter of the total male population of the United Kingdom belongs to these groups. By far the greatest percentage of the students studied (46%) had parents who came from the intermediate professions, technical occupations, teaching and social work. It is also clear that, as in the graduate population as a whole, students originating in the working class were under-represented. On the other hand, the percentage of working class PGCE students seems roughly in line with the percentage of working class undergraduates in universities. What is clear, however, from Table 2, is the higher percentage of men than women originating in the working class. As with other studies, we show the predominance of females entering teaching originating in the middle classes.

Regardless, however, of their social origins and previous experiences, all PGCE students undertake the three main features of PGCE courses, teaching practice, method work and the study of education. In turn, we examine each of these aspects of the PGCE course in order to provide some insights

into the working of courses and the nature of the students'
experience of them.

Table 2

SOCIAL CLASS AND SEX OF STUDENTS

	Male %	Female %
Social Class		
I	15.9	18.3
II	43.8	48.5
IIINM	11.9	10.1
IIIM	19.2	17.7
IV	7.1	4.0
V	2.1	1.4
Total	100.0	100.0

N - male: 1775, female: 2355. Missing cases - 220

TEACHING PRACTICE

Central to the students' experience of teacher training is, of
course, teaching practice. Despite the centrality of teaching
practice to the students' experience, institutional
differences remain significant. Thus, Table 3 shows the ways
in which the 30 different departments organise the temporal
aspects of teaching practice. The differences and variations
are immediately apparent.

Table 3

TEACHING PRACTICE STRUCTURES
(based on initial linkmen interviews)

Structure	Number of Departments
- 1 long practice (10-12 weeks)	11
- 1 long and 1 short or vice versa (e.g. 1 x 10 + 1 x 2)	6
- 2 approximately equal (e.g. 1 x 5 + 1 x 7)	9
- 3 practices (e.g. 1 x 2 + 1 x 7 + 1 x 4)	2
- 3 days per week for 2 terms	1
- 3 structures within 1 department	1
Total	30

INITIAL POSTGRADUATE TEACHER EDUCATION

In addition to the formal periods of teaching practice, most
students also have other opportunities to visit schools or to
work in various capacities with teachers and children. But, as
we shall show, these arrangements similarly differ
significantly between departments.

It is clear from Table 3 that the structure of teaching
practice offers the possibility that students might undertake
teaching practice in more than one type of institution. We
know that these opportunities are frequently accepted.

Table 4 shows the details of the students' teaching
practice schools for those 3350 students who completed our
final questionnaire at the end of their course.

Table 4

TEACHING PRACTICE SCHOOLS

	Number
Primary	981
Middle (9–13, 11–14)	294
Comprehensive (11–18, 11–16, 14+)	2718
Grammar (Direct Grant or Maintained)	187
Independent	235
Sixth Form College	76
Secondary Modern	59
Further or Higher Education College	167
Other	63

N>3350. Responses >3350 because many students went to more
than one type of institution.

Note
632 (18.9%) students did not go to a comprehensive school. Of
these:
243 went to a primary school
138   "   " " middle school
 99   "   " " grammar school
132   "   " " independent school
 19   "   " " sixth form college
 28   "   " " secondary modern school
 83   "   " " further/higher education college
 23   "   elsewhere.

Responses >632 because many students went to more than one
type of institution.

Certain points should be made at once. The numbers
undertaking teaching practice in primary schools, middle
schools and colleges of further or higher education are larger
than the numbers of students formally registered for such
courses. The difference arises because some students who train

43

to teach in secondary schools undertake part of their teaching practice in primary schools, middle schools or colleges of further education. What is clear is that an extremely high percentage of PGCE students in universities (81.2%) undertake part of their teaching practice in comprehensive schools.

It is also clear from the data that relatively small percentages of the students experience teaching practice in grammar schools, independent schools or sixth form colleges. These already small percentages fall more dramatically if the criterion applied is that of exclusivity. Thus, only 70 students (2.1%) did teaching practice in nothing but a grammar school; only eight students (0.2%) did teaching practice in a sixth form college only; and 97 students (2.9%) did teaching practice exclusively in an independent school.

To a limited extent, students' teaching practice experience reflects their own educational backgrounds. Students who had been educated at independent schools were more likely to have undertaken at least part of their teaching practice in an independent school than were those who had been educated at another type of school. Similarly, those who had been educated in colleges of further education were more likely to have undertaken teaching practice in such a college than were other categories of student.

It is clear that students spend differing amounts of time on teaching practice. 17.7% of the students spend less than 50 days on teaching practice throughout the academic year. By contrast, 11% spend 70 or more days. Table 5 shows the number of days that the students spend on teaching practice. Although the mean was 57 days, the range and the broad differences are immediately apparent. There were differences by main method subject with respect to the days spent on teaching practice. A greater proportion of primary and middle students tended to spend longer on teaching practice than students whose main method work was in, say, social science or physical education (P.E.), where the higher percentages tended to have spent less than 60 days on teaching practice.

Table 5

DAYS SPENT ON TEACHING PRACTICE

	Number	%
Less than 50	588	17.7
50–59	1129	34.0
60–69	1240	37.3
70 and over	364	11.0
Total	3321	100.0

Missing cases – 29

When the data are recoded by type of institution it is clear that there are again interesting differences relating to the length of time that students spent on teaching practice. Those in the New universities and at Oxbridge seemed to do more teaching practice than, say, the students in the University of Wales. No doubt the heavy representation of the Sussex students partially explains the former point. The Oxbridge case is somewhat different, as the longer teaching practices at the ancient universities seemed largely determined by the fact that some students who did practice away from the universities were encouraged to spend the whole of the school term on practice, and the school term is invariably longer than the university term.

The number of days that students spend in schools is, however, only part of the teaching practice story. Students differed considerably in the access they were given to direct teaching experience while on practice. Table 6 gives the overall picture.

Table 6

PROPORTION OF WEEK SPENT TEACHING ON TEACHING PRACTICE

Proportion of week	First institution N	%	Second institution N	%	Third institution N	%
25% or less	437	13.3	153	8.6	58	20.4
25% – 50%	486	14.8	222	12.5	34	11.9
About 50%	998	30.4	477	26.8	48	16.8
50.% – 75%	987	30.0	664	37.3	78	27.4
Over 75%	379	11.5	265	14.9	67	23.5
Missing	63		1569		3065	
Total	3350	100.0	3350	100.0	3350	100.0

Considering the first teaching practice, over 28% of the students spent less than 50% of their week teaching classes, with just over 60% spending between 50% and 75% of the week teaching. By the time of the second teaching practice, these figures had changed somewhat and just 21% of the students were spending less than half of the week teaching and over 64% were teaching for between 50% and 75% of the week. It should be noted, however, that over 40% of the students never experienced a second teaching practice. Only 40 students (1.2%) taught for only 25% of the time or less on all of their practices, and a quarter of these were in one department which had a relatively high proportion of P.E. students. When these data were examined by main method group, it emerged that students in further education colleges did the least teaching, while the P.E. students and the primary and middle students tended to do the most teaching. Obviously this has something to do with school and classroom organisation which enables select groups to be allocated to students. There were no important differences between the major secondary areas such as science, languages or arts.

Over recent years many universities and colleges have made arrangements with teachers to undertake special responsibilities for students on teaching practice. Sometimes these arrangements are of a very formal kind, with specifically named 'teacher tutors' being employed who are sometimes paid an honorarium. On other occasions the arrangements take a looser form, with perhaps a specially designated teacher having oversight of a group of students. Almost 85% of the students were allocated to a teacher tutor or to a specially designated teacher on at least one of their practices. It is important to realise, however, that there were variations within university departments of education with respect to the employment of teacher tutors. In all 30 institutions some students were exposed to the arrangements that we have described, but it does not follow that all students would be. Thus, in five of the departments we studied, fewer than 70% of the students had a teacher tutor or specially designated teacher, whereas in two other departments over 99% of the students were attached to a teacher tutor. There were, however, no differences in the use of teacher tutors by university staff in the different method areas. Variations appear to be entirely departmental or individually idiosyncratic.

Supervision of Teaching Practice

We also attempted to gather information about the more qualitative aspects of teaching practice supervision.

Table 7

PROCEDURES USED BY MAIN METHOD STAFF TO INFORM STUDENTS
OF THEIR PROGRESS ON TEACHING PRACTICE

	Number
− None	136
− Discussion/tutorial immediately after observation	2747
− Written comments (all types)	2030
− Collective discussions	441
− Weekly discussions/tutorials	614
− All others	88

N=3350. Responses >3350 because students could tick more than one procedure.

We were particularly interested in the mechanisms employed by university and school staff to convey information to students, and also in the nature and range of information that was transmitted. Table 7 shows the procedures used by method staff to inform students of their progress on teaching practice.

It should be noted that any one tutor might have employed more than one of these procedures. When no information seems to have been transmitted by the main method tutor, it was usually because the tutor had not visited the student. Nevertheless, about 2% of students claimed that they had been visited by their main method tutor but given no feedback. As can be seen from Table 7, the great majority of students were given information about their progress on teaching practice immediately after their lessons were observed and, in many cases, such reporting was followed up by written comments. Other methods used by tutors included collective discussions and weekly tutorials. The information that we have relating to the methods used by other university staff who visited students shows clearly that they tended to use the same kinds of procedures as the main method tutors.

None of what has been described above has so far given much intimation about the kind of problems that students faced on teaching practice and about the kind of criticisms that were made of them. We invited a sub-sample of the students to indicate the criticism most commonly made of them, only to find that relatively low percentages of students appear to have been criticised on any particular item. The students' view of the criticism most commonly made of them related to their main method tutors' view of their speech or voice. Yet even this criticism was noted by only 26.1% of the students.

No other criticism from any other source reached even this low figure. Quite simply, despite the evidence for extensive feedback and discussion as a result of student observation, the students did not seem to perceive much criticism. It is possible, of course, that the students chose not to admit to us that they had been criticised. We do not think that this is a major factor as in open-ended questions, interviews and diaries the students were frequently cruelly frank about their difficulties. We are forced to the conclusion, therefore, that either criticisms were not made or, more possibly, that they were made in such a way that the students did not perceive their true nature. Further, it is always possible that, by individual negotiation, students were able to prevent tutors witnessing their worst performances.

All of that said, it is possible to note that the university main method tutors were most frequently critical of students' speech or voice; of the ways in which students questioned pupils in class; of the students' classroom management; and of their use of the blackboard. Other frequent criticisms (and here it must be remembered that we are dealing with small numbers) were to do with lesson preparation;

teaching practice files/books; attempting to teach too much in too short a space of time; classroom discipline; and using materials unsuitable for the ability of the pupils.

The criticisms voiced by the teacher tutors or specially designated teachers were similar to those of the main method tutors. In order of frequency, the most numerous criticisms were made of the students' questioning of pupils; their speech or voice; their use of the blackboard; and their classroom discipline. Thus, classroom discipline appeared fourth on the teachers' list, whereas it was seventh on the university main method tutors' list.

STUDENT PROBLEMS ON TEACHING PRACTICE

As well as student perceptions of criticism, however, another way of looking at teaching practice is to invite students to reflect upon the problems which they believed they faced. We did this for the main sample of 3350 students. The students were given a list of eleven items which might have caused them problems on teaching practice and were invited to say whether these indeed had been a major problem, some problem or no problem.

In general, the students did not seem to perceive the existence of many major problems. Indeed, it was only the difficulties arising from teaching practice schools being a long way from the university which brought the percentage of complainants into double figures (13.8%). After that, the ordering of responses to the perception of major problems was: university tutors not having enough time to visit students (7.2%) and students finding it hard to communicate with school staff (6.9%). Only 5.6% admitted having major problems in their ability to control difficult classes. All of these details are set out in Table 8.

If we then turn to the rank order of percentages admitting some problems, there is a decisive change. Thus, 49.2% admitted to some problems with respect to their ability to control difficult classes, and 41.5% said that being given difficult classes presented some problems. These two items, with percentages of over 40%, are far ahead of the percentages confessing to some problems on any other item, none of which reaches 30%. It follows from what has already been said that the percentages claiming to have no problems were reasonably high. The item on which the smallest percentage of students admitted having no problems was with respect to controlling difficult classes (45.3%). This was followed by the 52.5% who said that they had no problems as a result of being given difficult classes. These data need to be seen in the light of our earlier discussion concerning the kinds of criticisms that were made of students and, most particularly, in relation to the criticisms on classroom control. It also needs to be

Table 8

STUDENT PERCEPTIONS OF PROBLEMS I

Problem	Ma... prob. %		
– Schoolteachers having insufficient time for supervising students	4.3		70.2
– Schoolteachers being unwilling to allow students to observe lessons	3.3	17.3	79.4
– Teaching practice schools being a long way from the university	13.8	29.4	56.8
– Students being given difficult classes	6.0	41.5	52.5
– University tutors not having enough time to visit students	7.2	27.2	65.7
– Students finding it hard to communicate with school staff	6.9	22.6	70.5
– Students finding it difficult to conform to norms and regulations of teaching practice schools	3.2	15.7	81.1
– Students not being welcomed in the staff room	3.1	13.4	83.4
– Students being unable to control difficult classes	5.6	49.2	45.3
– Students being given too many classes each week	2.2	11.3	86.5
– Students not being given enough teaching to do	1.4	12.4	86.2

remembered that these data are based on the students' self-perceptions of the problems which they faced in schools. As a result, it is inevitable that they will, up to a point, be representative not only of the problems that emerged, but also of their own expectations and of the general standards pertaining in the teaching practice schools.

ACTIVITIES ON TEACHING PRACTICE

We gathered from our main sample at the end of their PGCE year details of the kinds of work that they had undertaken while on teaching practice. Table 9 presents a list of eight such activities and shows the number and percentage of students who undertook each activity. From Table 9 it can be seen that over

ers of the students taught mixed ability classes,
60% gained experience of work with pupils being
pared for '0' level examinations and `CSE` examinations.
beyond those areas of work, however, less than half the
students undertook what might be thought to be important
activities. Thus, only a third experienced multi-racial
classes; just over 20% worked in special units with remedial
or disruptive children; and less than half taught pupils being
prepared for 'A' levels. Only just over a quarter of the
students had been asked to teach subjects for which they were
not properly equipped. As we have seen, however, this kind of
teaching produced many student problems.

When this material was analysed by sex, we found that a
greater proportion of females than males had gained some
experience of working in special units. Students who had
undertaken teaching practice in large schools (defined as over
1000 pupils) were found to have done more examination teaching
and were slightly more likely than other students to have
taught multi-racial classes. By contrast, those students who
taught in smaller schools were more likely to have had the
opportunity to work with small groups of pupils, and were more
likely to have taught subjects which did not match their
original academic qualifications. To some extent, these
findings are influenced by the predominance of primary schools
in the small school category.

Table 9

ACTIVITIES ON TEACHING PRACTICE

	Number	%
— Teaching mixed ability classes	2581	77.0
— Teaching pupils being prepared for '0' level examinations	2075	61.9
— Teaching pupils being prepared for 'A' level examinations	1535	45.8
— Teaching pupils being prepared for `CSE` examinations	2053	61.3
— Teaching small groups of pupils (less than ten, not sixth form)	1247	37.2
— Teaching multi-racial classes	1104	33.0
— Working in a special unit, e.g. for disruptive/remedial pupils	722	21.6
— Teaching subjects for which your degree, PGCE course or special interests have not equipped you	957	28.6

N=3350. Responses >3350 because students could tick more than
one item.

INITIAL POSTGRADUATE TEACHER EDUCATION

Students' experiences on teaching practice varied
according to the type of secondary school in which they had
been placed. Those who went to grammar schools, independent
schools and sixth form colleges were more likely than other
students to have experience of teaching 'O' and 'A' level
classes, but less likely to have taught in special units.
Students doing practice in comprehensive schools, by contrast,
were more likely to have taught `CSE` classes and worked in
special units.

Thus, we have tried to present a broad overview of the
kind of activities undertaken by PGCE students on teaching
practice, and of their perceptions of it. Such an overview,
however, cannot be considered in isolation. It must be seen in
the context of the method work undertaken by the students
during their PGCE course.

METHOD WORK

It is clear from our study that method work is a major part of
the student experience while on their PGCE courses - although
there has been little previous research on this important
matter. Overall, staff and students in our enquiry agreed that
students spent between six and ten hours each week in main
method work. There was, however, a very great difference in
time spent by the students following different method courses.
It was, for example, the P.E. students in our sub-sample who
spent the most time on method work, over 82% claiming to
attend such classes for more than eleven hours per week. On
the other hand, history students seemed to do less method work
than any other category. 50% of these students spent fewer
than six hours per week on method work, whereas not a single
physics or P.E. student spent less than six hours in method
work.

We have evidence from both diaries and interviews that
the students were sometimes uneasy about the differences that
existed within their own departments and about the different
demands that were made upon students pursuing different
courses. These differences were not always explicable in terms
of the nature of the subject, its procedures and
methodologies. Indeed, anxieties amongst students were
frequently sharpened by the appearance of formal equality and
uniformity in departmental timetables (where, for example, a
whole day might be set aside for method work and where,
nevertheless, the students found different tutors choosing to
utilise very different proportions of that day). Sometimes
students found that method work took up more time than the
timetable suggested, as the following extract from the diary
of a female modern language student indicates:

The demands made on our time by the method course are all so much greater than the original timetable would seem to have implied. We have all had to teach once or twice a week as well as preparing lessons to present to the method group and undertake written assignments. As we are expected to teach and prepare lessons in groups we have to arrange many extra working meetings amongst ourselves.

We were also interested in finding out as much detail as possible about the content of the method courses experienced by the students. It was recognised, of course, that different universities had different organisational structures, and that certain areas of work might in one department be included in a method course and in another be studied separately. The students were given a list of 30 topics, including such items as 'the law as it relates to teachers'; 'the use of the blackboard'; 'the preparation of pupils for "O" level examinations'; and were asked whether each of the 30 items was included in their main method course, was considered elsewhere during their PGCE year, or not included at all. The students were also invited to indicate whether they found the tuition that they had received useful on teaching practice. We have such information for the students completing the end of year questionnaire, though not all students answered each question and consequently there is some variation in the responses for the items. Table 10 presents the percentages of students claiming to have undertaken the various topics in main method, on some other part of the PGCE course, in both method and elsewhere, or not at all.

From Table 10 it is possible to see, firstly, those items that the students believed were not included at all. Thus, almost 65% of the students claimed not to have undertaken any work on team teaching, and around the same percentage had not done anything related to microteaching or interaction analysis. Despite the recommendations of the Warnock Committee, 60% claimed to have done nothing on the special educational needs of children with handicaps. Just over half had done nothing on the preparation of pupils for 'A' level examinations, and around a half had done nothing on the preparation of pupils for 'O' level and `CSE` examinations. Given the frequently made criticism that PGCE courses are too readily oriented towards work with pupils preparing for public examinations, the relatively high percentage of students who had not undertaken any such work is worthy of further comment. Obviously our figures include students pursuing primary courses, art, P.E. and the like, where public examinations may be thought to be less relevant. Nevertheless, it was clear from interviews with staff that many regarded work relating to public examinations as expendable in a busy PGCE programme. It was their feeling that good honours graduates were likely to need more help with topics like mixed ability teaching.

Table 10

LOCATION OF TOPICS WITHIN PGCE COURSES

Topic	Main method %	Elsewhere %	Main method and elsewhere %	Not included %
– The preparation of materials for teaching	65.2	9.5	15.9	9.3
– The use of school textbooks	52.9	7.8	7.6	31.7
– The use of prepared school materials	47.0	10.6	7.7	34.7
– Team teaching	23.1	10.6	1.8	64.5
– Voice projection and diction skills	18.4	20.6	3.5	57.4
– Project work in schools/colleges	39.4	11.1	5.3	44.3
– Teaching children of below average ability	31.3	26.7	14.3	27.7
– Syllabus planning	43.3	10.0	7.1	39.6
– Lesson planning	68.0	5.3	21.2	5.5
– Methods of assessment and evaluation	49.8	19.4	19.7	11.2
– Mixed ability teaching	43.1	19.4	21.0	16.4
– The preparation of pupils for 'A' level exams	43.5	2.7	1.9	51.9
– The preparation of pupils for 'O' level exams	44.7	3.4	3.9	48.1
– The preparation of pupils for 'CSE' exams	41.8	4.3	3.7	50.3
– The organisation of fieldwork for pupils	27.7	8.8	1.9	61.6
– The organisation of laboratory work for pupils	22.1	6.3	4.7	67.1

Table 10 (cont'd)

Topic	Main method %	Elsewhere %	Main method and elsewhere %	Not included %
- The skills involved in questioning pupils in class	49.3	15.7	15.2	19.8
- Varied methods of teaching your subject(s)	65.5	4.7	14.8	15.1
- The use of the blackboard	49.6	15.6	9.3	25.5
- The use of audio-visual aids	53.1	20.7	18.9	7.4
- Classroom management and organisation	38.1	24.0	24.0	13.8
- Control and discipline in the classroom	31.1	32.7	26.0	10.2
- Microteaching	28.2	6.5	2.1	63.3
- Interaction analysis	9.2	21.2	2.6	67.1
- The special educational needs of children with handicaps	4.0	35.0	1.1	59.9
- The government and management of schools	5.8	49.5	1.6	43.0
- Pastoral care and counselling in schools	5.5	62.6	3.1	28.8
- The law as it relates to teachers	6.7	48.4	2.6	42.3
- The use of language across the curriculum	16.0	51.1	12.5	20.3
- Moral education	6.4	43.4	2.9	47.3

In fact, during teaching practice substantial percentages of students gained no experience of teaching pupils being prepared for the various levels of public examination. With regard to voice projection and diction skills, almost 60% of the students appeared to have done nothing, despite the fact that it was on this item that they claimed to have received most criticism from their method tutors while on teaching practice.

Table 10 repays careful scrutiny. It is clear that items which students have covered in detail are those that relate strongly and directly to practical classroom work such as the preparation of materials for teaching, methods of assessment and evaluation, varied methods of teaching and the use of audio-visual aids. The students were, in addition, invited to indicate whether they had spent 'a lot of time' on a topic, or merely 'some time'. These results are not presented in tabular form but, in general, it is fair to say that where a high proportion of students seemed to have covered a topic, it was also one upon which individual students claimed to have spent a lot of time.

It is interesting to examine the material contained in the answers expressed in Table 10 by subject method group. In this way it is possible to consider differences that emerge between the experiences that students in different subject areas obtained. It is clear, for example, that the modern language students were more likely than all other groups to undertake the study of the use of school textbooks, a topic which was less frequently considered by primary and middle students or by social science students. It was also the middle school students and the social science students who were less likely to have undertaken tasks relating to the preparation of materials for teaching than were students in other groups. As might be expected from the last decade of development and dissemination of prepared school materials for science teaching, it was the science students more than any other category whose work included the use of such materials.

As has been noted above, the study of voice projection and diction skills was one of those activities which were frequently omitted from courses. Where it was undertaken, however, our data suggest that P.E. students were more likely to have pursued the subject. The same groups also paid more attention to syllabus planning, an area where primary work seemed relatively deficient. Where the primary and middle students did seem to gain more experience than other groups was in project work and (along with biology, geography, and history students) in the organisation of field work. Though the study of methods of assessment and evaluation was widely considered on PGCE courses, our evidence is that the primary and middle school students, along with the social science students, undertook less of it than did other groups. Indeed, a smaller proportion of the social science students than other groups spent time on mixed ability teaching; the skills involved in questioning pupils in class; classroom management; control and discipline in the classroom; moral education; and the law as it relates to teachers. Some of these are surprising omissions given that many social science graduates are likely, in schools, to be teaching integrated subjects such as humanities and social studies.

We pointed out earlier that many of the students had undertaken no work relating to the preparation of pupils for public examinations. What is clear from our analysis by subject, however, is that the modern language students were more likely than all other groups to have covered this work. They were similarly more likely to have undertaken a study of the skills involved in questioning pupils; the use of the blackboard; microteaching; and the use of audio-visual aids. As we have already noted, the study of the special educational needs of children with handicaps was not widely undertaken within PGCE courses but, overall, it was the primary students who gained more experience of this than did the others. Paradoxically, it was the same group of students who less frequently experienced work in pastoral care and counselling.

Some of the differences that have been noted in the above discussion are, of course, partly determined by different departmental practices. Where, for example, a department had a relatively high proportion of, say, primary students or modern language students, then what appeared characteristic of the experiences of primary or modern language students are more readily attributable to differences in departmental practices. It is therefore important that we go on to consider such departmental differences.

INSTITUTIONAL DIFFERENCES

There can on occasion be quite extreme individual differences between departments. Consider, for example, the item relating to mixed ability teaching. In one department in a large northern university, 36% of the students claimed never to have undertaken the study of mixed ability teaching compared with just 4% in another university. There were also differences by department with respect to the parts of the course in which various topics appeared. Thus, considering the same item (mixed ability teaching), in one Midlands university only 17% of the students had undertaken the study of the subject in method work alone, whereas at a Northern university almost 70% considered the topic in method work alone. The former university, however, provided the students with the opportunity to learn about mixed ability teaching in a specially constructed course, which brought the overall total pursuing that topic in the university to 96%.

The somewhat capricious nature of the PGCE course can be well illustrated by the study of the special educational needs of children with handicaps. As noted above, 60% of the students never pursued the topic, but in one Midlands university with special interests in the field, 90% of the students did study special educational needs. In this university, four fifths of the students undertook a special course on this subject.

We re-organised the data relating to the 30 topics under consideration in such a way that they could be considered by type of department – London, Oxbridge, Wales, Old Civic, Young Civic, New and Former College of Advanced Technology (CAT). Certain patterns emerged. There seems little doubt, for example, that students at London and at Oxbridge universities were more likely than students at other institutions to pursue those topics that might be said to relate to the more formal aspects of education. Thus, a higher proportion of the students at those institutions claimed to have spent time on topics such as the use of school textbooks and preparation of pupils for 'A' levels. A greater proportion of the Oxbridge students than of those in other universities seemed to have done more on a range of topics, including the teaching of children of below average ability; mixed ability teaching; voice projection and diction skills; control and discipline in the classroom; moral education; pastoral care and counselling; and the use of language across the curriculum. Generally, there is also evidence that where a high proportion of students undertook a topic individual students spent a lot of time in its study.

A smaller proportion of students at the University of Wales than at the other universities appear to have spent time studying team teaching or the use of school textbooks. The students at Wales also seemed less likely to do courses relating to the use of language across the curriculum. In general terms, it was the students at the New universities and the former CATs who seemed less likely to pursue any work relating to the various levels of public examinations, and these universities also appeared not to offer many of their students the opportunity to study moral education. A smaller proportion of students at the New universities also claimed to study topics relating to the law and the government and management of schools. The items considered above are those that showed the most marked differences between categories of department. The differences with respect to other items are less notable, with the relative proportions for each type being close to the average on each item.

PEDAGOGY

Finally, we need to consider all the work in the PGCE courses that is not obviously method, and not obviously teaching practice. It was in this area of work that the university departments differed most, and in which individual students within one department could have different experiences depending upon the choices which they made from the options offered by the department. Further complications in describing this work arise from the fact that not only did the departments offer a range of choice to their students, but they also differed significantly from each other in the nature and organisation of their courses. It should be noted that we have already acknowledged these differences in our earlier discussion of the kinds of topics students studied on their courses, and most particularly when we showed that important topics might be considered either in method work or in non-method parts of the PGCE.

Disregarding for the moment detailed differences between departments, a major structural distinction can be made between those departments that purported to offer separate specialised theoretical courses and those that purported to offer integrated theoretical courses. Overall, the majority of departments offered integrated courses. When a department offers an integrated course it does not necessarily mean that a great deal of highly developed conceptual re-organisation has informed its construction. Rather, the staff have been concerned to relate the course to practical work and policy-related issues in the field of education and classroom work. The approach, therefore, in an integrated course was most likely to be through topics, issues, and themes. Such methods maximised the opportunity to utilise both staff and student experience. It appeared, on the evidence from staff interviews, that integrated courses were more likely than other courses to involve relatively large numbers of staff – particularly method tutors. It was felt by some tutors that this increased the practical orientation of the non-method courses and enabled staff to make explicit the links between method work and the more theoretical elements of the course.

A further variation between departments was the extent to which whole courses or parts of courses were common to all students. Departments differed greatly in the degree of choice characterising their courses. In some departments little or nothing was common, and students had a range of options from which they might choose. In other departments there were clearly marked out common courses, which all students were expected to attend. Regardless, however, of the form of organisation, attendance expectations and attendance regulations also differed between departments. It is clear from our data that the 'holding power' of the non-method course was very different from that of method work, and student attendance levels, as reported by the students, were considerably lower at non-method than at method classes.

The students were asked to name the courses, other than method, that they had attended. Unfortunately, it has not always proved possible in the analysis to distinguish from the student responses detailed and named areas of work that students undertook as part of an integrated course. About a third of respondents gave only the broad title on an integrated course (e.g. 'Children and society'), whereas other

Table 11

TOPICS STUDIED IN NON-METHOD COURSES

Topics offered by many departments
- Psychology
- Sociology
- Aspects of science education (including science in the primary school, computing in education)
- P.E., games, recreational courses
- History of education
- Audio-visual aids, film-making, television in education
- Language - use and acquisition
- Philosophy
- Learning
- Comparative education
- Counselling and careers education
- Curriculum studies (including curriculum development and philosophy)
- Multi-cultural education
- Health and social education
- First aid
- Reading
- Education system/administration

Topics offered by few departments
- Childrens literature
- Museums and education
- Map work
- Behavioural techniques
- Alternative education, de-schooling
- Juvenile delinquency
- Youth and community education
- Photography
- Small group dynamics
- Greek for beginners
- Speech training
- Politics and education
- Computer-assisted learning
- The middle school
- Libraries and resources
- Educational statistics
- Calligraphy
- Aesthetic education
- Education of gypsies
- Women's studies
- Slow-learning children
- Special education

students took the opportunity in the question to provide more detailed information. It is impossible, therefore, to quantify with precision the numbers pursuing topics in the non-method area. Table II is intended to illustrate the array of courses that students claimed to have pursued. What is clear from the table, which is by no means a comprehensive list, is the diversity of work available on PGCE courses, and the availability of topics for study which seemingly bear little relation to each other, and which differ significantly in the extent of their attachment to theory, method, and empirical data. No doubt, these facts were as much influenced by the range of interest of staff as by other considerations.

The students were also asked which topics they found intellectually stimulating. The most favoured courses in this respect were, in rank order: psychology, sociology and philosophy. When asked, however, about the topics that contributed to their professional development, philosophy and sociology were much less well received, but psychology still headed the list, followed by various aspects of science education; control and discipline; and the use and acquisition of language.

We have more detailed information about non-method courses from the 460 students in the seven departments of education involved in the sub-sample. A close analysis of their responses to the parts of the inquiry which dealt with the more theoretical aspects of the study of education provides further insight into the nature of the courses offered; the work associated with them; the time spent on them; and the students' responses to them. The pattern which emerged from the sub-sample was both similar and dissimilar to that found in the main sample. Many respondents mentioned general education courses, as four of the seven departments had integrated theory arrangements. Apart from these, the courses most commonly named were in psychology, philosophy, and sociology, with substantial numbers also taking courses in language; learning; history of education; management; organisation and administration; examinations and assessment; and special education. Other topics, such as discipline and adolescence, were frequently subsumed in general, integrated courses. The non-method courses were taught in a variety of ways but it is clear that the lecture method still predominated, though it was frequently supported by seminars and/or tutorials. The staff inquiry offered further confirmation of the dominance of the lecture in non-method courses, though staff in many departments claimed that the amount of lecturing had been substantially reduced in recent years.

Table 12 shows the students' estimate of the average number of hours per week that they spent attending educational theory courses. Over a third said that they attended such courses for four hours or less, while over 40% claimed to spend between five and eight hours, and a fifth nine or more hours.

Table 12

AVERAGE NUMBER OF HOURS PER WEEK SPENT ATTENDING EDUCATIONAL THEORY COURSES

	Number	%
4 or less	159	35.3
5 - 8	199	44.2
Over 8	92	20.4
Total	450	100.0

Missing cases - 10

We also invited the students to give the titles of the essays, papers and dissertations which they undertook as part of their theory courses. Not unexpectedly, the general direction followed by the written work reflected the pattern of the courses attended. Thus, the PGCE students in the sub-sample were twice as likely to have written an essay on the psychology of education as on any other field. Other popular themes, in descending order, were: mixed ability teaching and alternative forms of grouping; discipline; topics in the sociology of education; comprehensive schools; aspects of the philosophy of education; language and learning. An attempt was made by some students to explore the relationship between aspects of method and theory. This was reflected in essay titles such as: 'The justification of maths in the curriculum'; 'Junior science teaching and Piagetian theory'; 'Teaching of science to the visually handicapped'; 'Language and history teaching'; and 'Social education - a biologist's contribution'.

The 460 students in the sub-sample appeared to have done an average of just over three essays each related to non-method work while on their PGCE courses, but they seemed to have had much less experience of giving papers or talks. Only about a third claimed to have undertaken this activity, and though there was a broad range of subjects covered, the numbers in each category were too small for any conclusions to be drawn. When dissertations or extended essays are considered, the proportions are reversed. About a third of the students were not required by their departments to undertake that kind of exercise. Obviously, students undertaking dissertations had a very free choice. Popular areas of work for dissertations were aspects of science education; aspects of english teaching; language; the history of education; careers education and counselling. This observation, however, tells us only part of the story. The most interesting point about the dissertations was the wide range of topics covered: sex roles; education in hospitals; truancy; women in education; the leisure activities of adolescents; financial cutbacks in education; and the transition from primary to secondary school. This diversity must be seen also in the context of the diversity associated with the non-method courses as illustrated in Table 11.

Diversity was also apparent in the range of books which students had read. It must be emphasised that students were not asked about their reading on the course, but were invited only to list those books which they had found most interesting and stimulating. When their responses were re-coded into categories, it emerged clearly that the students responded best to books dealing with various aspects of behaviour problems, remedial and special education and disadvantage. This category included works by authors such as Holt, Gulliford, Furneaux and Kellmer-Pringle. Fewer students were impressed by books relating to disciplines such as psychology, sociology and philosophy, though authors such as Hargreaves, Marland, Lacey, Stones, Morrison and McIntyre, Simon, Hirst and Peters were frequently mentioned. Relatively few students seem to have had their interest caught by books on subjects such as the history of education, evaluation and assessment, reading, the curriculum and race.

CONCLUSIONS

There is little doubt that university departments of education have suffered within their own institutions from being the 'poor relations'. To a large degree this has come about because of the practical and functional orientation of university departments of education which has established a tradition that does not always sit comfortably with the liberal, scholarly and detached values of the academy. University departments have suffered from being too close to the schools, and have been disadvantaged because the origins of state schooling in England and Wales must be seen in terms of making provision for the 'undisciplined' urban working class! Historically, students in schools of education have not been of the highest calibre and that, too, has affected relationships with the parent institution. What has also been of great significance, however, has been the relative failure of those who work in departments of education to develop a body of theory and a set of concepts which can adequately describe and inform the professional task of teaching. As a result, the work of university departments of education has frequently lacked focus and coherence.

Thus, even though some of the disadvantages under which university departments have laboured have now disappeared, many problems still remain. The students, for example, as our study has shown, are now intellectually strong and professionally committed; yet they are inducted into teaching in an unsystematic fashion – which produces differences not only between universities and departments, but within the same department. The inadequacies of the theories of teaching and learning encourage a situation where it is easy for courses to grow piecemeal, representing contemporary fashion, ideology or the enthusiasms of staff, and where students are encouraged to 'shop around' in elaborate option schemes representing different, and sometimes conflicting, intellectual traditions. It is for these reasons, also, that the work of university departments of education is so readily affected by changes in political will and educational rhetoric. Those who practice teacher education find it difficult to resist such changes by opposing them with a worked-out and agreed theoretical stance supported by relevant empirical data. It is in this context that the consequences of the liberal and progressive prescriptions and recommendations of the 1960s must be seen but, more importantly now, it is in this context that the current conservative and traditional prescriptions must be faced. In the end, arguments and policies which emphasise teachers' personalities, subject training and assessment, are only pre-empting one ideological stance at the expense of another. It must be the duty of those who work in teacher education, or, at least, of those who remain uncommitted to any particularist standpoint, to recognise that the patterns of teaching and learning emerge slowly and unclearly. The progress of all teachers and some learners is hard and does not bear comparison with the rapidity of the advance of social movements or the seductive attractions of new and old ideologies.

REFERENCE

Bernbaum, G., Patrick, H. and Reid, K. (1982) The Structure and Process of Initial Teacher Education within Universities in England and Wales, Leicester: University of Leicester School of Education.

Chapter Five

THE POSTGRADUATE CERTIFICATE OF EDUCATION,
TEACHING PRACTICE AND THE PROBATIONARY YEAR

Ken Reid

Although teaching practice and the probationary period have
received much attention, the literature dealing with students'
perceptions of these topics is sparse. This chapter is based
on SPITE (The Structure and Process of Initial Teacher
Education within Universities in England and Wales, Bernbaum,
Patrick and Reid, 1982) data and reports on a series of
student perceptions on teaching practice, probation and
induction. These findings suggest that:
1. Similarities betweeen student experiences on
   teaching practice and the probationary year appear to
   be limited.
2. The nature of student concerns changes between
   the initial and probationary period.
3. The majority of postgraduate student teachers
   were well satisfied with the amount and quality of
   the supervision which they received from both their
   method tutors and designated teacher tutors on
   teaching practice. Conversely, a high proportion of
   new teachers received comparatively little and/or
   uneven help from promoted and unpromoted colleagues
   alike during their first year in schools.
4. Far more postgraduate students gained experience of
   primary schools on teaching practice than eventually
   taught in one of these kinds of schools.

BACKGROUND

The first or probationary year (Rudd and Wiseman, 1962; Clark
and Nisbet, 1963; Cornwell, 1965; Edgar and Warren, 1969;
Taylor and Dale, 1971; Otty, 1972; Hill, 1975; Hannam et al,
1976; Bradley and Eggleston, 1978; Durner, 1979; DES, 1982;
Patrick, Bernbaum and Reid, 1983) and induction processes
(Baker, 1976; 1978; DES,1977; McCabe, 1978; Bolam et al, 1979;
Davis, 1979) have been extensively studied from a variety of
standpoints. Interest in these topics has been encouraged by

dissatisfaction with initial teacher education programmes; debates on the merits of continuing initial teacher training into the probationary period; recruitment procedures; employment opportunities; and early in-service provisions both nationally and within individual local education authorities (LEAs).

A reading of the literature suggests that many probationary programmes remain in their infancy. Lacey (1977) considered research into the first year of teaching to be 'too idiosyncratic to give a reliable picture', while induction schemes are difficult to evaluate because they are dealing with the rather ill-defined areas of personal and professional development and with the long-term effects of these upon attitudes, teaching performance and benefits to schools and children (Bolam, 1981).

The aim of this chapter, therefore, is to provide up-to-date evidence obtained from a comparison of some of the SPITE postgraduate student teacher data with data on the probationary year, focusing specifically on aspects of the relationship between teaching practice and the first year of teaching. Issues covered in the chapter include the link between:

1. Student teachers' educational backgrounds, teaching practice and probation.
2. Teaching practice supervision and help given to new teachers in schools.
3. Student problems on teaching practice and beginning teachers' difficulties in their schools.
4. The postgraduate certificate of education (PGCE) curriculum and academic needs by the end of the probationary year.

Detailed evidence on the probationers' teaching responsibilities (match and mismatch) and career perceptions have already been reported elsewhere (Patrick, Bernbaum and Reid, forthcoming). It should be noted that some of the earlier information presented in chapter 4 on teaching practice (time spent in schools; activities on teaching practice; teaching practice structures; schools; and so forth) provides further support for the arguments discussed hereafter.

Of the full cohort (N=4350), 2675 probationary teachers responded to the SPITE questionnaire towards or at the end of their first year in teaching (61.5%). Each university type (e.g. Oxbridge, New, former college of advanced technology) was represented in approximately the same proportions as in previous questionnaires used in the SPITE study. The tables presented in this chapter show the precise number of respondents to each question or each item as appropriate.

STUDENT-TEACHERS' EDUCATIONAL BACKGROUNDS, TEACHING PRACTICE
AND PROBATION

Table 1 shows the type of school or college in which the SPITE
cohort spent their last two years of secondary education
compared with their teaching practice institutions (schools or
colleges) and first appointments. Although the primary and
middle school categories are excluded from the first column
for obvious reasons, these data indicate that more than three
times as many new teachers commenced work in comprehensive
schools as attended them as pupils. Owing to the
Principality's early adoption of the system, far more students
from Wales than from England experienced comprehensive
education as pupils and teachers. By contrast, a higher
proportion of students from the North of England than
elsewhere came from grammar school backgrounds.

Table 1

DISTRIBUTION OF THE STUDENTS' EDUCATIONAL BACKGROUNDS,
TEACHING PRACTICE AND FIRST APPOINTMENTS

Type of institution	Students' secondary education N	%	Teaching practice institution N	%	First appointment N	%
- Comprehensive schools (all types)	1107	25.7	2719	81.2	1693	70.8
- Grammar schools (all types)	2008	46.6	187	5.6	90	3.8
- Independent schools	348	8.0	235	7.0	223	9.3
- Further education colleges	300	7.0	167	5.0	48	2.0
- Sixth form colleges	233	5.4	76	2.3	45	1.9
- Secondary modern schools	98	2.3	59	1.8	45	1.9
- Others	221	5.1	63	1.9	110	4.6
- Primary			981	29.3	89	3.7
- Middle schools			294	8.8	48	2.0
Total	4313	100.0			2391	100.0

For teaching practice institutions N=3350; reponses >3350
because many students went to more than one type of
institution.

Perhaps much greater significance should be given to the
fact that approximately eight times as many students undertook
primary teaching practices as eventually obtained posts in
primary schools. Similarly, roughly four times more students

undertook a teaching practice in a middle school as eventually started their careers in one. Only 18.9% of the postgraduate student teachers did not go to a comprehensive school on any teaching practice; a higher proportion of these students trained at Oxbridge than elsewhere.

HELP DURING PROBATIONARY YEAR

Table 2 shows the people from whom the probationers received help in schools during their first year of teaching. It should be noted that the totals are taken as a percentage of 2397 respondents - the number of probationary teachers who were employed. The total percentage is greater than 100 because many respondents received help from more than one person.

Table 2

DISTRIBUTION OF PEOPLE FROM WHOM PROBATIONERS RECEIVED HELP

	N	%
Nobody	132	5.5
Headteacher	420	17.5
Deputy Headteacher(s)	843	35.2
Head(s) of Department	1750	73.0
Pastoral Head(s) of year	652	27.2
Other Teacher(s)	1693	70.6
Local education authority (LEA) adviser(s)	530	22.1
Her Majesty's Inspectorate of Education (HMI)	81	3.4
Someone else	204	8.5

Not surprisingly, new teachers were most likely to say that they had received help during their probationary year from heads of departments and from other teachers. Over 70% had recieved help from each of these categories, while over a third had been helped by a deputy headteacher. Only 5.5% said that nobody had helped them. Those teaching science subjects and physical education (P.E.) were least likely to have had no help, while those teaching in independent schools and in colleges of further or higher education were among those most likely to have had no help. To some extent the people from whom new teachers received help varied according to the type of school in which they taught. Those working in primary and middle schools tended to get help from the head or deputy headteacher, while those in comprehensive schools, grammar schools and sixth form colleges were more likely to have been helped by heads of department. LEA advisers seemed most often to have been of help to P.E. and primary teachers.

Respondents were also asked whether they had attended any induction or in-service courses for probationary teachers. Nearly half (47.6%) had done so. Those teaching P.E. and primary and middle school subjects were most likely to have done so, as were those teaching in primary, middle and comprehensive schools. Teachers in independent schools and colleges of further and higher education were less likely than their colleagues elsewhere to have had the benefit of such courses. Many respondents gave no specific details of the courses they attended, noting only that they consisted of general discussions or talks organised by an LEA adviser. Courses on individual teaching subjects tended to be taken by those teaching the relevant subjects. Apart from specific subjects, other topics on which courses were attended by relatively high numbers of probationers included counselling and pastoral care; the use and management of resources; remedial education; assessment; the organisation and administration of the education system; discipline; the role of the teacher; language; teaching methods; visits to other schools and to places other than schools; the teacher and the law; and safety. Courses in remedial education tended to be taken by english and maths teachers, while those on safety were attended almost exclusively by science teachers.

The probationary teachers were also asked whether their schools made any special arrangements for the induction of new teachers. Just over two fifths (41.6%) said that they did. Those teaching primary and middle school subjects and those teaching in independent schools were less likely than other groups to report that special arrangements were made. Such arrangements took a variety of forms, the most commonly mentioned being a senior member of staff with responsibility for all probationers in the school. Many probationers attended meetings specially arranged for new teachers. Some had fewer teaching periods than other members of staff or were relieved of tasks such as playground duty. Other arrangements mentioned were short courses in the school before the term began to introduce new teachers; opportunities to observe other teachers at work; and a requirement to submit lesson plans to the head of department or other senior teacher.

As they neared the end of their first year of teaching, the probationary teachers were also asked whether there were any topics on which they would now like a course. In all, 975 (40%) of those employed as teachers noted at least one area on which they would like a course. Most wanted a course on some aspect of their own teaching subject or on some closely related subject. English teachers, for example, might want a course on drama; mathematicians on computing; and primary teachers on reading. Beyond this, the topics most commonly mentioned, in order of frequency, were remedial education (including the teaching of slow learners, under-achieving pupils and the less able); discipline and control; pastoral

; mixed ability teaching; the organisation and
of education; various teaching methods; the use
.including audio-visual aids and libraries); the
.eacher; sixth form teaching; multicultural
.nd first aid.

PROBATIONARY YEAR PROBLEMS

The SPITE probationers were asked to indicate which, from a
list of ten items, had caused them some or major problems
during their first year of teaching. Table 3 shows that the
issue which caused problems to more teachers than any other
was difficulty in controlling individual pupils. 63.5% had
some problems with this, and 14.0% had major problems. This
was followed by difficulty in controlling classes, with which
57.0% had some problems and 7.6% had major problems. 63.0% had
some or major problems with the amount of marking required.

Table 3

DISTRIBUTION OF BEGINNING TEACHERS' PROBLEMS

Problem	None %	Some %	Major %	N/A %
- Teaching subjects for which your training has not equipped you	33.0	36.4	4.2	26.4
- Amount of marking required	34.7	53.7	9.3	2.3
- Lack of non-teaching time	47.7	40.8	8.8	2.7
- Lesson preparation	41.8	50.6	7.0	0.6
- Difficulty in controlling individual pupils	21.8	63.5	14.0	0.6
- Difficulty in controlling classes	34.4	57.0	7.6	1.0
- The administrative tasks associated with teaching	58.1	35.8	3.7	2.4
- Inadequate school textbooks	33.4	42.4	20.2	4.0
- Inadequate audio-visual resources	49.3	30.8	13.6	6.4
- Lack of clear direction from established staff	46.2	39.2	11.8	2.8

Although only 42.4% said that inadequate textbooks had caused some problems, 20.2% said that this had caused them major problems - a higher percentage than for any other item on the list. There were few differences between the sexes with regard to the problems they had encountered, but the women were slightly more likely to have difficulty in controlling both individual pupils and classes, and the men were slightly more likely to have difficulty with the administrative tasks associated with teaching.

Not unexpectedly, teachers of different subjects tended to encounter different problems. Relatively few modern linguists had problems arising from teaching subjects for which their training had not equipped them, but this did cause problems for relatively high numbers of primary teachers, as did a lack of non-teaching time. Primary teachers, however, were less likely than their colleagues in other subjects to have problems arising out of most of the other items on the list. The amount of marking caused problems for teachers of arts subjects, while the social scientists suffered from the problems of teaching subjects for which their training had not equipped them; a lack of non-teaching time; inadequate audio-visual resources; and a lack of clear direction from established staff. On most items the science teachers did not seem particularly prone to problems. They were slightly more likely than were teachers of other subjects to have problems in controlling classes, but comparatively few had problems with regard to inadequate audio-visual resources or the lack of clear direction from established staff. P.E. staff were also relatively fortunate, being less likely than their colleagues in other subjects to have problems with the amount of marking required; lesson preparation; controlling individual pupils or classes; inadequate textbooks; or audio-visual resources. They did have problems, however, with the administrative tasks associated with teaching and with a lack of clear direction from established staff.

Teachers working in different types of schools faced, to some extent, different problems. As might be expected from the preceding paragraph, those teaching in primary and middle schools were more likely than their peers in other schools to have problems because of teaching subjects for which their training had not equipped them and because of a lack of non-teaching time, but comparatively few had problems in the other areas listed. Those working in comprehensive and secondary modern schools were among those most likely to face problems because of difficulty in controlling individual pupils, difficulty in controlling classes, and inadequate school textbooks, while a higher proportion of those in secondary modern schools than in any other type of school or college suffered from a lack of clear direction from established staff. Those teaching in grammar schools tended to have problems because of audio-visual resources but, apart from

this, teachers in grammar schools, sixth form colleges and
independent schools were no more likely than their colleagues
elsewhere to have problems with most of the items listed, and
were comparatively unlikely to have problems with regard to
lack of non-teaching time, and controlling classes and
individual pupils. Relatively small proportions of those
working in independent schools faced problems because of the
administrative tasks associated with teaching, inadequate
school textbooks or inadequate audio-visual resources.

INSTITUTIONAL TRAINING, TEACHING PRACTICE AND FIRST POSTS

We now turn our attention to the link between subject training
on PGCE courses, teaching practice and the probationary year.
In this book, tables 10 and 11 in chapter 4 show some of the
topics covered by students on the PGCE by course component.
Tables 4, 5 and 6 in this chapter show the percentage of
students who found these topics useful on teaching practice;
the probationers' opinions of the usefulness of these topics
in their first posts; and the probationers' retrospective
opinions on the topics on which it would have been useful to
have spent more time during their initial training year.

Table 4 lists the percentages of those who undertook
study on each item who found it useful on teaching practice.
Higher percentages of students found the following practical
topics useful: lesson preparation; questioning skills;
preparing materials; various methods of teaching; use of
blackboard; classroom management and organisation; control and
discipline in the classroom; and the use of audio-visual aids.
In addition, these were frequently the topics on which the
students claimed to have spent a lot of time during their
courses. It is also the case that there are several items for
which a high percentage of those studying them found them
useful but which we know were not widely studied in
departments. A clear example in this category is the study of
voice projection and diction skills which, though not widely
undertaken by students, was found useful by 68.0% of those who
were able to study the topic. The items that were not found
very useful tend to be those of a more general nature, such as
moral education. The fact that only a third of the students
who undertook work relating to the preparation of pupils for
'A' level examinations found it useful is almost certainly
explained by the relatively small proportion of students who
had the opportunity to teach 'A' level classes while on
teaching practice.

There were also differences by subject with respect to
what the students found useful while on teaching practice. The
students teaching in primary schools, for example, seem to
have found slightly less useful than all other students those

items that head the list in Table 4 and, perhaps unexpectedly, they were well below the overall average figure for their

Table 4

STUDENTS' PERCEPTIONS OF THE USEFULNESS OF COURSE TOPICS
FOR TEACHING PRACTICE

	% of students who found topics useful on teaching practice
– Lesson preparation	91.0
– The skills involved in questioning pupils in class	89.2
– The preparation of materials for teaching	82.5
– Varied methods of teaching your subject	81.2
– The use of the blackboard	80.5
– Classroom management and organisation	80.1
– Control and discipline in the classroom	76.9
– The use of audio-visual aids	76.5
– Voice projection and diction skills	68.0
– The organisation of laboratory work for pupils	66.9
– Teaching children of below average ability	61.4
– Mixed ability teaching	60.6
– Methods of assessment and evaluation	55.6
– The use of prepared school materials	55.3
– Project work in institutions	51.4
– The use of language across the curriculum	50.8
– The use of school textbooks	50.3
– The preparation of pupils for 'O' level examinations	46.7
– The preparation of pupils for 'CSE' examinations	45.9
– Microteaching	43.0
– Interaction analysis	43.0
– Syllabus planning	39.0
– Pastoral care and counselling	34.3
– The organisation of field work for pupils	33.5
– The preparation of pupils for 'A' level examinations	33.3
– Team teaching	27.6
– Moral education	27.0
– The special educational needs of children with handicaps	22.7
– The government and management of schools	17.0
– The law as it relates to teachers	3.1

appreciation of the benefit of audio-visual aids. They seem, however, to have found the study of voice projection and diction skills; preparatory work in the use of language across the curriculum; and project work more useful than did other students. The science students (including mathematics) claimed to benefit less from those topics available on courses which might be said to relate to the more modern and progressive developments in education than did other students. Relatively low proportions of science students found topics such as varied methods of teaching; teaching children of below average ability; mixed ability teaching; methods of assessment and evaluation; project work; the use of language across the curriculum; and the special needs of children with handicaps; useful on teaching practice. More than other groups, however, the science students found the work done on the preparation of pupils for 'O' level examinations useful. This was not the case with 'A' level examinations, where their proportion was similar to that of all other secondary groups apart from the social scientists.

It is interesting to note that a greater proportion of the social scientists than any other group found the work done in preparing pupils for 'A' level examinations useful, and also found useful the work done relating to children with special educational needs and the teaching of children of below average ability. This apparent polarisation in the responses of the social science students is probably explained by the nature of their teaching practice experience, since they were more likely than students in other subjects to have taught 'A' level classes and to have worked in special units. Social science groups are likely to include a relatively high proportion both of those teaching exclusively 'O' and 'A' level classes in schools and further education colleges, and of those whose training in the social sciences is thought to give them a special insight into children with various forms of disadvantage.

This lengthy discussion on course topics and their perceived usefulness on teaching practice has further highlighted the different practices and arrangements in the various university departments. These differences also manifest themselves when consideration is given to the perceived usefulness of the various items categorised by individual department, or by type of department. It would be too easy to draw the erroneous conclusion that perceived usefulness is a measure of the effectiveness of courses. In fact, such a simplistic position cannot be sustained. Perceived usefulness might well reflect other factors such as the nature and organisation of local teaching practice schools and the access which students had to different experiences on teaching practice.

Finally, there were also differences with respect to courses studied and their perceived usefulness for teaching

practice when the students were considered
undergraduate qualifications. These differ
largely reflect other differences in the st
have already been considered above. Discussi
students, for example, is largely a discussi
language students.

Included in the questionnaire completed by
towards the end of their PGCE year was a list o........pics
which might be included in a PGCE course (see ch..ter 4). This
list was also used in the probationary year questionnaire.
Respondents were asked to indicate how useful they had found
each topic in their teaching so far, and whether it would have
been useful to have spent more time on each topic during the
PGCE course (tables 5 and 6).

Table 5

TEACHERS' PERCEPTIONS OF THE USEFULNESS OF COURSE TOPICS
IN THE PROBATIONARY YEAR

	Very use- ful %	Some use %	No use %
— The preparation of materials for teaching (e.g. worksheets)	53.8	41.3	4.9
— The use of school textbooks	24.3	55.4	20.3
— The use of prepared school materials (e.g. Nuffield science)	15.4	44.7	39.9
— Team teaching	5.8	20.8	73.4
— Voice projection and diction skills	21.0	47.5	31.5
— Project work in institutions	17.2	48.3	34.5
— Teaching children of below average ability	39.7	38.9	21.4
— Syllabus planning	23.8	45.6	30.6
— Lesson preparation	56.3	39.4	4.3
— Methods of assessment and evaluation	35.4	53.0	11.6
— Mixed ability teaching	31.9	44.1	24.1
— The preparation of pupils for 'A' level examinations	22.3	26.4	51.2
— The preparation of pupils for 'O' level examinations	28.1	38.4	33.5
— The preparation of pupils for 'CSE' examinations	26.9	35.8	37.4
— The organisation of laboratory work for pupilsupils	15.4	16.1	68.5

5 (con't)

	Very useful %	Some use %	No use %
- The skills involved in questioning pupils in class	42.0	50.9	7.1
- Varied methods of teaching your subject	44.7	45.4	9.9
- The use of the blackboard	28.4	57.1	14.5
- The use of audio-visual aids	34.2	54.6	11.2
- Classroom management and organisation	43.2	47.7	9.1
- Control and discipline in the classroom	47.0	43.3	9.3
- Microteaching	6.0	25.1	68.9
- Interaction analysis	6.8	35.8	57.4
- The special educational needs of children with handicaps	7.7	26.4	65.9
- The government and management of schools	4.2	36.9	58.9
- Pastoral care and counselling	24.5	49.6	25.9
- The law as it relates to teachers	10.4	54.0	35.6
- The use of language across the curriculum	20.4	51.4	28.2
- Moral education	8.6	45.9	45.6

Table 6

TEACHERS' PERCEPTIONS OF TOPICS
ON WHICH IT WOULD HAVE BEEN USEFUL TO HAVE SPENT MORE TIME

	Yes %	No %
- The preparation of materials for teaching (e.g. worksheets)	63.7	36.3
- The use of school textbooks	50.0	50.0
- The use of prepared school materials (e.g. Nuffield science)	36.3	63.7
- Team teaching	30.2	69.8
- Voice projection and diction skills	34.6	65.4
- Project work in institutions	56.0	44.0
- Teaching children of below average ability	84.4	15.6
- Syllabus planning	60.1	39.9
- Lesson preparation	49.0	51.0
- Methods of assessment and evaluation	64.2	35.8
- Mixed ability teaching	67.4	32.6

Table 6 (con't)

	Yes %	No %
- The preparation of pupils for 'A' level examinations	60.1	39.9
- The preparation of pupils for 'O' level examinations	67.7	32.3
- The preparation of pupils for 'CSE' examinations	66.4	33.6
- The organisation of fieldwork for pupils	31.7	68.3
- The organisation of laboratory work for pupils	22.6	77.4
- The skills involved in questioning pupils in class	66.3	33.7
- Varied methods of teaching your subject	71.8	28.2
- The use of the blackboard	36.9	63.1
- The use of audio-visual aids	44.4	55.6
- Classroom management and organisation	65.5	34.5
- Control and discipline in the classroom	71.8	28.2
- Microteaching	18.3	81.7
- Interaction analysis	25.0	75.0
- The special educational needs of children with handicaps	36.6	63.4
- The government and management of schools	27.9	72.1
- Pastoral care and counselling	61.5	38.5
- The law as it relates to teachers	47.3	52.7
- The use of language across the curriculum	41.2	58.8
- Moral education	33.4	66.6

There were six topics which over 60.0% of the respondents had found very useful. These were lesson preparation, the preparation of teaching materials, control and discipline in the classroom, varied method(s) of teaching their subject(s), classroom management and organisation and the skills involved in questioning pupils in class. Between 30.0% and 40.0% had found the following topics very useful: teaching children of below average ability; methods of assessment and evaluation; the use of audio-visual aids; and mixed ability teaching. All these topics, with the exception of lesson preparation and the use of audio-visual aids, also came high on the list of topics on which probationary teachers believed it would have been useful to have spent more time during the PGCE course. Over 60.0% would have liked more time on them. Other items on which over 60.0% of the teachers would have liked to spend more time were syllabus planning; the preparation of pupils for 'A' level, 'O' level and 'CSE' examinations; and pastoral care and counselling.Clearly, therefore, there were some topics which teachers had found very useful but which they would have liked to pursue even further, whereas they felt they had learned enough on other aspects, such as the use of audio-visual aids, which they had also found very useful.

Topics which teachers tended to have found of little use included team teaching; microteaching; the organisation of laboratory work; the special educational needs of children with handicaps; the organisation of field work; the government and management of schools; and interaction analysis. These were also topics on which comparatively few teachers (under 40.0%) believed it would have been useful to have spent more time. Other items on which less than 40.0% would have liked more time were the use of prepared school materials; voice projection and diction skills; the use of blackboard; and moral education.

Some of the items which the majority of teachers had not found useful were of a general nature (e.g. the government and management of schools), but others were clearly subject specific. Thus, most P.E. teachers had not found topics such as the use of the blackboard and the use of textbooks useful, but did tend to find the study of voice projection and diction skills and mixed ability teaching useful. Not surprisingly, although most teachers found that laboratory work was not a useful topic, over 40.0% of science teachers had found it very useful. A comparatively high proportion of modern linguists found the use of textbooks and the skills involved in questioning pupils in class very useful, while the topics found very useful by many primary teachers were team teaching; project work; teaching children of below average ability; mixed ability teaching; the use of language across the curriculum; classroom management and organisation; and control and discipline in the classroom. Social scientists tended to have found very useful, topics as varied as teaching children of below average ability; mixed ability teaching; the special educational needs of children with handicaps; team teaching; project work; and the preparation of pupils for 'A' level, 'O' level and 'CSE' examinations. Compared with teachers in other subjects, the social scientists were also more likely to have found the more general topics included in the list very useful (e.g. moral education; the government and management of schools; interaction analysis; and pastoral care and counselling).

When the teachers were grouped according to their main teaching subjects, they tended to believe it would have been useful to have spent more time on the topics they had found very useful. Thus, for example, a higher proportion of the primary and middle school teachers than any other subject group had found the teaching of children of below average ability very useful and would have liked to have spent more time on it. There were, however, some exceptions to this. The social scientists, for example, more than any other group, thought that the preparation of pupils for 'O' level examinations had been a very useful topic, but were actually less likely than the languages, arts and science teachers to think it would have been useful to spend more time on it.

The kinds of schools in which teachers were working also affected, to some extent, their views on what had been useful and what it would have been useful to have spent more time on. Sometimes these differences simply reflected the secondary/primary split. This was true, for example, of the usefulness of topics such as preparing pupils for all levels of public examinations, which, not surprisingly, teachers in primary and middle schools were less likely than their secondary school colleagues to have found useful.

Among those in secondary schools, there were further differences. Teachers in grammar schools, independent schools and sixth form colleges were more likely than those in comprehensive or secondary modern schools to have found the preparation of pupils for 'A' level examinations a very useful topic, whereas teachers in comprehensive and secondary modern schools were more likely than their secondary teaching colleagues in other types of schools to have found the preparation of pupils for 'CSE' examinations very useful. The degree of selectiveness of different types of schools also emerged in this context. Teachers in primary schools, middle schools and secondary modern schools were likely than their colleagues elsewhere to have found very useful the teaching of children of below average ability and mixed ability teaching. These topics had been found very useful by only a small minority of teachers in grammar schools, sixth form colleges and independent schools. On these, as on some other issues, teachers in secondary modern schools resembled their colleagues in primary and middle schools rather than those in other types of secondary schools. Along with teachers in primary and middle schools, teachers in secondary modern schools were among those most likely to have found very useful such topics as classroom management and organisation; control and discipline in the classroom; language across the curriculum; and project work. In general, the topics found very useful by teachers in different types of school were also those on which they believed it would have been useful to spend more time.

There was a tendency for a greater proportion of women than of men to claim that they had found almost every item useful. Exceptions to this were five topics on which there was no difference between men and women: the use of prepared school materials; team teaching; voice projection and diction skills; the law as it relates to teachers; and moral education. Three topics which slightly higher proportions of men than women had found very useful were: the organisation of field work; the organisation of laboratory work; and the government and management of schools.

CONCLUSIONS

Most student teachers and probationers receive help in schools to a greater or lesser extent, depending upon such factors as need, school organisation and staff interest. The SPITE data suggest, however, that help is much more readily forthcoming and structured on teaching practice than in the first year of teaching. Evidence from the SPITE probationary year diaries showed that new teachers often value the help they receive from their junior colleagues as much as from senior staff. Similarly, the kind and degree of help given by such people as deputies and heads of department differs by school. Whereas student teachers are largely satisfied by the amount of help and supervision afforded to them on teaching practice, probationary teachers' views are more extreme depending upon their personal experiences. Whereas postgraduate student teachers were found on teaching practice to have received approximately five visits from their main method tutors alone, for example, substantial proportions of new teachers claimed not to have been given any advice or help by (amongst others) their headteachers, deputies, heads of departments, heads of year and LEA advisers.

Despite some differences between the categories used in tables 4 and 5 and the dates when the data for tables 4, 5 and 6 were collected, a comparison of them shows that there is a strong similarity in students' perceptions of topics found useful on teaching practice and during the probationary year. It seems that students feel that they require courses to put a greater emphasis on the practical skills required for teaching in the classroom.

The similarities between the SPITE and HMI (DES, 1982) surveys are striking despite the different way in which the work was conducted. 'The New Teacher in School', for instance, also comments on the comparatively little or uneven help which many probationers receive from senior and junior staff in schools and of the inequality of induction provision.

One further point stands out. The SPITE data provide evidence which shows that in 1979/80 many PGCE courses were already heavily school focused and practically orientated, if not exactly school based or utilising the skills of practising teachers within the training institutions. On average, students spent approximately 40.0% of their time on all forms of school experience.

Finally, after a period of development, recent cutbacks have severely restricted research activity into the probationary year, induction schemes and early in-service. The time may fast be approaching when, in the wake of recent developments in initial teacher training courses, far more concerted attention will have to be given to the crucial first year of teaching.

REFERENCES

Baker, K. (1976) 'A Review of Current Induction Programmes for New Teachers', British Journal of In-Service Education, 2, 179-86.

Baker, K. (1978) 'Survey Findings From LEA Induction Programmes', British Journal of In-Service Education, 4 (3), 151-60.

Bernbaum, G., Patrick, H. and Reid, K. (1982) The Structure and Process of Initial Teacher Education within Universities in England and Wales, Report to the DES, Leicester: University of Leicester School of Education.

Bolam, R., Baker, K. and McMahon, A. (1979) The Teacher Induction Pilot Schemes Project National Evaluation Report, Bristol: University of Bristol School of Education (mimeo).

Bolam, R. (1981) 'Evaluative Research. A Case Study of the Teacher Induction Pilot Schemes Project', Journal of Education for Teaching, 8 (1), 70-83.

Bradley, H.W. and Eggleston, J. F. (1978) 'An Induction Year Experiment, Educational Research, 20 (2), 89-98.

Clark, R.P. and Nisbet, J. (1963) The First Two Years of Teaching, Aberdeen, Department of Education.

Cornwell, J. et al. (1965) The Probationary Year, Birmingham: University of Birmingham Institute of Education.

Davis, O. J. (1979) The Liverpool Induction Pilot Scheme: A Summative Report, Liverpool: University of Liverpool School of Education (mimeo).

DES (1977) Teacher Induction: Pilot Schemes' Progress, Report on Education No 89, London: Department of Education and Science.

DES (1982) The New Teacher in School, London: Her Majesty's Stationery Office.

Durner, V. (1979) 'The Induction Year - A Confrontation with Reality', Cambridge Journal of Education, 9 (2 and 3), 145-52.

Edgar, D. and Warren, R. (1969) 'Power and Autonomy in Teacher Socialisation', Sociology of Education, XLII, 47.

Hannam, C. et al. (1976) The First Year of Teaching, Harmondworth: Penguin Books.

Hill, D. (1975) 'Experiments in Induction: New Approaches to the Probationary Year', British Journal of Teacher Education, 1, 29-40.

Lacey, C. (1977) The Socialisation of Teachers, London: Methuen.

McCabe, C. (1978) 'A New Look at Problems of the Probationary Year', British Journal of In-Service Education, 4 (3), 144-50.

Otty, N. (1972) Learner Teacher, Harmondsworth: Penguin Books.

Patrick, H., Bernbaum, G. and Reid, K. (1983) The Probationary Year: An Interim Report, presented at the DES/University of Leicester Conference on Teacher Education, Oxford.

Patrick, H., Bernbaum, G. and Reid, K. (forthcoming) 'The PGCE and the Probationary Year', British Journal of In-Service Education.

Rudd, W.E.A. and Wiseman, S. (1962) 'Sources of Dissatisfaction Among a Group of Teachers', British Journal of Educational Psychology, 32, 45ff.

Taylor, J.K. and Dale , I.R. (1971) A Survey of Teachers in Their First Year of Service, Bristol: University of Bristol School of Education.

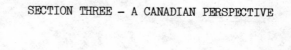

SECTION THREE — A CANADIAN PERSPECTIVE

Chapter Six

CHARACTERISTICS OF FACULTIES OF EDUCATION

Marvin F. Wideen

INTRODUCTION

In the current period of economic decline, teacher education
in Western Europe and North America is under tremendous
pressure. The problems facing those who prepare teachers,
however, are not only economic. Like the schools for whom they
train teachers, faculties of education have failed to respond
to changes in society. The much heralded experiment of moving
the preparation of teachers from the normal school to the
university has not yet fulfilled its promise. Time may be
running out.

Advocacy for change in education generally, and for
faculties of education in particular, is not in short supply.
What appears to be lacking in the case of faculties of
education is an understanding of how to manage the change
process in order to bring about the reforms needed in response
to societal pressures. Before that process can be understood,
more must be known about the characteristics of faculties of
education as organisations. It is strange, indeed, that while
schools have been examined extensively through case studies
and sociological analysis, those institutions that prepare
teachers have been almost totally ignored.

This chapter aims at identifying some of the
characteristics of faculties of education and discussing their
ability to cope with the change process in the light of those
characteristics. I begin with the context of the workplace
focusing on one of the key tensions that members of an applied
faculty face. The discussion then deals with the
characteristics of faculties of education under seven
headings: goals, activity, instruction, rewards, climate,
leadership, and influence structure. The concluding section
returns to the question of how well faculties can be expected
to deal with the change process given these particular
characteristics.

The basis for this chapter comes primarily from two large
scale studies of teacher education. The more recent of these,

completed in 1983, was a national one involving ten english-speaking Canadian teacher training institutions (see note 1 at end of chapter) In that study the Guide to Institutional Learning was administered to 504 faculty members and 1443 students to obtain their opinions on a range of characteristics and issues related to the way faculties of education operate and respond to environmental pressures. Specifically, questions were asked about activities such as goals and instructional practice, faculty activity, leadership, and climate. Faculty members were also asked to comment on the issues they saw as important in teacher education, particularly those dealing with how their institution planned for change. The data from this questionnaire were supplemented by interviews with a small sample of faculty members and students in each institution. Further, data were generated during a second phase of the study. This involved case studies of self-initiated change resulting from information being fed back to ten institutions in an attempt to encourage problem solving. This intervention, though very limited in organisational development terms, contributed greatly to our understanding of how faculties of education operate as organisations because, as Bronfenbrenner pointed out in his 1978 address to the annual meeting of the American Educational Research Association, to understand how an organisation functions, one should try to change it.

The second study, conducted in 1978 by IMTEC (see note 2 at end of chapter), involved 16 teacher training institutions in six countries. I was involved in examining the data from these institutions and discussing it with representatives from them. These data were gathered using a questionnaire which was the forerunner to the one used in the Canadian study. In addition, that study was followed up by an intensive examination of four institutions which had attempted to implement a major innovation. Interviews I held with the people who attended the IMTEC seminar in Gaaustablek, Norway in 1979 added greatly to the data base supporting the discussion that follows.

CONTEXT OF THE WORKPLACE

Faculties of education, like all organisations, possess a set of norms unique to the beliefs, aspirations and activities of those who work in them. As Sarason (1971) has pointed out, the behaviour of individuals must be seen and interpreted within the context of such group norms. Frequently, however, individuals find themselves operating within different sets of norms arising from different contexts. The university community provides an academic setting for teacher education. The schools for which faculties of education prepare teachers have contrasting opinions regarding the 'ideal' nature of teacher education. These two contexts create conflicting sets of normative expectations.

All faculties examined in the two studies were university based. This fact is the result of one of the most significant changes to occur in teacher education – the move of teacher education from the single college (normal school in many jurisdictions) to the university. Beginning in North America around the turn of the century (Cushman, 1977), the movement has occurred in Europe mostly within the past two decades. In European countries the basis for the change was to attract better faculty members and students and to obtain more time and attention for research and development (Ford, 1975; Gwyn, 1976). Both were considered necessary for the new teacher who had to cope with the complex problems of the 1970's, and both were considered a task beyond the means of smaller colleges. In one jurisdiction in North America, the justification for the move rested on the conviction that 'the university provides a setting and an atmosphere in which fundamental issues can be examined critically, fresh alternatives can be explored, and promising, imaginative programmes can be developed' (Myers and Saul, 1974). Thus, the move of teacher education to the university generated high expectations for the preparation of better teachers, the development of knowledge and ideas, and the examination of educational issues and concerns.

The task of adjusting to the academic norms of the university has been a difficult one for teacher education. Cushman (1977) describes the problem in these terms.

> Throughout any review of the history of teacher education and the structures in higher education to facilitate such education, there appears again and again the theme that the preparation of teachers, and of school personnel generally, even including educational leaders, is somewhat beneath the dignity of a university whose primary purpose is research, especially research in the academic disciplines.

As Cushman and other historians point out, however, the problem is deeper than merely adopting a new set of norms. The problem lies in the different perceptions held about effective teacher education. The academic tradition provides the basis for the 'liberal arts' view of teacher education which argues that formal education is centred in the world of knowledge and is aimed at the development of the mind. The 'professional' view places much more emphasis on the learning process and interprets that process in a way that extends it far beyond intellectual and academic learning (Woodring, 1975). The former view is more prevalent in academic departments; the latter typical of the teachers college. Cushman argues that a main function of faculties of education within a university is

to reconcile these viewpoints to achieve the best of both
worlds. Teacher education, however it is conducted within
university settings, is continually struggling with this
problem in one way or another.

University departments of education are also faced with
reconciling viewpoints which are external in origin (Howsam,
1977). Most people who teach in faculties of education spend a
great deal of time in direct or indirect contact with the
schools. This orientation is a practical one – teachers and
students demand ideas that can be applied in the classroom,
where tacit knowledge and anecdotal information are perceived
to be far more useful than abstract theory. Such contact
supports the professional view of education referred to
earlier. Other external groups such as school systems and
professional teacher organisations encourage faculties of
education to pursue activities and conduct their affairs in
ways that would cause them to become more practical. While
this relationship with the 'field' takes different forms in
different jurisdictions, it represents an important part of
the context of teacher education. Follow-up studies have been
done where graduates have been asked to assess their teacher
education preparation. The results have not been encouraging
(Bessai and Edmonds, 1977; Flanders, 1980; Unruh, 1981).
Teachers do not look back on their teacher preparation,
particularly the input on campus, as having had much impact on
them.

A second external group (which has legal authority in
many jurisdictions) is the national, provincial, or state
legislature. Cushman (1977) indicates that in the United
States faculties of education are far more controlled in this
regard than are most other applied faculties. Because such
groups control certification they can, if they wish, exercise
enormous influence. Generally, the nature of that influence
tends to be of a professional kind not unlike that pressure
which comes from the schools.

A third external community to which teacher education is
accountable, and which generates a quite different set of
expectations, is the university itself. The encouragement here
is toward an academic, liberal arts perspective in which
theoretical thoughts and writing are likely to be rewarded
more than those activites of a more professional nature.

The influence of these three different constituents poses
a number of theoretical and practical problems for those who
train teachers, raising issues about what teacher training
ought to be. In this debate it is useful to consider the
perspective of those principally involved in the teacher
education process – faculty members and students.

It is, however, a difficult (and indeed presumptious)
task to attempt to suggest the `character` of faculties of
education which are spread across two continents and which
occupy a wide range of settings. Consequently, the discussion

that follows will not be without exceptions, and
generalisations beyond the institutions examined in the two
studies cited earlier and the literature I draw upon, will be
made with caution.

GOALS: CONFUSED IN PERCEPTION, CONSERVATIVE IN PRACTICE

An examination of programmes developed in faculties of
education and analyses and reports from different
jurisdictions, suggest that insufficiient attention is given
to goals, purposes and conceptualisations that would direct
practice. In those cases where analysis has been done at the
national level (McLeish, 1971; Peterson, 1974) the conclusions
are that faculties of education, in terms of statements that
make arguments as to how the young become teachers, lack
focus. What appears most commonly in the planning of teacher
education programmes, is that coursework forms the building
blocks that are put into place by committees concerned more
with vested interests than sound argument. What is missing in
such plans is the conceptual framework that provides a
programme of teacher preparation which works towards some
purpose. Even when more systematic attempts have been made to
develop programmes, certain underlying assumptions have never
been examined in great depth. What is even more rare is a
critical examination of such models (Apple, 1972).
This lack of focus is institutional. Individuals appear,
on the surface at least, to be able, within specific contexts,
to be much more precise about their goals. Interviews with
teacher educators, however, do not usually reveal conceptual
underpinings supporting statements of objectives. When they
do, they are usually individualistic and not shared on an
institutional level, resulting in a confused array of opinions
relating to the goals of teacher education. Such differences
are most in evidence when groups within a faculty are asked to
identify goals and objectives. People who teach in curriculum
areas, for example, have opinions which are enormously
different from those of teachers in the foundation areas.
Given such diversity, are there any common goals in teacher
education? In the Canadian study, we asked those in faculties
of education to indicate the importance being assigned to each
of eight goals and the importance that ought to be assigned to
them. The mean response of 507 faculty members and 1443
students is shown in Table 1. Several observations can be made
from the table. First, faculty members and students agree in
terms of what is being emphasised and what they would like to
see emphasised. (Of the 18 possible comparisons on similar
items, 14 show differences of less than 10%). Second, sizeable
discrepancies appear in perceptions of what exists and in
opinions regarding what ought to exist. Both faculty members
and students indicate that most importance is currently being

Table 1

OPINIONS OF FACULTY AND STUDENTS ON THE IMPORTANCE OF THE GOALS OF TEACHER EDUCATION

Question
In your opinion, of what importance
are the following goals?

To prepare teachers who:
- Are knowledgeable in subject or content areas
- Can adapt to, and work within, existing school
  systems
- Have effective interpersonal skills
- Can integrate theory and practice
- Have the perceptions and skills to implement
  changes in the schools
- Have skills in various teaching techniques
- Deal effectively with the individual
  differences of students
- Have the ability to analyse critically
  the existing school system

Faculty Response

None   Very
Little   Great
1 2 3   4 5

Student Response

None   Very
Little   Great
1 2 3   4 5

———— Real   – – – Ideal

given to the preparation of teachers who are knowledgeable in subject areas; can work within existing school systems; and have skills in teaching techniques. Such goals support the status quo in education. Much less importance is given to those goals which imply changes in the schools (e.g. the preparation of teachers who have skills to implement changes in the schools and can analyse critically the existing school systems).

Preparing teachers for schools as they exist, assumes that a good teacher is one who can cope with what currently goes on in schools. Apple (1972), who analysed several programmes in the United States, points out the essential conservatism in this approach. He argues that the criticisms of current educational practice are too potent to be ignored. Relying on what exists, he continues, is more suited to a static society than to one that is rapidly changing. Clearly, students and faculty members in the Canadian sample had quite different perspectives in relation to the 'ideal' of what teacher education ought to be. These ideals, however, were not fulfilled in practice. This apparent contradiction is probably linked to, or may even be the cause of, the conservatism in approach referred to by Apple. The lack of well developed conceptualisations of how teachers should be trained leaves most instructors in faculties of education essentially isolated. Pressure from the students to provide them with information that is practical and will help them survive is far more compelling than the ideals they may have about what ought to be taught. Thus, while individuals may have goals which are very idealistic, without the benefit of an overarching theory in which to express those ideals, their practice is very conservative.

I have argued that faculties of education lack a focus in terms of meaningful conceptualisations that would direct practice. Also, opinions of what goals should be vary considerably. Those goals that are being achieved, as perceived by faculty members and students, are likely to maintain the status quo. Interestingly, neither faculty nor students see such goals as being ideal.

This lack of institutional focus was a theme which ran through our data in both the IMTEC and Canadian studies. It did not appear, however, to lead to much diversity across or within institutions. As one professor of education remarked: 'Despite the fact that none of us know what we are doing, we all tend to do it in the same way.' What was intended as a humourous line carried with it more than a grain of truth.

FACULTY ACTIVITY: THE PRIMACY OF INSTRUCTION

In both the Canadian and IMTEC studies of teacher education, faculty members and students were presented with activities

Table 2

OPINIONS OF FACULTY AND STUDENTS ON FACULTY ACTIVITIES

Question
How do you use (real) and how do you
feel you should use (ideal) time?

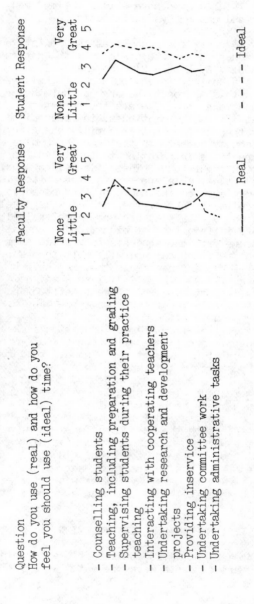

Faculty Response   Student Response

None   Very   None   Very
Little   Great   Little   Great
1 2 3 4 5   1 2 3 4 5

— Counselling students
— Teaching, including preparation and grading
— Supervising students during their practice
  teaching
— Interacting with cooperating teachers
— Undertaking research and development
  projects
— Providing inservice
— Undertaking committee work
— Undertaking administrative tasks

——— Real   - - - Ideal

and asked to indicate how much of their time was used on each. Data from the Canadian study are provided for both faculty members and students in Table 2. It can be seen that faculty members reported spending by far the greatest amount of time on teaching, which included preparation and grading. Less time is reported to be spent on counselling, supervising, and carrying out committee work. Thus, apart from committee work, the three activities occupying faculty members' time dealt either directly or indirectly with instruction. The activity placed lowest on the five point scale was carrying out research and development projects. Providing in-service teacher education and interacting with co-operating teachers were ranked slightly higher. Similar results were obtained in the IMTEC study.

The student data provides an interesting set of check points, and may offer some suggestions as to why faculty members report as much emphasis on teaching as they do. As in the case of faculty members, students perceive most emphasis placed on teaching, although they do not perceive the amount to be as great as do faculty members. The significant datum, however, is the ideal state. Students, it appears, would like to see much more faculty time spent on teaching! From an ideal point of view, and compared with faculty members, students rank research quite low.

The written comments of both students and faculty members suggested a conflict: faculty members expressed the need to do more research and be more involved in activities related to their own professional development; students expressed the concern that faculty members were frequently too preoccupied with research to devote sufficient time to them. This is a strange perceptual conflict given the limited amount of time faculty members see themselves spending on research.

INSTRUCTION: A PRIMARY BUT RHETORICAL FUNCTION

Instruction can be viewed in terms of the amount of time it occupies in the lives of people within a faculty and also in terms of how it is done. We saw in the previous section that faculty members perceive themselves as spending a comparatively great deal of their time in instruction related activities. Why is the nature of the instruction valued so highly by faculty members? One word can be used to sum up the instructional process in faculties of education: 'lecturing'. This finding was consistent both in the IMTEC and Canadian studies. Certainly, some institutions appeared as exceptions. In one case examined, where a deliberate attempt had been made on the part of the head of the institution to change the pattern of teaching in his institution, a much different pattern of teaching was in evidence. This institution was, though, the exception among the 25 examined in the two

Table 3

PERCEPTIONS BY FACULTY AND STUDENTS ON THE AMOUNT OF TIME SPENT ON DIFFERENT FORMS OF INSTRUCTION

Question
The following questions relate to several forms of classroom instruction. Please indicate the general practice in your courses.

- Listening to lectures, or watching demonstrations.
- Discussing topics and issues.
- Working in groups.
- Having the opportunity to try out a variety of teaching methods.
- Working individually on issues and problems, which the student organized or initiated.
- Receiving instruction through audio-visual, printed or other self-teaching materials.
- Engaging in role playing or other simulation exercises.
- Engaging in instructional activities outside the faculty setting (other than practice teaching).

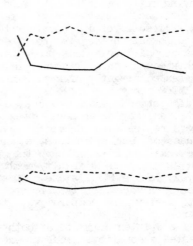

Faculty Response   Student Response

None   Very   None   Very
Little   Great   Little   Great
1 2 3   4 5   1 2 3   4 5

————— Real   — — — Ideal

studies. The most common pattern is illustrated in Table 3 which provides a summary of results from the Canadian data.

It can be seen that, in the view of both faculty members and students, more lecturing occurs than is ideal, and that many of the student oriented types of learning experiences receive little attention. There is nothing novel about these data. Hoetker and Ahlbrand (1969) have used the phrase 'persistence of recitation' to describe teaching in schools. From these data it appears that the same can be said of those who teach in faculties of education. What appears curious is that this particular approach to teaching is not an ideal either in the minds of faculty members or of students; both expressed a preference to see more time devoted to modelling and the presentation of a variety of teaching methods. This is similar to the case of goals and objectives, where we saw one set of goals being achieved when another was seen as ideal. Clearly, there is a link between the two. My contention is that part of the problem lies in resolving the problem of theory and practice in most faculties of education – a question taken up elsewhere in this book. This question of theory versus practice is not unrelated to the point about the lack of conceptualisation so evident in teacher education.

REWARDS: INTRINSICALLY ORIENTED

The reward structures within an organisation are of major importance both for maintaining stability and encouraging change. If an institution wishes to shift its priorities or bring about some type of reform, then the reward structure is one means that it has at its disposal. Of equal importance, however, are the rewards that those in the organisation see as important. How do faculty members in teacher training institutions view the importance of various reward structures? In the IMTEC study, faculty members from 11 institutions in four different countries were presented with six means by which they might be rewarded within their institution, and were asked to rank them in terms of importance. The data are presented in Table 4 where the results have been aggregated for each of the four countries.

Respondents ranked their own 'sense of achievement' as their primary source of reward; in each of the 13 institutions in the study this item was ranked highest. Peer support was ranked second and administrative promotion last. The greatest variability in ranking occurred with item 3, monetary compensation, and item 4, recognition and praise by supervisors.

The type of reward structure evident in these data is of a 'flat' type. No external factors rank high in terms of what might be offered as rewards by the institution. One's own 'sense of achievement' can mean many different things in a

Table 4

METHODS BY WHICH FACULTY MEMBERS FEEL MOST REWARDED

Ranking

Top 1 2 3 4 5 6 Lowest

Item
- Own sense of achievement
- Recognition and praise by peers
- Monetary compensation
- Recognition and praise by supervisors
- Academic promotion
- Administrative promotion

• Norway × United States □ Great Britain o Canada

faculty of education which houses many different kinds of people aspiring to many different goals. Such systems are not readily amenable to change when the rewards are extrinsic.

Another aspect of the data reported in Table 4 is the consistency of results that occur across institutions within and across countries. This consistency of response was typical in both the IMTEC and Canadian studies.

CLIMATE: NEGATIVE AND SUSPICIOUS

The climate of an organisation is usually defined in terms of how members in that organisation perceive themselves in relation to others and the prevailing organisational norms. Positive climates are usually seen as those in which people feel productive and connected to their work and clients in meaningful and useful ways. Negative climates typically imply alienation, isolation and feelings of anomie. While the concept is sometimes slippery to define, no one doubts its importance because it is linked to so many other facets of organisational development and growth. Most schools of management agree that positive climates tend to foster growth, innovation and productivity; negative climates work against the achievement of goals. In both the Canadian and IMTEC studies, we attempted to examine the climate of the institutions. The results from both studies were roughly similar - in both cases we found that climate was linked to other aspects of faculty life in very essential ways.

Table 5 provides data from the Canadian study which used a scale that sampled the quality of communication; the clarity of philosophy; and receptiveness to ideas. The data shows a very clear pattern. Faculty members feel productive, informed, and able to communicate with others (items a-f). All these items were written in the first person, indicating that for individuals the climate was positive. In the case of the last two items on that scale (involving clarity among faculty as to their philosophy and to what that philosophy means in practice), a noticeable shift occurs to the negative side of the scale. We also used a semantic differential to determine how faculty members perceived their institution along continua such as trusting or suspicious; collaborative or individualistic; and innovative or routine. Perceptions were that the institutions were individualistic rather than collaborative; suspicious rather than trusting; and routine rather than innovative.

These data suggest that, while individual faculty members can communicate (with one another and with administrators) and feel productive as individuals, they are suspicious of collaborative effects. Written comments offered by faculty members in the Canadian study confirmed this. Apparent in such comments was an undercurrent of dissatisfaction with the

Table 5

PERCEPTIONS BY FACULTY MEMBERS OF FACULTY CLIMATE

Question
Please indicate what the current climate is
in your faculty (as you experience it)
with regard to the following statements

Response

None Very
Little Great
1 2 3 4 5

- I feel professionally productive in this faculty.
- I receive adequate information concerning the changes
  which affect me in this faculty.
- Faculty members are receptive to my ideas and suggestions.
- I feel free to express to the faculty administration my
  opinion about issues which concern me.
- The quality of communication I have with faculty members
  is satisfactory.
- There is clarity among most members about what the
  faculty's philosophy is.
- There is clarity among most faculty members about what
  this philosophy means in practice.

prevailing general faculty climate. Mistrust between departments; feeling of insecurity; a lack of confidence; and competition arising from individual promotion were cited as examples.

These findings are highly problematic in regards to the collaborative efforts that are needed to address many of the problems facing faculties of education. Sustained institutional thrusts are required to provide focus for institutional efforts to clarify goals and to develop conceptualisations. Activities of the individual entrepeneur will not be sufficient. In a climate of suspicion and individualism, though, such efforts are working against the norm.

LEADERSHIP: CUSTODIAL AND BENIGN

Leadership within a faculty of education can be perceived as part of the overall governance system of the university. Cushman (1977) defines governance as a highly complex process by which decisions affecting behaviour are determined. He cites Baldridge (1971), who provides a three group classification for decision making in university governance: bureaucratic, collegial, and political. Decision making in the bureaucratic model is rational and formal, but in the collegial system it is shared among professional equals. In the political model, decision making takes the form of a negotiation or bargaining process among individuals or groups. Leadership in education, however, has connotations that go beyond decision making – it also implies the notion of how much a dean or department head encourages a faculty to make change, and the extent to which he/she provides direction in instruction, research, or in-service teacher education to the field. Within these boundaries, what characterises leadership in faculties of education?

It was quite clear from the Canadian study that decision making in the institutions was perceived to be a fairly smooth process well managed by the deans and directors. Faculty members indicated that decisions tended to be made and carried out in a reasonably 'businesslike' way. In that regard, the reality of the situation and the ideal perceptions of faculty members were very similar. Also, the data were in agreement with Baldridge's suggestion that decision making tends to be a political/social process in which a great deal of bargaining and negotiation occurs. The leadership role in this situation was largely that of a custodian or manager of a continuing political process.

Additional insight into the characteristics of leadership emerges from the data in Table 6 in which faculty responses to the question 'How do the formal leaders in your faculty do the following things?' are summarised. Clearly, the leaders'

Table 6

PERCEPTIONS BY FACULTY MEMBERS OF FACULTY LEADERSHIP

Question
Please indicate the extent to which
the formal leaders in your faculty
with whom you interact do the following things

Response

A great deal   Not very much
1   2   3   4   5

- Maximise the different skills found in the faculty.
- Display a strong interest in improving the quality
  of the educational program.
- Run conferences and meetings in an organized fashion.
- Procrastinate in decision-making.
- Co-ordinate effectively competing interests in the faculty.
- Show a real interest in the welfare of faculty members.
- Develop a sense of common purpose in working with members
  of the faculty.

ability to run conferences and meetings in an organised way are rated high by the respondents. Also, they show a strong interest in the welfare of faculty members and in improving programmes. They are perceived, though, as poor decision makers and to only occasionally maximise potential, develop a sense of purpose, and co-ordinate competing interests.

In the Canadian study, these data were followed-up by interviews. Further probing revealed that, for the most part, the leaders were well liked by faculty members - mostly because the type of leadership being offered was what they wanted. The decisions that were being managed by the leadership were not, however, of a substantive nature. They rarely involved goals, programme alternatives, or change in teaching practice. Deans themselves, when interviewed, did not perceive themselves as leaders in the sense of taking the faculties in a particular direction. Rather, they perceived themselves as managers. Paraphrasing the response of one particular dean reflects the opinion of most of those interviewed. He was quite emphatic that deans should not provide academic or instructional leadership. This, he argued, was counter to the ideals of a university faculty. Faculty members were the experts who should provide the leadership. When he left his dean's position and resumed the role of a faculty member he did not wish to have anyone attempting to lead him. Those deans who did see themselves offering leadership indicated that the way they would do it would be to encourage initiatives that they saw as important.

INFLUENCE STRUCTURES: INTERNAL AND EXTERNAL

In the earlier discussion of context, reference was made to Howsam's (1977) conceptual framework for analysing the collaborate efforts of governance. The potential influence of three external groups were noted. The perceptions that faculty members have of these groups and how well they communicate with them reflects the character of faculties of education as organisations. In both the Canadian and IMTEC studies, faculty members were asked about factors influencing them as individuals and about factors influencing programmes and goals.

The data provided in Table 7 is based on faculty perceptions of the internal influences on the instructional programme. It can be seen that, in practice, faculty committees and administrators are perceived to be the most influential, followed by faculty members themselves. Students are perceived to have the least influence on the instructional programme. The internal influence structure therefore suggests something of a hierarchy within the organisation in which administrators who manage faculty committees are seen to exert

Table 7

PERCEPTIONS BY FACULTY OF INFLUENCE ON INSTRUCTIONAL PROGRAMME

Question
The following items relate to influences on the instructional programme by groups internal to the faculty. Please indicate what influence the following individuals or groups have (real) and ought to have (ideal)

- Faculty committees or councils in the faculty
- Administrators in the faculty
- Faculty members
- Student council/government or other formal student groups in the faculty
- Students in general

Response

None   Little   Very Great
  1   2   3   4   5

——— Real
- - - Ideal

Table 8

INFLUENCE OF EXTERNAL GROUPS AS SEEN FROM TWO PERSPECTIVES

Question

To what extent should goals and practice
be consistent with these groups?
(———)

How important are these groups on your daily work?
(— — — —)

Response

No importance 1 2 3
Very important 4 5

- Ministry of education
- University community
- Local school board
- Teachers
- Students

most influence on the programme. Students at the lower end of the hierarchy are perceived to lack influence.

Questions regarding external influence were asked in both the Canadian and IMTEC studies, but in somewhat different ways. Those in the Canadian institutions were asked the extent to which goals and practices are, and should be, consistent with various groups. The results are represented in Table 8 by a solid line. It can be seen that a fairly reasonable balance of influences exists among the university, the schools, districts, and central authorities (the three categories identified by Howsam). In contrast to what we saw in Table 7, however, students appear much more influential.

The same external influence groups were presented to those in the IMTEC study, but the question asked was somewhat different. In this case, faculty members were asked the extent to which these groups influenced their daily work. The results are represented in Table 8 by a broken line. Here a very different picture emerges. It can be seen that students now represent the most important influence, while other groups rank behind.

Thus, when the influence is on programme, then students rank low in influence; when the influence is upon faculty members themselves, then students rank as high in influence.

The role played by the central administration of the university appears to offer a conundrum for faculty members. As we have seen, they perceive the central administration as being a most influential factor, both upon themselves and on the programme. Yet, when asked to identify those groups with whom they had most difficulty in communicating, they identified the central administration of the university. When asked to identify key issues in their faculty, a surprising number identified a lack of respect and credibility within the university community. These data point to a type of 'inferiority complex' possessed by many within faculties of education in repect to the rest of the university.

SUMMARY AND CONCLUSIONS

The argument proposed at the opening of this chapter was that faculties of education must become more adaptable if they are to adequately provide for their students and, indeed, if they are to survive as institutions. How well, given the characteristics discussed, do they appear to be structured to respond to such a challenge?

The data on which this chapter is based indicated that goals in faculties of education are vague, poorly defined, and diffuse (different people hold varying opinions about what goals ought to be). Perhaps it should not be surprising, therefore, that the goals that are in practice being achieved support the status quo in education. The conceptualisations that might support alternatives and, thereby, changes are not well defined.

The goals of faculties of education as represented in these findings do not well equip them for change. New approaches to the training of teachers are unlikely to arise in organisations where goals are vague, poorly defined, and diffuse. In the absence of conceptualisations to mobilise collaborative thrusts, the efforts of individuals tend to cancel each other out. Consequently, faculties of education tend to prepare teachers for schools as they currently exist. Certainly, many would argue that this is precisely what they ought to do. That is not, however, the role that faculty members wish their institutions to play nor is it likely to lead to reform.

We saw that faculties of education (at least those examined in the two studies) are primarily instructional institutions. The time to reflect and to research new models of teacher preparation is unlikely to occur in faculties of education in which little time is spent on research. Further, this limited amount of time being devoted to research does not fulfil the charge given to faculties of education when they became part of the university structure. Instruction, the most prevalent activity, is of a very traditional nature involving mostly a lecture approach. Such a pattern of instruction is unlikely to lead to alternative approaches to teaching which break the induction cycle through which the young become teachers. Again, as was the case with goals, this is not the ideal situation for the majority of faculty members.

Thus, in terms of the goals and instruction being achieved, faculties appear poorly equipped to change or to deal with that process. What is curious, and perhaps optimistic, is the fact that neither the types of goals being achieved, nor the instruction being carried out, are perceived as ideal by faculty or students.

The stability of faculties of education is supported by the type of reward structures that faculty members are likely to respond to. One's own 'sense of achievement' (which was rated highest) can mean different things to different people. Organisations wishing to take certain courses of action cannot, therefore, use rewards as a means to that end.

The climate of the institutions examined in the two studies was seen on an individual basis to be very positive; it was, however, seen as quite negative when collaborative efforts were involved. In short, people felt good about themselves, but very suspicious about groups. Such a climate is unlikely to produce the type of collaborative efforts required to initiate and sustain the change that is required for major reform in teacher education. However it does not exclude individual innovation.

Those in leadership positions are managers of procedure but non-commital with regard to programmatic leadership. Their role is typically that of negotiation and the balancing of competing interests in a faculty.

Thus, the character of faculties of education is such that it supports individualistic initiatives but not collaborative efforts. Put in practice, many of these are oriented toward the status quo. Positive change in faculties of education is unlikely to occur at the institutional level without enormous expenditures of time, money and effort, simply because so many factors augur against it. If faculties of education are to respond to the many environmental pressures, this is likely to be through the efforts of individuals or small groups. However, as such initiatives begin to impact upon the institutional structures, then these too will fall the victim of institutional pressures which frustrate reform. Institutions, and the leaders within them, must learn to provide and shelter the conditions necessary for such initiatives to grow. Indeed, if some teacher training institutions survive while others do not, the survivors are likely to be those who meet this challenge.

The themes running through this chapter point to an educational institution equipped to preserve the status quo rather than one able to produce innovation. The lack of focus augurs for stability in a very subtle and persistent way. While innovations may emerge, their individualistic nature tend to cancel out and nullify such ideas. A result is that there may appear to be change when, in fact, there is no change. With the primary activity revolving around instruction, faculty members rarely step back to consider just how that task may be more effectively accomplished. The instruction itself is very traditional and not likely to lead to the development of new insights or new patterns for teaching. The climate also augurs against innovation and change because of its negative and suspicious nature. When one suspects one's neighbour, one is unlikely to hold out bold new ideas. One might expect some initiative from the leadership, but this is simply not the case. As we saw, leaders manage the details and activities of the faculty, they do not provide new programmatic thrusts. The negativeness of the climate, and the feelings of inadequacy that arise from the context in which faculty members find themselves (e.g. at the nexus between theory and practice) provide a potential stimulus for change – if for no other reason that it is bound to create dissonance.

One conclusion that might be drawn from this analysis is highly negative. Faculties are completely incapable of dealing with the changes which must come in the years ahead. We must not forget, however, that the move to the university has improved the quality of the people who occupy positions in our teacher training institutions. Also, the pressures for change are there – in fact they are enormous. Also, a number of innovative programmes have emerged in teacher education over the last several decades. The history of mankind has shown that periods of uncertainty are frequently among the most productive. Hopefuly, faculties of education can capitalise on this uncertainty.

Notes

1. This study which sampled all regions in Anglophone Canada was completed in 1983. A copy of the four volume report is available from the author of this chapter at a cost of $10.00 Canadian at this address: Faculty of Education, Simon Fraser University, Burnaby, B.C. V5A 1S6, Canada, or from the editors at the West Glamorgan Institute of Higher Education, Townhill Road, Swansea SA2 OUT, West Glamorgan, South Wales. Throughout this chapter this study will be referred to as the Canadian study.
2. IMTEC stands for International Movement Toward Educational Change, an internal network centrally located in Norway, Dr Per Dalin, director.

REFERENCES

Apple, M. (1972) 'Behaviorism and conservatism: The educational views in four of the "systems" models of teacher education', in B. Joyce & M. Weil. Perspectives for reform in teacher education, Englewood Cliffs, N.J.: Prentice Hall.

Baldridge, J.V. (ed.)(1971) Academic governance: Research on institutional politics and decision making, Berkeley, Ca: McCutcheon.

Bessai, F. and Edmonds, E. (1977) Student opinions of student teaching, Toronto, Ont.: Canadian Education Association.

Cushman, M.L. (1977) The Governance of Teacher Education, Berkeley, Ca: McCutcheon.

Flanders, T. (1980) The professional development of teachers, (A summary report for the Professional Development Division) Vancouver: British Columbian Teacher Federation.

Ford, B. (1975) 'Universities and teachers colleges: A study of changing relationships in some European countries', in Institutions Responsible for Teacher Training, Paris: Organisation for Economic Co-Operation and Development.

Gwyn, R. (1976) Current Trends in Teacher Education, Strasbourg: Council for Cultural Co-operation, Committee for Higher Educational Research.

Hoetker, J. and Ahlbrand, W.P. Sr. (1969) 'The persistence of recitation', American Educational Research Journal, 6, 145-167.

Howsam, R.B. (1977) 'A conceptual framework for analysis of

collaborative efforts in governance', in M.L. Cushman The Governance of Teacher Education, Berkeley, Ca: McCutcheon.

Myers, D. and Saul, D. (1974) 'How not to reform a teacher education system', in D. Myers and F. Reid (eds) Educating Teachers: Critiques and Proposals, Toronto: OISE, Symposium Series £4.

McLeish, J.A.B. (1971) 'Teacher Education for the seventies', Teacher Education, 4, 76–84.

Peterson, G.K. (1974) 'The case for reform in teacher education', Teacher Education, 7, 3–16.

Sarasan, S.B. (1971) The Culture of the School and the Problem of Change, Boston: Allyn and Bacon.

Unruh, W. (1981) Evaluation of the Faculty of Education, (Evaluation Report 1978–1981), Faculty of Education, University of Calgary.

Woodring, P. (1975) 'The development of teacher education', in K. Ryan (ed.) Teacher Education (74NSSE Yearbook), Chicago: National Society for Studies in Education, 1–24.

Chapter Seven

DRIFT AND THE PROBLEM OF CHANGE IN CANADIAN TEACHER EDUCATION

David Hopkins

Change in educational systems is a highly complex yet little
understood phenomenon. This is particularly true in teacher
training institutions (TTIs), which appear especially
resilient and unamenable to change. Contemporary attempts to
conceptualise educational change have generally failed to take
account of the culture within which educational institutions
are embedded, and within which their members act. This myopia
has resulted in models and characterisations of change that
bear little relationship to empirical reality. Consequently,
there is a need for theories of educational change which take
into account the environments in which change takes place, and
which also reflect the involvement of those implicated in the
change process itself. In short, there is a need for theories
of change which are applicable to and within educational
scenarios. First, this chapter presents a naturalistic
analysis of Canadian TTIs, which had as its impetus an attempt
to understand and analyse the reasons why change is so
problematic in those institutions. Second, from this analytic
description, a 'grounded theory' of 'drift' as change in
teacher education is proposed.

A Note on Methodology
This chapter is based on data gathered during a research
project which explored the management of change in Canadian
teacher education. The sample for this funded project was a
representative sample of ten anglophone Canadian TTIs. During
the course of the project (which was mainly concerned with
gathering information on the organisational functioning of
TTIs and in assessing the impact of an organisation
development intervention), data was also collected on the
change process in, and ecology of, contemporary Canadian
teacher education. These data were derived from three sources:
extant documentation, interviews and participant observation.
The data was collected from each institution in the sample.
    Because of its essentially qualitative nature, I have
woven the data into an argument about the nature of change in

teacher education. This is somewhat different from the
traditional approach to research, where an hypothesis is
stated, data gathered, and conclusions drawn. Here the data is
used to generate hypotheses rather than test them, but this
does not imply that the methodology is any the less rigorous
than that of the normative paradigm. Researchers adopting a
more ethnographic approach to educational research have had
their canons laid down by Becker (1958), Glaser and Strauss
(1967) and Hamilton et al (1977), rather than Campbell and
Stanley (1963). The important point is that the standards of
validity and reliability which are expected are the same
whether the data be quantitative or qualitative.

Following the conventions established by Becker (1958)
the data was searched for categories, and when these were
established they were tested against the data. When there was
sufficient evidence to saturate a category it became a working
hypothesis, which was eventually woven into the narrative. The
evidence that supports the argument is presented in this way:
first an hypothesis is outlined and discussed; examples from
the data are then given to support the contention and 'flesh
out' detail. The data was initially coded - each quotation
used in the text has a code number which relates it to the
mass of material from which it is derived. For ease of
exposition, the code numbers have been omitted in this paper
and some of the quotations summarised. The chapter then
presents a series of hypotheses about the nature of change in
teacher education which are based on categories derived from
the data.

THE IMPLEMENTATION PROCESS IN TEACHER EDUCATION

There was a plethora of apparent change in Canadian teacher
education during the 1970s. The transfer of the teacher
training function from colleges to universities was completed,
and fundamental programme change occurred in virtually every
institution e.g. the introduction of the extended practicum
(see chapter 8). Declining enrolments and budgetary restraints
necessitated changes of a different kind. Despite this
catalogue, little appears to have changed in the behaviour of
those closest to the innovations. Schools, teachers, students
and professors carry on in much the same way as they did ten
years ago and the same concerns are raised about the
effectiveness of teacher education programmes. This paradox
can be explained by two themes that emerge from the literature
on educational change: that structural change is a function of
the power of external influences acting on TTIs, and that
little change in practice is testimony to the inability of
TTIs to react effectively to change (Hopkins 1984).

An example will illustrate this point. There were a
number of programme changes in TTIs which occurred as a result

of the introduction of the extended practicum. Most of these changes attempted to make programmes relate theory more appropriately to practice. The response in one TTI took the form of the introduction of block programming for on-campus courses. The idea was that groups of professors would work with groups of students on a regular basis instead of individually teaching half-courses or leading specific study groups. By teaching and collaborating with colleagues, and by being associated with the same group of students over an extended period, the intent was to engender a personalised form of education and to more effectively bridge the theory-practice gap. The change was approved, block programmes appeared on the timetable and professors and students were asigned to particular groups. After a period of dissonance and subsequent hiatus, however, professors returned to teaching as they had done previously (i.e. individually to discrete groups), yet the block programmes still appeared on the timetable and in the calendar.

This example supports the contention that structural change is not necessarily reflected in practice. This implies a delinquency in the process of implementation. Implementation is a topic which has recently received much attention (q.v. Berman and McLaughlin, 1976; Fullan and Pomfret, 1977; Fullan, 1982). When implementation is regarded as a process, rather than as an event, there is the realisation that structural change is only one component in a highly complex and dynamic situation. There are five components to the implementation process, viz: structure, materials, role and/or behaviour change, knowledge utilisation, and internalisation. Not only do structural alterations have to be made and accompanying materials produced, but the changes have also to be understood, roles and behaviours altered to complement the change and, finally, those involved in the change have to internalise it. What commonly occurs is that structure and materials are provided (sometimes also knowledge utilisation), but it is increasingly rare to find internalisation and role behaviour change catered for in implementation strategies. This is certainly the case in the example cited above.

There are a number of sets of reasons why change is difficult to institutionalise in teacher education: there are certain barriers or impediments to change; there are certain contemporary influences which may or may not continue to exist; and, because of these two groups of phenomena, certain cultural myths develop within institutions which serve to define their collective behaviour. These three complex and interrelated issues account for the inability of contemporary teacher education to be more effective at carrying through change.

BARRIERS TO CHANGE

From the data, a long list of barriers to change were identified (see Table 1). The conceptual scheme fits well into the typology suggested by the literature on change in higher education, with barriers existing at the systemic, organisational and individual levels (Baldridge, 1971; Lidquist, 1974). As the research progressed, it became obvious that a number of the barriers to change were perceived rather than actual or, if not perceived, were a reality that had little empirical support. This necessitated an extension to the scheme to include perceived barriers, which is reflected in the table. Many of the barriers listed in Table 1 correspond to those which one would have expected to find from a reading of the literature on educational organisations. As a result, only those barriers which have received little attention in the literature (numbered) are discussed below.

1. Autonomous pluralism
   The barrier refers to the norm that faculty members pursue their own interests without reference to the goals of the institution as a whole. Because of the resulting fragmentation within the faculty there is little knowledge about other people's attitudes and stances on various issues, which makes it difficult to build a consensus for change. One professor, for example, maintained that despite being in an institution for ten years he did not know the people who were innovative or would support change. He spoke to only a few colleagues and not to the other 90 or 100 faculty. This he perceived as being a major barrier to change.

2. Discontinuity of personnel
   The academic year is only fully functioning for some seven months of the year, and even during that time the ranks are depleted by sabbaticals. Consequently, it is often difficult for an individual to see a proposed change through the time frame normally required for its successful implementation. One interviewee highlighted the problem this way: 'Although policies get made they do not often get implemented because the people who implement the policies keep changing.'

3. Inertia
   This refers to a generalised resistance to change evidenced in the institutions sampled. It reflects an acceptance of the status quo because that condition offers the most comfortable life style, and the least dissonance. This thought was put starkly by one interviewee:

   Most people have etched out for themselves a fairly comfortable role in the college which allows them to

Table 1

BARRIERS TO CHANGE IN TEACHER EDUCATION

Systemic

Real barriers	Perceived barriers
- Economic factors	- Inertia
- Political pressure (government)	- Future uncertainty
- Vulnerability (environmental constraint)	
- Central university administration	- Bureaucratic myth
- Tradition	

Organisational

Real barriers	Perceived barriers
- Lack of clear mission (goal variability)	
- Incongruent reward system	- 'Top-down' approach to change
- Poor communication	
- Absence of linking structures (low interdependence)	
- Autonomous pluralism(1)	- Teachers' college legacy
- Complexity of decision making process	
- Inadequate implementation	- Recent history of change
- Discontinuity of personnel(2) (academic year, sabbaticals, retirement)	
- Inertia(3)	

Individual

Real barriers	Perceived barriers
- Poor leadership(4)	
- Tenure system	
- Pluralism of roles	- Emotional resistance to change
- Socialisation into a discipline(5)	- Too busy(6)
- Incompetence	- Tendency to externalise(7)
- Innovative fatigue	- Innovative fatigue

complain about the state of affairs which, in reality, is quite comfortable. Change may result in losing the comfortable niche which they have established for themselves.

One dean saw this inertia as the most important barrier to change:

> A real [barrier to change] is the general feeling by many individuals that once you take something and find that you are able to do it you do not want to change. Nobody likes to move from comfort to discomfort.

Inertia appears to be a very prevalent barrier to change and reference was made to it by interviewees in each institution during interviews or informal discussion.

4.   Leadership

The quality of leadership in faculties is often seen as a barrier to change – particularly by those not in administrative positions. In six of the institutions where data was collected, those interviewed pointed to ineffective or non-collaborative leadership as being a major barrier to change. Many of those interviewed felt that without clear leadership faculties tended to take on all sorts of activities and projects, without having a clear purpose.

5.   Socialisation into a discipline

There is a strong theoretical and empirical argument (e.g. Bernstein, 1971; Evans, 1968) which maintains that allegiance in higher education is vertical (i.e. to one's discipline) rather than horizontal (i.e. to the faculty). The academic socialisation process revolves around disciplines rather than institutions, and so provides a barrier to concerted action. This phenomenon was well displayed in the sample. One respondent maintained that: 'Allegiance is to a subject group, a discipline group, and to other groups outside the faculty, rather than across the institution.'

6.   Too busy

In conversation with individual faculty members, a common characteristic became very evident. Virtually everyone talked to or interviewed considered themselves as being busy. Whether this was true or merely perceived varied from individual to individual but, true or not, the norm tended to reinforce itself. Consequently, those interviewed tended to consider that they were too preoccupied with the day-to-day press of the work place to have much time to spend on planning, initiating or implementing change:

> One factor is time, it has become a status symbol to be busy, but it does not have to be productive. That norm

has a great deal to do with inhibiting change, because it means that people no longer sit back and ask any fundamental questions.

7. Tendency to externalise

The tendency to externalise – to blame others – contributes in some way to the inertia which is prevalent in teacher education. During interviews many faculty members convincingly 'explained away' the need for individual change, despite almost overwhelming evidence to the contrary. As one faculty member put it: 'I really do think we externalise in that we think that what happens to us is outside of our control.'

Although the list in Table 1 is much longer, this discussion has highlighted those barriers to change which have not received much attention elsewhere. These barriers (viz: autonomous pluralism, discontinuity of personnel, inertia, poor leadership, socialisation into a discipline, the norm of busyness, and the tendency to externalise) are, with the possible exception of inertia, the norm of busyness and the tendency to externalise, not exclusive to TTIs. Although they present a formidable catalogue of inhibitions to change, they also characterise many other departments and institutions of higher education. I wish to argue that TTIs have a specific pathology when it comes to the implementation of change. If these barriers reflect the situation in other organisations as well, it is important that the distinctive features of the contemporary situation in TTIs are articulated and analysed. This I hope to do in the following section.

THE ECOLOGY OF CONTEMPORARY TEACHER EDUCATION

A major problem with TTIs is that they have not satisfactorily come to terms with their new role. Although the move to universities has been completed in a physical or structural sense, there are still a number of unresolved tensions which hamper the functioning of TTIs. These tensions revolve around three major and interrelated issues: university norms, the role crisis of TTIs, and TTIs vulnerability to the environment.

1. University Norms

When the teachers' college moved onto the campus it became subject to the norms of the university. In particular, they become subject to the university's tenure and promotions criteria, which place almost exclusive emphasis on research and publication. It is well established that education professors are, in general, not prolific publishers (Guba and Clark, 1978). This immediately puts them at a disadvantage when compared with their colleagues in other departments and faculties. Similarly, the major funding agencies in Canada (e.g. Social Science and Humanities Research Council [SS and HRC]) tend not to support the type of research that large numbers of education professors could engage in. They tend to favour 'pure' research rather than 'action' research and, even less, developmental projects or applied curriculum research. The lack of research being carried out in faculties of education, and the dilletantism associated with what is done, reflects the sample as a whole.

The lack of emphasis on research has had two major outcomes in the institutions surveyed. First, because the teachers' college tended not to match the academic faculties in terms of the traditional criteria for promotion and tenure, they are regarded as the poor relation on campus – tolerated because they are 'family' but still not quite acceptable. Second, the existence of these norms has encouraged many education professors to forsake their traditional roles and tasks and concentrate on activities (allegiance such as pure research) that are somewhat tangential to the main purpose of teacher preparation.

2. Role Crisis

The role crisis in TTIs is fed by three influences, viz: plurality of roles, quasi-professionalism, and the teachers' college legacy.

The no-win situation created by the university norms is compounded by the plurality of roles that education professors have to fill – mention has already been made of their teaching, research, counselling, supervision and administrative load. The great majority of faculty members interviewed complained not only of the workload, but also of the diversity of roles they had to fulfil. They also maintained that this diversity inhibited the pursuit of excellence in any one field of endeavour. One dean put the dilemma this way: 'We have certain commitments to meet; there are students who have to be taught; and we have a prescribed programme that has to be offered. One cannot do other things without having met these requirements first'. Another compounding factor is the 'quasi-professionalism' (to use Sieber's 1975 term) of most education faculties. Although I have no hard data to support the contention, I suggest that the majority of faculty members in TTIs are still teachers' college staff. Although this claim does not necessarily call their competence into question, it means in practice that the traditionally high entry standards required of university professors are not always reflected in education faculties. This situation is unlikely to be remedied in the near future, because the majority of these people were granted tenure when the college moved to the university.

Besides inheriting the staff of teachers' colleges, the TTIs also took the teachers' college legacy with them into the universities. This point has been made to on several occasions, and it is a powerful influence in Canadian teacher education. The national character of the phenomenon was well caught by one interviewee: 'We are all in the same bind – survival: but typical of Canada, as opposed to the U.S.A., we are haunted by the normal school approach rather than the academic research orientation of the colleges in the States.' The following extract from field notes illustrates how powerful the legacy can be in the case of individual institutions:

Up until 1969 the dean was a joint appointment of the Ministry of Education and the University. This tells one a great deal about the orientation of the faculty. People I talked to felt that the administrators saw the faculty very much in terms of a school and the dean ran the faculty much as a principal would run a large school.

The compounding of these factors (viz: the plurality of roles in teacher education, its quasi-professional character, and the teachers' college legacy), engenders a sense of anomie and rootlessness in TTIs. There are a large number of role tensions which are keenly felt: they are of the university, yet not part of it. This dissonance appears to inversely affect their capacity to 'carve out' a unique role for themselves.

The difficulty in 'carving out' a unique role for the institution is well exemplified in two contrasting examples taken from the sample. In one institution, great emphasis had been placed, since the reforms of the early 1970s, on the practical nature of their teacher education programme. A vocal, energetic and persuasive minority of faculty members proposed a model of field based teacher education. Because this approach lies outside the norms of traditional university departments, the group conflicted with the central university administration. There was no formal conflict, but their advocacy of a field based role for themselves led to innumerable frustrations – particularly in terms of funding, promotions, tenure, and the general status of the faculty. This conflict is so pervasive that a number of the group, particularly those in senior administrative positions in the faculty, regret the move of the college to the university. They desire a return to their previous situation where they could exercise their professional autonomy without recourse to the criteria imposed upon them by a central university administration.

The second example is that of a department of education in an old established university. This faculty consciously regards education as an academic discipline rather than a profession. They purposefully teach about education, at the expense of preparing student teachers in methods and teaching skills. Field experiences are minimal and, on occasion, even these opportunities are used to illustrate theories about education, rather than to demonstrate and refine teaching skills. In this way the department is seen to be conforming to the norms of a traditional academic role, and a number of faculty members have international academic reputations. Because they do this, however, the department has lost favour with the local school board, the ministry of education and the teachers' federation. Even worse, their enrolment has drastically reduced, which now seriously affects their position within the university.

These two cameos represent the extremes of the sample, and well illustrate the 'double-bind' in which TTIs now find themselves. There is another characteristic response to this predicament found within the sample, and it takes two forms. The most common is to separate the teacher education function from the study of education as a discipline. In some faculties, persons (usually practising teachers) are brought in on a temporary basis to supervise and instruct trainee teachers. This allows faculty members to teach theory courses and supervise graduate students. In the other situation, some faculty members (usually the teachers' college personnel) are permanently assigned supervisory tasks, while others (the more 'academic' faculty members) teach only theory courses.

In each of these three instances there is a dichotomy betweeen the theoretical and practical aspects of teacher education. Many regard the lack of integration between theory and practice as the most critical problem facing teacher education. This analysis unfortunately suggests that it occurs as the result of entrenched structural factors not readily amenable to change.

3. Vulnerability to the environment

It could be argued that Canadian teacher education is in its present state because the move to the university was a major innovation; that it takes time to institutionalise; and that, given experience, the situation will right itself. Be this as it may, the luxury of time is not available. A consistent theme emerging from interviews and observations is the vulnerability of teacher education. The reasons behind this (declining enrolments, increased accountability, budgetary restraints, and acceleration in the pace of social change) are well known and have been discussed elsewhere. The impact of this vulnerability has served to heighten the feeling of anomie experienced by many TTIs in the sample. Declining enrolments have occasioned reduction in staffing and heavier workloads, and in eastern Canada some TTIs have even been closed. In all institutions expansion is a thing of the past and a static professional population is now the norm.

The majority of the interviewees specifically talked about the political, economic, and social vulnerability of their institution. They also expressed concern about what this meant for their future, and the future of teacher education in general. All saw little mobility in the job market; most saw increasingly little room for flexibility in their roles.

Not only has there been contraction, but increased pressure for change. The inability of most TTIs to cope with demands has produced a malaise and a condition of 'innovative fatigue'. It is not an exaggeration to describe many of the institutions in the sample as being 'tenured in and changed out'. Referring to his own faculty, one dean commented:

> We have been engaged in substantial programme change for three and a half years. We still have another year or so to complete the overall revision of our programmes and I think that people are (1) tired and (2) extremely busy – there is a feeling of 'Oh my God... I have got too much on my plate already, I am involved in all these programme revision committees and I just can't take any more of this'.

This section has analysed a number of factors which are defining the present character of Canadian teacher education. The move to the university, the role crisis in TTIs and their vulnerability to their environment, have created a situation where there is a general ambivalence and uncertainty as to their prime function. This uncertainty in its turn has led to a generalised reduction in effectiveness of many of the TTIs surveyed in the study. Despite this assessment, however, some institutions were functioning admirably; others, less so. What accounts for these individual differences, and what is their character, is the topic of the next section.

IMAGES, MYTHS AND SAGAS

The specification of the barriers to change, and the defining features of contemporary Canadian teacher education, are supported by the data. But they do not explain the individual variability which exists in the sample. Clark's (1975) concept of 'saga', a cultural artefact that defines the character of an institution, may be useful here. His definition of saga includes the lengthy historical development which one associates with certain Ivy League institutions and Oxbridge, and this tends to limit the utility of the concept. When it is applied in conjunction with the concept of 'images of change' (Runkel et al., 1979), it may, however, be able to explain the analytical similarity and practical differences existing in TTIs.

DRIFT AND THE PROBLEM OF CHANGE

Over the past 10 to 15 years there has been a continuing pressure for change in TTIs - which has been resisted. This resistance, coupled with the enervating experience of change that has occurred in most institutions, has resulted in a cumulative perceived resistance moderated through the unique character of each institution. The perceived cumulative resistance manifests itself in a 'quasi-institutional' saga which creates a set of meanings owned by many faculty members. The saga comprises the single most powerful and sustaining barrier against change in TTIs. The concept of saga provides a satisfactory way of explaining the gap between the technical capacity of an institution to change (despite all the real barriers that have been articulated) and its emotional capacity to change which is, of course, the determining factor.

I suggest that all institutions possess such a saga: a collection of perceptions which has grown out of the dynamic between the pressure for and resistance against change. Obviously, the power of these sagas to inhibit change varies across institutions, as a result of each institution's own unique character and its unique interaction with the environment. In creating a taxonomy of these sagas within the sample it was found that they fell into five fairly discrete and evenly distributed categories:

1. The state of institutional retrenchment is one where there has been continued and prolonged pressure for change which has (for whatever reason) been largely resisted. The promise of change, followed by a lack of implementation, has resulted in a disillusionment so pervasive that it is no longer a matter for contention. The result is an institution where faculty members are rarely concerned about change, are content to fulfil their normal duties and have little contact with faculty members other than their immediate peers. This saga is so entrenched that it is difficult to see how the institutions concerned can remedy the situation. This is especially true if they are very large, well established institutions, with a preponderance of tenured faculty members. I regard this particular saga as the most entrenched and least open to change of all those presented here.

An appreciation of what this saga entails can be gauged from this quotation:

> I detect this feeling throughout the place and what we have now is really good. Let us hang in there and not change anything. We have been like this for 50 years or however long the place has been running and let us not mess around with it.

2. Paralysed into inaction describes a situation where a faculty is simply overwhelmed by the external forces acting

118

upon it and feels powerless to do anything in reply. As a result, faculty members do nothing until action is forced upon them. This is potentially more serious than institutional retrenchment where programmes continue, students graduate, and funding continues much as it always has. Institutions who are 'paralysed into inaction', however, are in a state of crisis. They have been subject to extreme criticism by external agencies and, as a result, have lost their credibility within and outside the university. This tends to disrupt normal operation, and forces the administration of the faculty into extreme action - which is usually regarded negatively by the faculty at large. Given the volatility of the situation, this particular predicament, although more serious, is probably easier to remedy than is institutional retrenchment.

An appreciation of the situation of TTIs caught in this saga is captured in the following interview extract:

> We are going through a time of uncertainty here. We are losing professors; fighting to keep some; fighting to get more; our chairmanship is in the process of changing over and we do not know who the chairman is going to be; the President of the University and the Dean of Arts are changing so we do not know who we will be dealing with and we do not know how they are going to regard us; ... our enrolment decline is 40% in the undergraduate programme this year, and that also has been a topic of concern among faculty members.

3. Innovative fatigue and suspicion describes a state which may well precede the one just described. The dialogue with change has been long, arduous and not consistently successful. Much of the impetus to change has come from sources other than the grass roots and, as a result, has engendered a sense of weary cynicism which faculty members now associate with change efforts. This attitude is probably the most destructive and negative of the five, for a faculty in the grip of this saga will treat even rational and well-meaning attempts at change with a suspicion and hostility that they do not warrant. The differences between this saga and the other two previously discussed are that it is a conscious situation (faculty members realize that they are weary and suspicious) and is not the result of external criticism (It appears to be the result of a history of poor change management within the faculty.). As with the previous saga, the pathology is not so extensive that it could not be changed by concerted action.

The following verbatim quotation from a conversation with a faculty member captures the essence of this saga:

> We have had a tradition of establishing committees to study a particular topic and then shelving the reports; it is a technique of handling people who want to bring

119

about change. This approach has produced a climate of
mistrust and people consequently feel alienated and
powerless.

4. Institutions whose development is slowed by 'myth' present
a mild form of inhibition. Here the recent history of the
faculty has had a relatively benign influence which, although
partially anachronistic in the contemporary situation, still
guides its present direction. The benign influence of the
recent past creates a myth of a 'glory' which still guides the
traditions and mores of the faculty. It is difficult to
persuade faculty members to relinquish a comfortable and
comforting status quo for an uncertain future.
　　Institutions living within this saga are usually regarded
as successful; particularly if they are either large or small,
not moderate in size. If large, the saga provides a buffer
which protects the institution from external criticism and
allows individual departments to pursue their own policies.
The fact that the saga is in place protects the institution.
In small faculties, the myth is pervasive and, as most faculty
members adhere to it, it normally exerts a benign influence.
In medium-sized institutions, however, the saga can have a
negative influence. This is because departments of moderately-
sized institutions may have differing interpretations of the
saga which, although not powerful enough to unite the faculty,
are pervasive enough to cause dissonance.
　　In general, this saga gives faculty members an identity
and self confidence which enables them to react effectively to
external pressure. A faculty member described it in this way:

> Change comes from pressures from various sources in
> response to perceived needs. I think that we have
> responded pretty well and reasonably intelligently to
> demands on the part of the school boards, trustees,
> public, and supposedly the students, that we develop more
> in-the-field competence in our training programme.

5. An institution that is relatively free to change is one
which is uninhibited by myth but is still constrained by the
organisational barriers and ecological constraints described
earlier. They are typically small, well integrated faculties,
with good relations with the field. They are aware of their
limitations and are 'businesslike' in their approach to their
everyday tasks and possible future directions. This 'down-to-
earth' attitude appears to be most conductive to change. The
characteristics most clearly associated with the institution
in this category were: open leadership; good relations with
the field; good internal communication; good integration into
the university; relatively small; an ability to diagnose; and
an ability to mobilise resources. An institution with this
saga is well able to implement change, and least displays the

pathological symptoms usually associated with change in teacher education.

A professor in an institution characterised by this saga described it thus:

> I think that we are a reasonably cohesive group of people, and we also have some very good teachers on staff. Consequently we are well accepted by the community of teachers around. We have credibility in the community and schools as the result of public relations work and our concern for education.

So far, a series of conceptual categories that provide an explanation for the paradox of 'change and no change' in Canadian teacher education have been described in some detail. The paradox of change and no change was resolved by pointing to delinquencies in the process of implementation. 'Implementation' is a multidimensional concept. Consequently, when change at the level of structure is not matched by changes in the behaviour of individuals associated with the innovation, there is the appearance (but not the reality) of change. Reasons for this lack of internalisation were sought at a number of levels. First, barriers to change in teacher education, both real and apparent, were described. Second, three major and interrelated issues (university norms, the role crisis in TTIs and vulnerability) were depicted as inhibitors to change. Third, individual differences between institutions were explained with the use of the concept of saga, which is a collection of perceptions that acculturate and partially control the milieu of TTIs. When taken together, these conceptual categories suggest a typology of change in teacher education that is non-linear and essentially unpredictable.

CONCEPTIONS OF CHANGE IN HIGHER EDUCATION

In his paper Organisational Change in Schools of Education, Giacquinta (1979) outlines three predominant conceptions of change which apply to TTIs. These are: the research, development and diffusion of innovations (R.D. and D.) model; the organisational self renewal model; and the organisational drift model.

The R.D. and D. model reflects an instrumental orientation to change which, at the behest of some authority figure, focuses on the adoption of 'packages' of ideas. This approach is most commonly associated with 'top-down' strategies of change e.g. the 'research, development and diffusion' model (Guba and Clark, 1965); the 'social interaction and diffusion' model (Rogers and Shoemaker, 1971); and the 'linkage' model (Havelock, 1973). These models reflect a linear approach to change, and tend to disregard the variables existing within the receiving environment.

'Organisation self renewal' is a generic label for a number of strategies which involve a self-learning and/or problem solving component. Most often, these strategies employ the services of an outside consultant in conjunction with internal change agents. Examples of this approach are, Argyris' (1970) 'intervention theory and method' approach; Lippitt et al's (1958, 1978) 'planned change' model; the research of Berman and McLaughlin (1975-1978), Emrick and Peterson (1978), Fullan, Miles and Taylor (1980); and the writings of Schmuck and Runkel (e.g. Schmuck et al, 1977 and Runkel et al, 1979). These models of change appreciate the environment in which they intervene, and their implementation demonstrates a concern for developing a capacity for change within the client system, rather than the adoption per se of a specific approach.

Giacquinta's third conception of change is 'organisational drift'. Giacquinta's (1979) sparse description of drift is a hypothetico-deductive construct which he describes in this way:

> Change occurs as a result of impersonal, non-deliberate change forces or conditions located in the environment of an organisation. These conditions impinge on an organisation in such a way that alterations in organisational goals happen, for the most part, haphazardly. In other words, this conception portrays an organisations's structure, at any point in time, as a function of pressing environmental forces.

Apart from Giacquinta's original mention of the concept, few (if any) studies have dealt with drift. This chapter, a short paper (Hopkins 1982) and the work from which they emanate (Hopkins 1980) are (to my knowledge) the only attempts to elucidate and apply the drift concept of educational change. My contention is that the problem of change is best understood through a notion of change that utilises drift as its central organising concept, rather than through the more traditional approaches.

DRIFT AND INSTITUTIONAL CHANGE

The paradox of change and no change in Canadian teacher education was earlier explained by the failure of implementation (the ability to change at the level of structure but not at the level of practice is a major aspect of drift). Change occurs as a result of sustained external pressure, but its result is essentially unpredictable because of the nature of the institutions concerned. There is no doubt that change occurs in TTIs, but when it does there is a considerable time lag between its initiation and institutionalisation. During this delay the intent of the change is often distorted. To summarise: there is an initial external impetus for change; when it is strong and persistent enough the change is reflected in some structural alterations, but rarely in the behaviours and commitment of those affected by the change; if the impetus for change can withstand this lack of internalisation and behaviour change then, over a period of time, the change becomes assimilated into the culture of the institution and it becomes an artefact which begins to condition the behaviour of the actors involved; it is a long enervating process which usually involves the breaking down of perceived barriers to change, and the gradual engendering of commitment towards it.

One example of this process stands out. The mid 1970s witnessed strong demands for a more practical teacher education programme. Most TTIs instituted an extended practicum, and some went further to initiate programme change (usually when forceful members of faculty, typically young new faculty members or those from non-academic backgrounds, pursued the innovation within the TTI). This was the case here. The change was resisted by a majority of faculty members for a number of years, until the pressure for this particular change became part of the institution's culture. With the realisation that the change would not go away, the faculty members who were previously opposed to the innovation decided to take part in the programme changes, to work with them, and to adapt these changes to match their own aspirations.

There appears to be a critical point in the process where change is accepted as an inevitability and so the line of least resistance is to go with it. This is the essence of the drift conception: if there is enough external pressure then real change will occur. This change will not be systematic but, rather, will be a reflection of the particular patterns of aspirations existing within the institution.

A THEORY OF DRIFT AS CHANGE IN TEACHER EDUCATION

The argument so far has been that traditional approaches to change in teacher education (viz: the R. D. and D. model and the organisation renewal model) are inconsistent with the reality of change. In the previous section it was proposed that the concept of drift provides a more satisfactorily explanation of the process of change in teacher education. Drift as a substantive theory of change in teacher education embodies the following principles:

1. Change in teacher training institutions occurs as a result of sustained external pressure.

2. The pressure is resisted by TTIs because of the organisational pathology (contextual variables); barriers to change which exist within the institution; the TTIs' uncertainty as to the contemporary situation; and, sometimes, because the change is pushing the 'wrong' way.
3. When the pressure of change is strong and persistent enough to be sustained over a period of time, it becomes assimilated into the culture of the organisation. Since the culture conditions the behaviour of organisation members, there results (on the part of institution members) a gradual commitment towards the change. This commitment is conditioned by the influence of the saga that acculturates the institution.
4. This commitment eventually results in the institutionalisation of the change. Because the change has been assimilated gradually its character is essentially unpredictable.

On what grounds is this claim to theory made? It is substantive because (at the present time) it applies only to teacher education, and grounded because it has been generated from the phenomena to which it applies. There are however, other criteria that have to be met.

In The Discovery of Grounded Theory, Glaser and Strauss (1967) outline the criteria upon which such a claim to theory must be based:

> The practical application of grounded sociological theory, whether substantive or formal, requires developing a theory with (at least) four highly interrelated properties. The first requisite property is that the theory must closely fit the substantive area in which it will be used. Second, it must be readily understandable by laymen concerned with this area. Third, it must be sufficiently general to be applicable to a multitude of diverse daily situations within the substantive area, not to just a specific type of situation. Fourth, it must allow the user partial control over the structure and process of daily situations as they change through time.

It is instructive to assess how well this substantive theory matches the criteria outlined by Glaser and Strauss. The criterion of 'fitness' reflects the congruence of a theory to the data from which it was generated. This is often difficult for the reader to assess without recourse to the field notes and an understanding of the machinations of the author's mind. The methodology, however, if employed correctly (Hopkins 1980) will ensure a degree of congruence.

The criterion of 'understanding' implies that a theory will make sense to people working in the substantive area – in this case teacher education. Does the theory of drift appear plausible to the reader? As long as it does, then this criterion will have been met, irrespective of whether it is eventually proven to be right. This is because the theory will have provided a new framework within which readers may refine and develop their own hypotheses.

The criterion of 'generality' implies that a theory is flexible enough to be applied to a wide variety of situations. Reference has already been made to a number of examples of recent events in Canadian teacher education. The example of the planned introduction of the extended practicum that only marginally affected the day to day life of schools students and professors, and the example of an institution where a small group of faculty members pressed for a change that was resisted until the pressure itself became institutionalised and the change occurred in a somewhat altered form, are both good examples of drift. They illustrate the incremental nature of change in teacher education; the internal resistance to change; and the inevitable, but unpredictable, nature of change when the pressure has been persistent and sustained over time.

The vexed problem of 'theory versus practice' is another example of the way in which drift helps illuminate contemporary issues in teacher education. In the SS and HRC project referred to throughout this chapter, data was collected on the goals of Canadian teacher education. The goal of preparing teachers to effectively integrate theory and practice was ranked the lowest but one in importance by the aggregate sample (The only goal ranked lower was 'to prepare teachers who have the perceptions and skills to implement changes in the schools'!). Yet, when asked an open-ended question, 'What are the foremost issues facing Canadian teacher education faculties today?' the majority of responses centered around the integration of theory and practice! One could speculate at length about the significance of this paradox. The data, however, suggests that faculties members realise that the integration of theory and practice is something not well done, yet important to do well. They feel, however, that they lack the ability to do anything about this problem. Their inability to tackle such a major problem is consistent with the theory of drift, for at least two reasons. First, the demand for resolution of the problem is not yet sufficiently strong to affect current practice. Second, the responses to the theory versus practice problem that have emerged reflect institutional style, rather than a rational attempt to consider the substance and complexity of the problem.

The notion of institutional style is also highly pertinent to the concept of drift. Earlier, I suggested that perceived cumulative resistance to change (which is an aspect of drift) manifests itself in a quasi-institutional saga which creates a set of meanings characteristic of the institution. The power of these sagas to condition change varies from institution to institution as a result of the institution's unique character and its interaction with the environment. This notion helps us understand why the pressure for change may result in different outcomes in different institutions.

The criterion of 'control' refers to the ability of a theory to assist decision makers in understanding the process of change in teacher education, and in planning and introducing change. Let me now examine the issues.

The major claim made for drift is that it is a substantive theory i.e. that it emerges from the data to which it pertains. In other words, the theory is grounded in the substance of teacher education. Because of this, drift as a theory of change has a great deal more power than conventional theories in explaining to practitioners why certain events occur as they do. A dean, for example, who is trying to understand why an initiative to introduce block-programming in a teacher education program has failed to 'take root', is likely to become very confused if he/she attempts to interpret events in the light of a R.D. and D. model of change. If, however, he/she is familiar with the assumptions of the drift theory, then what initially appeared confusing becomes more intelligible - the dean realises that the outcomes of 'top-down' change efforts are usually unpredictable and incremental. This knowledge empowers the dean, and is one aspect of gaining control over the change situation.

The second aspect involves the planning and introduction of change. Although a detailed methodology of a drift change process has yet to be worked out, certain guidelines are fairly obvious. First, existing change strategies (e.g. R.D. and D. and organisation renewal) are not comprehensive enough in their concept of change. Second, the ecology both within and without an institution needs to be considered. Third, when change does occur it is likely to be incremental and unpredictable, insofar as it faithfully resembles the planner's original intent. Given this, change efforts conceptualised within a theory of drift should be based on a system of participatory democracy, be sensitive to environmental and ecological factors, avoid being too specific about product outcomes, and should concentrate more on the process of change. Such an approach, it is suggested in the literature (e.g. Runkel et al, 1979), would enhance an institution's capacity for problem solving and thus make it more responsive to change initiatives.

It is in ways such as this that drift as a substantive theory of change has utility and pertinence for teacher educators, and for those interested in organisational structure, theory and change. It is, however, an essentially fluid concept. This is theory in process – the analysis has utility only if it is used and refined, for grounded theory is applicable in situations as well as to them. In this way, the concept of drift explains the problem of change in teacher education and, further, points to ways of resolving it.

SUMMARY

Drift is the name given to a substantive theory of organisational change in teacher education. It is predicated on the interaction between the environmental impetus for change, and the internal constraints inhibiting change. When the pressure for change is sustained over a period of time, and is moderated through the saga of the institution, the resulting pattern of change is essentially unpredictable. The theory of organisational drift was derived from a sociological analysis of ten Canadian teacher training institutions over a two year period. As such, the theory is grounded in, and is consistent with, the political and ecological environments in which teacher education occurs. As a substantive theory of change, drift has the power to resolve, analyze, explain and predict aspects of the process of change in teacher education.

This chapter is based on papers previously published in the Canadian Journal of Higher Education, 12 (2), 1982, 17-31, and the Higher Education Review, 16 (2), 1984, 51-60. Permission to reprint is gratefully acknowledged.

REFERENCES

Argyris, C.A. (1970) Intervention theory and method, Reading, Mass: Addison-Wesley.

Baldrige, J.W. (1971) Power and conflict in the university, New York: John Wiley.

Becker, H.A. (1958) 'Problems of inference and proof in participant observation', American Sociological Review, 28, 652-660.

Berman, P., and McLaughlin, M.W. (1976) 'Implementation of educational innovation', The Educational Forum, 40, 345-370.

Berman, P., and McLaughlin, M.W. (1975-78) Federal programs supporting educational change (8 vols), Santa Monica, Ca: Rand Corporation.

Bernstein, B. (1971) 'On the classification and framing of educational knowledge' in M.F.D. Yound (ed.), Knowledge and control, London: Collier Macmillan.

Campbell, D.T. and Stanley, J.C. (1963) 'Experimental and

quasi-experimental designs for research on teaching' in
N.L. Gage (ed.), Handbook of Research on Teaching,
Chicago: Rand McNally.

Clark, B.R. (1975) 'The organizational saga in higher
education' in J.V. Baldridge and T.E. Deal (eds),
Managing change in educational organization, Berkeley,
Ca: McCutchan.

Emrick, J.A., and Peterson S.M. (1978) 'A Synthesis of
findings across five recent studies in educational
dissemination and change' (rev. ed.) Educational
knowledge dissemination and utilization, Occasional Paper
Series. The National Institute of Education. San
Francisco: Far West Laboratory.

Evans, R.I. (1968) Resistance to innovation in higher
education, San Francisco: Jossey-Bass.

Fullan, M. (1982) The Meaning of Educational Change,
Toronto: Oise Press.

Fullan, M. and Pomfret, A. (1977) 'Research on curriculum
and instruction implementation', Review of Educational
Research, 47 (1), 335-397.

Fullan, M., Miles, M.B. and Taylor, G. (1980) 'Organization
development in schools: The state of the art', Review of
Educational Research, 50 (1), 121-183.

Giacquinta, J.B. (1979) 'Organisational change in schools of
education: A review of several models and an agenda of
research' in D. Griffith, D. Griffith, and D. McCarty
(eds), The dilemma of the deanship, Interstate.

Glaser, B.C., and Strauss, A.L. (1967) The discovery of
grounded theory. Chicago:

Guba, E.G., and Clark, D.L. (1965) 'An examination of
potential change roles in education' quoted in Strategies
for Educational Change, Newsletter No. 2, Columbus: Ohio
State University.

Guba, E.G., and Clark, D.L. (1978) 'Levels of R. and D.
productivity in schools of education. Educational
Researcher, 7 (5), 3-9.

Hamilton, D., MacDonald, B., King, C., Jenkins, D., and
Parlett, M. (eds) (1977) Beyond the numbers game.
Berkeley, Ca: McCutchan.

Havelock, R.G. (1973) The Change Agents Guide to Innovation
in Education, Educational Technology Publications.

Hopkins, D. (1980) Survey Feedback and the Problem of
Change in Teacher Education. Unpublished Ph.D. Thesis,
S.F.U. ERIC Document ED 202820.

Hopkins, D. (1982) 'Politics, Ecology and Drift: Change in
Teacher Education', Education, Management and
Administration, 10, 166-9.

Hopkins, D. (1984) 'Change and The Organisational Character
of Teacher Education'. Studies in Higher Education. 9
(1), 37-45.

Lidquist, J. (1974) 'Political linkage: The academic

innovation process', Journal of Higher Education, 45, 323-343.

Lippitt, R., Watson, J., and Westley, B. (1958) The dynamics of planned change. New York: Harcourt Brace.

Lippitt, R., Hooyman, G., Sashkin, M., and Kaplan, J. (1978) Resourcebook for planned change, Ann Arbor, Mich.: Human Resource Development Associates.

Rogers, E.M., and Shoemaker, F.F. (1971) Communication of innovations: A cross-cultural approach, London: Collier Macmillan.

Runkel, P.J., Schmuck, R.A., Arends, J.H., and Francisco, R.P. (1979) Transforming the schools' capacity for problem solving, Eugene, Oregon: Center for Educational Policy and Management, University of Oregon.

Schmuck, R.A., Runkel, P.J., Arends, J., and Arends, R. (1977) The second handbook of organisation development in schools. Palo Alto: Mayfield.

Sieber, S.D. (1975) 'Organizational influences on innovative roles' in J.V. Baldridge and T.E. Deal (eds), Managing change in educational organizations, Berkeley, Ca: McCutchan.

Wideen, M., Fullan, M., Hopkins, D., Eastabrook, G., and Holborn, P. (1983) The management of change in teacher education: Final report to the S.S. and H.R.C., Simon Fraser University, Vancouver B.C. Mimeo, S.S. and H.R.C. grant no. 410-77-01459-21.

SECTION FOUR - TEACHING PRACTICE

Chapter Eight

MAKING PERFECT? – FORM AND STRUCTURE IN TEACHING PRACTICE

David Hopkins

The old adage tells us that 'practice makes perfect'. My
dictionary tells me that practice: 'is to exercise or perform
one's skill regularly in order to achieve greater command'.
Although this definition embodies the essence of
professionalism, it fails to add that the behaviours practised
may be in and of themselves valuable and important. The value
of practice in teaching (as in medicine) lies not in the end
result, the achievement of a 'one off' superlative and
virtuoso performance, but in the gradual improvement of one's
everyday performance. Practice in teaching and medicine,
unlike practice in snooker and tennis, does not consist of
'practice shots'. Here lies the basis of a professional ethic
for teaching. Although the case has been put (e.g. Stenhouse,
1975), the consideration of teaching as a profession still
falters at the definition. Unfortunately, there is in
education an implicit assumption that during initial teacher
training certain skills are mastered 'once and for all' and
that further practice (albeit desirable) is not necessary. In
this respect teaching is unlike medicine, snooker or tennis –
albeit for different reasons. This is paradoxical, because
teaching is one of the most practical of activities. The
situation is further confused because until recently, and in
some localities still, the practice element in teaching was
short and was unrelated to the theoretical studies of
disciplines (other than education) that comprise much of the
curriculum of student teachers. Even today in some parts of
the United Kingdom the Dip.H.E./B.Ed. route for teacher
training advocated in the James Report, and implemented in the
reorganised teacher training institutions from the mid 1970s,
sometimes under-plays the importance of teaching practice.
    In this chapter I do not intend to put the case for
practice as the central component of teacher education
programmes but, rather, I wish to examine aspects of the
teaching practice experience. In particular, the nature of the
teaching practice, the quality of supervision and the role of
the teacher in whose class the student is placed (variously

called the host or co-operating teacher, or the school associate) are discussed. The purpose of the discussion is not simply to review the literature on the topic but to make an argument around two themes: the first is that initial training is only a start, and teachers need to practice their craft to become expert through long experience; the second is that both students and teachers need to try out new ideas in a systematic, intelligent, self-conscious way and thereby take more responsibility for their professional development. It should also be added that these aims are a function more of the form than the structure of teaching practice - a distinction that will become clearer as the chapter progresses. Much of the literature reviewed and experience quoted here is North American and, more specifically, Canadian in origin. This reflects my background, and is a limitation of my scholarship rather than a comment on the North American or British scene. The ideas presented, though, are intended to be applicable to both contexts.

TEACHING PRACTICE

In North America in general and in Canada in particular, one of the major innovations in teacher education during the 1970s was the introduction of the extended practicum.

The term 'practicum' refers to that period of time student teachers spend in the classroom observing and practising teaching. The use of the qualifier 'extended' is indicative of an innovation that occurred when the traditional time allocation for practice teaching was extended from some 30 days to 13 weeks. This increase of the time allowed for practice teaching was intended to provide the neophyte teacher with greater classroom experience and skills prior to entering the teaching profession. In the Professional Development Program at Simon Fraser University, for example, one third of the year is devoted to classroom observation and seminars on curriculum and teaching skills, another third is devoted entirely to classroom practice (the extended practicum) and the final third given over to academic course work. This is not unlike the balance of many existing postgraduate certificate of education (PGCE) courses in the United Kingdom. This innovation occurred in many North American universities during the 1970s, but is still not evident in some localities.

Although, in many instances, the introduction of the extended practicum was preceded by intense public debate and internal deliberation, the innovation is not currently regarded as being entirely successful. The literature is at best equivocal on the ability of the extended practicum to produce 'better' teachers, and there remain popular concerns over the quality of recent teaching graduates. The extended practicum was introduced because of a widespread conviction that teachers required more 'on-the-job' training. This is an easy banner under which to rally and the extended practicum was a convenient shelter to protect teacher educators from criticisms of their work. They could now point to increased teaching practice as being a committment to the integration of theory and practice and to the improved teaching performance of new teachers. The underlying assumption was that increased time in the classroom during initial training would produce more 'effective' teachers - practice would make perfect. Happily, it was this assumption that provided the focus for much of the subsequent research.

RESEARCH ON THE EXTENDED PRACTICUM

There was an initial spate of studies that related a student's practicum experience to scores on self concept tests. Clifton and Covert (1977) evaluated the effects of an experimental programme (i.e. extended practicum) on the motivation and self concept of a group of student teachers. They concluded that:

> the amount of productive time a student teacher spends in school and the integration between what is observed and practised there and what is taught in educational institutions has a significant effect upon the development of his motivation to become a teacher and his self-concept as a teacher.

In another study (also conducted in a single institution), Kaufman and Shapson (1977) identified an overall tendency for students to either maintain or improve their scores on self concept and attitude measures. Their conclusion, however, is equivocal and represents an ongoing theme in many studies which suggest that self concept and motivation do not necessarily increase as a result of an extended teaching practice. Gregory and Allen (1978) reviewed a number of studies that reported decreases in professional self concept as a consequence of the practicum. They conclude, however, on the basis of their empirical work, that 'the generally found decline in self concept after student teaching is not inevitable'. Covert and Clifton (1981) are less optimistic, particularly as regards the student teachers' professional attitude. They comment:

> Much of that recent research [we have] referred to about the length of practica and its effect on professional attitudes is not very encouraging. For example, Walberg (1967) found that student teachers' professional self-concepts declined as a result of their practice teaching experience. Furthermore, Kropp and Anderson (1963) state as a result of their study that 'the increasing semester

does not seem to be an especially fruitful time during
which to develop attitudes about the role of the
teacher'. And more recently Cohen, Peters and Willis
(1976) state that: 'the general consensus regarding the
impact of the practicum experience is that it has little
or no effect on the most ingrained educational beliefs of
student teachers'. Altman and Castek (1971) in their
review of research state the following: 'Kinard (1968),
Watson (1964) and Castek (1970), in separate studies,
found no overall positive significant difference in
student teachers' attitudes after one semester of
practice teaching', and summarise their findings in this
way: 'From the studies reviewed, it appeared that not
only could the practice teaching experience be described
as being questionable in terms of developing a positive
attitude toward teaching, but more seriously, as one with
the potential for having a detrimental effect upon the
teacher trainee.'

They further conclude that 'attitudes towards teaching,
motivation to become a teacher and self concept may all be
adversely effected by prolonged practice teaching
experiences'. Tatersall (1979) monitored student self concepts
throughout a practicum and concluded that 'had the practicum
ended after three weeks the student teachers would have left
the classroom less anxious', and that 'It takes a minimum of
nine weeks for student teachers to achieve desirable and
durable decrements in teaching anxiety, and twelve weeks for
positive trends and significant changes in professional self
concept to appear.'
    Taken as a whole, these studies do not add much credence
to the widely held belief that extending the length of
teaching practice necessarily results in more effective
teachers. The inference that can be drawn from the equivocal
nature of the research is that although the extended practicum
can provide positive effect, simply lengthening the practice
teaching experience is of itself not a sufficient condition.
As Wideen and Holborn (1983) put it:

It appears that while length of practicum may be
important, a longer practicum alone is insufficient to
produce higher levels of motivation and self concept or
lower levels of anxiety among student teachers ... the
combination of specific program characteristics with a
larger practicum experience may be necessary for
significant change to occur.

For, as Tattersall (1979) points out:

Studies before 1969 claimed that the practicum was
associated with lowered professional self concept and

undesirably high levels of teaching anxiety. Since 1969, studies have reversed these findings for programmes which prepare student-teachers adequately, offer them a gradual introduction to the classroom, and provide skilled support throughout the experience.

It would appear important, therefore, to identify those programme variables that contribute to an effective practicum experience. Various researchers have written about this. Allen (1976) suggests that the practicum could be improved by more effective use of differentiated staffing, supervision techniques, teacher self-evaluations, and sequencing of programme components. Gregory and Allen (1978) argue that self concept can be enhanced during the extended practicum if conditions which provide a high level of support exist. These conditions include the quality of interaction and supervision, speed of induction and school context factors. Glassberg and Sprinthall (1980) point to structured role taking, peer supervision, coaching and microteaching, a supportive learning environment and the use of subjective journals as the important elements in teacher education programmes. Terry (1980) in her interviews with co-operating teachers, found that they wanted better prepared students in terms of teaching skills and more support from the university. Marble (1982) noted that during the extended practicum he studied, supervision and feedback by school associate qua student decreased over time. This may have been the cause of the lack of change in teacher effectiveness variables exhibited by students during the practicum.

Hopkins (1982) identified five variables that he researched during his attempt at 'enhancing the extended practicum'. These were:

1. Support for school associate and training in supervision skills.
2. Reduction of anxiety and stress by the use of stress workshops.
3. Monitoring the student teacher's subjective experience, through the use of log books and 'teacher as person' tasks.
4. Sharing of common experiences by students through the means of a retreat.
5. reduction of stress during practicum by the rephasing of the teaching practice experience.

So, the major point to be derived from this review is that the extended practicum can be an effective tool in the preparation of student teachers if it is combined with other programme variables. The literature reviewed suggests a wide range of such variables. These can be sorted into three major categories. The first category is called 'structural', because the variables in that category are the result of negotiations between school and university over a period of time. The second category contains 'environmental' variables and reflects the milieu in which the student teacher operates. The third category 'operational' refers to those variables under the control of the faculty supervisor. A full list of these variables is given in Table 1.

Table 1

VARIABLES THAT APPEAR TO AFFECT THE QUALITY OF THE PRACTICUM EXPERIENCE

Structural
- Primacy of S.A. selection.
- Closer university liaison with school.
- Faculty teams.
- Clustering.
- Sequencing.
- Integration of practicum with school year.
- Quality/speed of induction.

Environmental
- Level of trust and support regularly given to student.
- Level of authority, responsibility and competence given to student.
- Sensitivity towards problems of induction, and the demands and reality of classroom life.
- Peer support.
- Stress caused by sequencing of practicum.

Operational
- Increase in quality and quantity of supervision.
- Increase in quality and quantity of feedback.
- Encouragement of self evaluation (external criteria).
- More tutor/lecturer contact.
- Use of student journals for personal reflection (internal criteria).
- Enhancement of conceptual level.

This is an extensive list that cannot be discussed in detail here, but it does provide an agenda for future research and consideration. For the purposes of this chapter the quality of supervision and the adoption of new roles will now be considered in more detail.

SUPERVISION

While preparing this chapter, I have also been involved in supervising student teachers on teaching practice. I have attempted to base the form of my supervision on the ideas and philosophy implicit in this chapter. I suppose I have been reasonably successful: my students appear to be happy with my supervision - they are all doing well in their teaching and we have an easy and positive relationship that permits (two-way) critical and constructive comments. I like to think that we all leave our Friday afternoon sessions feeling good about ourselves and each other, and that the students will end teaching practice as more competent and confident teachers. This is all well and good, and not in the least spectacular (the positive outcomes enjoyed by my students may have little [I suspect] to do with me or my methods). Given the limited amount of time and energy that I am giving to teaching practice, though, it is fairly satisfactory. On reflecting on this situation and that of my students, I am struck by a number of contrasts. Principally, I am able only to influence the form and not the structure of teaching practice. I can introduce innovations (e.g. clinical supervision and video analysis) to my own students, but not to others. It is very difficult at the moment to affect the school/college variables and the normative practice of colleagues - this normative practice is deeply rooted and pervasive. The traditional mode of supervision involves a tutor entering a student's classroom with or without prior warning, observing the lesson, making detailed (or not so detailed) comments, and (either then or later) discussing the comments with the student. Much of this work is done conscientiously and caringly but, generally, places the students in a reactive role where they are subject to advice and criticism without being involved in the process of establishing judgement. Much supervision appears to be of this well-meaning, but perhaps somewhat misguided, type. As far as the structure of teaching practice is concerned, schools and colleges appear to have, in general, an uneasy relationship. Although teacher tutors are appointed in some schools their role tends to be ill-defined and equivocal.

Canadian research supports these somewhat subjective observations. Flanders' (1980) controversial report on the professional development of teachers maintains that 'university teacher education was universally alleged to have been useless in preparing teachers for the realities of the classroom experience.'

Marble (1982), in a rather different type of empirical study, found no change in the range of teacher effectiveness variables on the extended practicum which he studied. Further, he observed that the rate and quality of supervision and feedback exhibited by the school associate diminished over time.

These studies suggest that it is the form and quality of supervision that is important. Joyce's work on training provides a clue to the design of programmes that are effective in enabling teachers to develop and enrich their teaching

skills. After reviewing about 200 papers on training, Joyce
and Showers (1980), concluded that:

> Whether we teach ourselves or whether we learn from a
> training agent, the outcomes of training can be
> classified into several levels of impact.
>
> Awareness - At the awareness level we realise the
> importance of an area and competence begins with
> awareness of the nature of inductive teaching, its
> probable uses, and how it fits into the curriculum.
>
> Concepts and Organised Knowledge - Concepts provide
> intellectual control over relevant content. Essential to
> inductive teaching are knowledge of inductive processes,
> how learners at various levels of cognitive development
> respond to inductive teaching and knowledge about concept
> formation.
>
> Principles and Skills - Principles and skills are tools
> for action. At this level we learn the skills of
> inductive teaching: how to help students collect data,
> organise it, and build concepts and test them. We also
> acquire the skills for adapting to students who display
> varying levels of ability to think inductively and for
> teaching them the skills they lack. At this level there
> is potential for action - we are aware of the area, can
> think effectively about it, and possess the skills to
> act.
>
> Application and Problem Solving - Finally, we transfer
> the concepts, principles, and skills to the classroom.
> We begin to use the teaching strategy we have learned,
> integrate it into our style, and combine the strategy
> with the others in our repertoire.
>
> Only after this fourth level has been reached can we
> expect impact on the education of children. Awareness
> alone is an insufficient condition. Organised knowledge
> that is not backed up by the acquisition of principles
> and skills and the ability to use them is likely to have
> little effect.
>
> Alone and in combination, each of these training
> components contributes to the impact of a training
> sequence or activity. (As we shall see, when used
> together, each has much greater power than when they are
> used alone). The major components of training in the
> studies we reviewed are:
>
> 1. Presentation of theory or description of skill or

strategy.
2. Modelling or demonstration of skills or models of teaching.
3. Practice in simulated and classroom settings.
4. Structured and open-ended feedback (provision of information about performance).
5. Coaching for application (hands-on, in-classroom assistance with the transfer of skills and strategies to the classroom).

In a later paper, Joyce and Showers (1984) explore the concept of peer coaching as a cost-effective means of developing teacher competence. The message from this body of work is clear: if new teaching behaviours, skills and competencies are to be passed on effectively to teachers, then it would appear that 'on-the-job' coaching and support can help students who are experimenting with different teaching approaches to adapt and widen their repertoire of teaching skills.

Systematic Supervision

The argument to this point is that supervision for developing teacher competence needs to be systematic, reciprocal and school based. In the United Kingdom, a number of books have recently been published that discuss this type of approach. Stones (1984), for example, suggests changing the role of supervisor from that of an adjudicator to one that involves co-operation along the lines discussed here. The largest body of work in this area, however, comes from the United States, where this approach is termed 'clinical supervision'. The type of role I envisage for the supervisor is somewhat broader than that implied by this title, so I prefer to use the generic term 'systematic supervision' to describe the supervisory role proposed in this chapter.

The primary emphasis in clinical supervision is on the improvement of the student teachers instructional performance. This approach was initially developed in Harvard in the early 1960s and is most closely associated with Cogan (1973) and Goldhammer at al (1980). Clinical supervision has subsequently become very popular in North America as a means for training teachers and has begat a wide literature. Interesting background to and perspectives on clinical supervision are, for example, found in Sullivan (1980), Grimmett (1981) and Sergiovanni (1982). Acheson and Gall (1980) have also published an eminently sensible and practical book entitled Techniques in the Clinical Supervision of Teachers. Rudduck and Sigsworth (1983) provide an extended example of clinical supervision.

In their book on supervision, Acheson and Gall (1980) point to three functions that comprise supervision. These are counselling, curriculum support and clinical supervision. Because clinical supervision has such a specific application, and tends to be defined narrowly by most teacher educators, it is useful to add a fourth function, 'general supervision'.

Counselling

For most student teachers the practicum is a time of great stress. There is anxiety about their ability to be effective in the classroom, and there is also the strain of teaching full time. Clifton (1979) has pointed to the problems student teachers have by being placed in 'marginal' situations (e.g. doing a teacher's job but not having the status) and sometimes not being fully accepted or appreciated by students and staff in the school. All of these influences produce stress and, consequently, supervising teachers may be able to provide reassurance and emotional support to their student teachers. By doing this, the supervisor is acting in the role of counsellor. On other occasions, supervisors may be in a position to give vocational advice (e.g. on applying for teaching positions, or further education).

> Jikja was a school associate with a student teacher, Mary, whom she believed to be overly anxious about her practicum. Jikja broached the topic with Mary and as a result of the conversation they compiled a list of seven areas of concern upon which they would concentrate. For her part Jikja read a number of texts and research papers, talked to the local school district consultant, and then devised a series of strategies for assisting Mary. The evaluation component was provided by a structured interview and a self-concept check list, administered both at the start and end of the project. Jikja's data and Mary's self report suggested that the strategies had been successful in enhancing Mary's self concept, reduced her anxiety and generally improved her practicum experience (Hopkins and Norman, 1982).

Curriculum Support

It often takes student teachers a considerable amount of time to become familiar with the curriculum and confident in the production and implementation of materials. In these situations the student teacher may well need the help of his/her supervisor. In this instance the school associate is acting in the useful and important role of curriculum consultant.

> Gwen was a school associate in a K-1 split class. David, her student teacher was having difficulties in coming to terms with the nebulous nature of the kindergarten curriculum. For one of her projects Gwen,

in consultation with David, developed a list of
objectives which served as a check list in planning an
integrated kindergarten unit. After the check list had
been developed, they used it as a tool to evaluate
their own lessons and other curriculum materials
produced for kindergarten classes (Hopkins and Norman,
1982).

Clinical Supervision

Although it is important to realise that counselling and
curriculum support are important and legitimate aspects of the
supervisor's role they must not be confused with the act of
clinical supervision which focuses on the student teacher's
instructional performance by observing actual teaching. It is
sometimes too easy to be caught up in emotional problems or
curriculum concerns and, consequently, avoid the discipline
that clinical supervision imposes.

Although Goldhammer et al (1980) and Cogan (1973) propose
five and eight stage models respectively, clinical supervision
has three essential phases: planning conference, classroom
observation and feedback conference. The planning conference
provides student teachers with an opportunity to reflect on
the proposed lesson, and this leads to a mutual decision to
collect observational data on an aspect of the student's
teaching. During the classroom observation phase the
supervisor observes the student teach and collects objective
data on the aspect of teaching that they earlier agreed on. It
is in the feedback conference that the supervisor and student
teacher share the information, decide on remedial action (if
necessary) and, often, plan to collect further observational
data. Variations on this process are put forward by different
writers on the topic, but all follow this basic pattern. It is
important, however, to realise that to be effective all three
phases of the process need to be gone through systematically
and sequentially.

Marsha had observed several of George's grade 7 social
studies classes and was generally pleased with his
performance, although both recognised room for
improvement. During a planning conference they went
over George's lesson plan on current events. Marsha
helped George clarify his objectives, one of which was
to involve as many pupils as possible in discussing a
particular news story. They decided to focus the
observation on the type of questions George asked and
the pupils' responses. Marsha suggested she use a
seating plan on which to 'tally' the voluntary and
solicited comments from the pupils. George agreed and
also requested that she jot down his questions,
verbatim. During the lesson Marsha recorded
information for the twenty minutes George had planned

for the discussion. Afterwards, as they went over the data, patterns began to emerge. George noticed that, although the discussion had been lively, only twelve out of twenty-eight pupils had participated (he had thought, during the lesson, that more were involved). As well certain types of questions tended to elicit more complete responses. They both decided that it might be useful if George sequenced his questions from factual types (to establish a common knowledge base) to more open-ended, opinion questions. Also, now that he knew which pupils were reticent, George would attempt to involve them more in class discussions. Marsha suggested a couple of techniques that worked for her, and George was excited about trying them out. The feedback conference ended with both agreeing to use the same observation focus in the near future to assess the impact of George's new strategies (Hopkins and Norman, 1982).

There are a number of principles that are also important to consider. First, the climate of interaction between student teacher and supervisor needs to be non-threatening, helping, and one of mutual trust. Second, the focus of the activity should be on improving instruction and the reinforcement of successful patterns, rather than on unsuccessful patterns or changing the student's personality. Third, the process depends on the collection and use of objective observational data, not unsubstantiated value judgements. Fourth, student teachers are encouraged to make inferences about their teaching from the data, and to use the data to construct hypotheses that can be tested out in future lessons. Fifth, each cycle of supervision (planning, observation, feedback) forms the foundation for succeeding cycles. Sixth, both supervisor and student teacher are engaged in a mutual interaction that can lead to improvement in teaching and observational skills for both.

General Supervision

I have borrowed Cogan's (1973) term 'general supervision' to describe a range of observation techniques that have a less specific application than clinical supervision. In North America, clinical supervision is regarded as the sine qua non of teacher education, often to the exclusion of other equally useful approaches. I have already described two other supervision roles, (curriculum consultant and counsellor), and three more can be envisaged. First, the school associate can also act as a 'resource' in terms of teaching methods – not only in terms of actual teaching styles (q.v. Joyce and Weil, 1980), but also as a 'diagnostician' (q.v. Good and Brophy, 1978). Second, the school associate can serve as a 'coach' to the student teacher when he/she is trying to master a new teaching technique (Joyce and Showers, 1984). Finally, and perhaps most importantly, the school associate can encourage in their student teachers a self-monitoring approach to teaching (Hopkins, 1984). This involves the student teacher taking more responsibility for his/her own supervision and utilising a specific set of self-monitoring skills. By engaging in these activities the school associate is also involved in a process that clarifies his/her own teaching and leads to increased professional development.

NEW ROLES

Change in the form of teaching practice, resulting from the adoption of these methods of supervision, necessitates a change in the roles of those involved. The following lists of role characteristics illustrate these changes.

The student will:
1. Review and adhere to the stated objectives.
2. Make him/herself available for regular planning and feedback sessions with the co-operating teacher and supervisor.
3. Meet with the co-operating teacher and supervisors in a four-way conference concerning his/her progress.
4. Attend faculty meetings, parent/teacher (PTA) functions and other school-related activities, in order to become acquainted with the total school programme.
5. Maintain ethical and professional relations with the school staff, parents and community.
6. Arrive at school and be prepared with the instructional materials and plans necessary for the day's activities.
7. Call the school and, if possible, the co-operating teacher, in the event of an absence due to illness or an emergency.
8. Attend all internship sessions, including seminars and team meetings.

The co-operating teacher will:
1. Accept the student as a colleague. It is important that the co-operating teacher accept the student as a professional colleague and that this attitude be conveyed to the student.
2. Plan with the student. Planning between student and teacher should take place at least once a week. In the initial weeks of the semester planning on a daily basis is appropriate and sometimes necessary. This is especially important when decisions concerning grouping, scheduling, and management are being made. It is the student's responsibility to plan the lessons

that he/she is responsible for, but the teacher's guidance may be solicited by the student.

3. Observe the student conducting instruction. The teacher should observe the student at least once a week. The student and teacher should schedule the time and discuss the lesson before the observation takes place. After the teacher observes, feedback must be provided.

4. Provide feedback for the student. Feedback is necessary not only after formal observations but also throughout the course of the day. For example:

> All the children had a big smile on their faces when you were reading the story a while ago.
>
> Angie stopped crying after you sat her on your lap and talked to her.
>
> Michael and Joe just told me how much fun they had playing the game with you.

The above examples of feedback are quick and 'on-the-spot', and serve as positive reinforcement for the student.

5. Evaluate the student. The teacher, along with the student and supervisors, will meet in a three-way conference to evaluate the student's progress at mid semester and also at the end of the semester. It is advisable that the teacher keep an ongoing record of the weekly formal observations for the purpose of student evaluation.

6. Acquaint the student with instructional materials. The student's experience in the classroom may be enriched with the exposure of a variety of materials made available to him/her.

The supervisor will:

1. Oversee the studentship.

2. Formally and informally observe the student. The supervisor, along with the student, will schedule observations and will be responsible for scheduled videotaping sessions.

3. Provide feedback for the student from formal and informal observations, and will help with the post video and audio tape sessions.

4. Evaluate the student at the end of the semester in a three-way conference.

5. Meet with the student to assist him/her accomplish objectives.

6. Conduct weekly seminars related to the practicum.

7. Serve as a resource person for the student.

8. Maintain a collegial relationship with the students.

Teaching practice and supervision occur within the context of a school. The adoption of roles like those just described may mean significant changes in the norms of the schools and teacher training institutions involved. Clifton (1979), for example, describes the typical student school placement as 'practice teaching as a marginal situation', and continues:

> the lack of legitimacy may be identified by two interrelated factors. First, student teachers do not have authority in the classroom, and secondly they do not know the rituals of the classroom. These factors are interrelated in the sense that not having authority means that the student teacher can never participate in forming all of the rituals which are continually being evolved as new situations arise. And because the student teachers never know all of the rituals, they are continually reminded of those they do not know by both pupils and co-operating teachers. This further illustrates their lack of authority.

Clifton argues quite reasonably that teaching practice must be better integrated into the school situation. This, however, is difficult to achieve. In a case study of a teacher education programme, Wideen and Hopkins (1978) pointed to the existence of two cultures that inhibit effective collaboration between school and college/university on teaching practice.

> The concept of the two cultures is one which has emerged from the interview data in this study and has general credence for teacher education. Simply put, the two cultures refers to the differing perceptions held by university and college teacher education departments and those held by teachers in the schools. To parody, the school perceives such departments as being out of touch with the reality of public education, hidebound by intellectual theorising and blissfully oblivious to the practical difficulties of classroom teaching. In the same way, the school is seen as having the monopoly of common knowledge when it comes to classroom practice and the initiation of student teachers into this folklore.

This is not an original observation. The quotation describes a common situation, yet one that seriously restricts the implementation of ideas such as those being presented here. In another paper (Hopkins, 1980), I pointed out that:

> The traditional goals of teacher education programmes in Canada are preparing teachers who can work within

existing school systems, who are knowledgeable in subject areas, and who have skills in various teaching techniques. These goals are at variance with the recognised need on the part of the schools for teachers who can integrate theory and practice, who have the ability to analyse critically, and who have perceptions and skills to implement changes. To enrich the practicum period to the mutual advantage of both students and cooperating teachers, teacher education programmes should develop practica that: (1) develop a closer philosophic match between school and university; (2) develop a clear understanding of the impact of intervention in the school by the university supervisor; (3) provide opportunity for mutual involvement in planning of practica; (4) use the practicum as a school-focused form of professional development for cooperating teachers; and (5) utilise the practicum as the core component in the teacher education process.

If the form of supervision that I have outlined so far is to be implemented then, of necessity, the relationship between the school and the college/university must also change in order to accommodate these 'new' ideas. The process of successful innovation involves much wider changes in the culture of the organisation than most people imagine, but this is a broader problem and some solutions have already been proposed (e.g. Fullan, 1982; Sarason, 1982).

Let us look more closely at the role of the co-operating teacher, for this is the most critical task in the whole teaching practice process. The co-operating teacher is the major influence on the student teacher, for no other reason than the student tends to assume the behaviours and style of his/her mentor. Seperson and Joyce (1981), in addition to their own empirical research, report on a number of studies that confirm a relationship between the teaching styles of student teachers and those of their co-operating teachers. A paper by Copeland (1979) suggests a more complex ecological relationship between student teachers and their mentors. Copeland's data suggests that teaching skills acquired by student teachers during initial training will be extinguished during practice teaching unless the co-operating teacher and his/her classroom also practice and accept these teaching styles. The implication from both these papers is that for the extended practicum to effectively complement and build on initial training there has to be a very close relationship between the teacher training programme, the co-operating teacher and his/her classroom.

What is even more interesting in this context is that the sponsor teacher is engaged in a reciprocal relationship with his/her student. In a previous study we examined the impact of the student teacher on the professional development of the host teacher (Wideen and Hopkins, 1984). We found that of all the various influences operating on the host teacher it was the presence of the student teacher that had the greatest impact on their professional development. Our data also suggested that if the student was prepared at an institution with a specific philosophy (e.g. 'child centered') then, over time, faced with a succession of students from the same institution, the host teacher's style would move in the direction of that philosophy.

These findings provide the 'other side of the coin' identified by Seperson and Joyce, and also by Copeland. They also underline the importance of the relationship between the student and the co-operating teacher and hint at the potential for professional development contained in that relationship. Conscious of this, Norman and I recently prepared a course handbook for co-operating teachers that aimed at improving the quality of supervision and providing an opportunity for further professional development (Hopkins and Norman, 1982). In this we stated that:

> The initial impetus for developing the course was our conviction that school associates or co-operating teachers play an increasingly important but neglected role in contemporary teacher education. We argue that although co-operating teachers now assume the pivotal role in many teacher education programmes, they are ill-prepared for such a role, and receive inadequate support for their endeavours. By adopting the co-operating teacher role, teachers become aware of tremendous professional development opportunities. The presence of a student teacher in the classroom has enormous possibilities for mutual professional development – but these possibilities are often not explored. We also feel that there is too great a distinction between pre and inservice teacher education. We hope that this course will help to break down that particular barrier and encourage teachers, administrators and professors to regard teaching as an endeavour that requires ongoing support and involves recurrent and self-directed learning.
>
> More specifically the course provides a unique opportunity for school associates to undertake Directed Studies in Education during the semester in which they are supervising student teachers. The aims of the course are two-fold:
>
> 1. to provide a rigorous yet flexible opportunity for school associates to enhance their professional development.
> 2. to increase the quality of the practicum experience for both student, teachers and school associates.

FORM AND STRUCTURE IN TEACHING PRACTICE

The course we developed is just an example of the opportunities available for collaboration between the school and college/university engaged in teaching practice. The possibilities for collaborative action are many and varied, but all depend on the breaking down of the two cultures and the adoption of new roles.

FORM AND STRUCTURE IN TEACHING PRACTICE

In this chapter I have suggested that merely extending the length of teaching practice is no guarantee that student teachers will be 'made perfect'. It is a necessary but not sufficient condition. A number of variables were identified that can enhance the quality of teaching practice (these were summarised in Table 1). Further consideration was given to the nature of supervision, and to the adoption of new roles by those involved in the teaching practice process - particularly the co-operating or host teacher. These two major suggestions were related to the quality of supervision and the role of the co-operating teacher. Both imply changes in structure and form. If a college/university is to conscientiously adopt a type of clinical supervision model then this may well have budgetary and time-tabling implications. If a school is to designate the role of co-operating teacher, then this person will have to spend more time with his/her students (with similar implications). These are structural changes that require negotiation through a political process; but even when new structures are set in place there is no guarantee that practice will change. For this to happen a change in form is required: the tutor has to become less of an instructor and more of a collaborator; the student has to become more self directed and proactive; and the host teacher has to develop a new set of skills and to assume and manifest responsibility that exceeds that of the tutor. These are difficult moves to make, yet are crucial to the successful implementation of the ideas presented here. They are also complementary to the notion of professionalism described at the beginning of the chapter and congruent with our best knowledge of how teachers learn and develop (Joyce et al, 1981).
    The implication of the previous paragraph is that if change is to be successful, change must affect both the systems and personal level. Unfortunately, it is often assumed that it is necessary for systemic change to occur first in order to lay the ground for personal change. Often this means that change is 'a long time in the coming' and, consequently, opportunities are missed. I want to argue, in conclusion, that despite the need for structural change, the prospect of building a new professional ethic in teaching is more dependent on personal change and committment. Irrespective of the system characteristics within which one works, the

individuals involved can significantly affect the quality and form of these relationships. Many of the procedures discussed in this chapter are of this type. Changes in form occur as a result of individuals, however hesitantly, trying out new ideas in a systematic, intelligent and self conscious way. This applies equally to tutors, students and teachers involved in teaching practice. Through adopting more systematic modes of supervision, and by involving the host teacher more specifically in the process, we stand a better chance of practice making perfect.

REFERENCES

Acheson, K. and Gall, M. (1980) Techniques in the Clinical Supervision of Teachers, New York: Longmans.

Allen, I (1976) 'Extending the Practicum: Problems in Intergrating Theory and Practice', Canadian Journal of Education, 1 (3), 43-51.

Altman, B. and Castek, J. (1971) 'A comparative evaluation of the effectiveness of student teaching, interning and micro teaching in undergraduate teacher training', ERIC document Ed 059-184.

Castek, J. (1970) Changes in attitudes, philosophical views and knowledge of secondary education during student teaching, Unpublished Ph.D. thesis, University of Nebraska.

Clifton, R. (1979) 'Practice teaching : survival in a marginal situation', Canadian Journal of Education, 4 (3), 60-74.

Clifton, R. and Covert, J. (1977) 'The effects of an experimental program on the motivation and self concept of student teachers', Canadian Journal of Education, 2 (2), 23-32.

Cogan, M. (1973) Clinical Supervision, Boston: Houghton Mifflin.

Cohen, A., Peters, D., and Willis, S. (1976) 'The effects of early childhood education student teaching on program preference, beliefs and behaviours', Journal of Educational Research, 70 (1).

Copeland, W. (1979) 'Student teachers and co-operating teachers: an ecological relationships', Theory into Practice, XVIII (3), 194-199.

Covert, J. and Clifton, R. (1981) An examination of the effects of extending the practicum on the professional disposition of student teachers, Memorial University, Newfoundland, Unpublished M.S.

Flanders, A. (1980) The Professional Development of Teachers, Vancouver: British Columbia Teachers' Federation.

Fullan, M. (1982) The Meaning of Educational Change, New York: Teacher's College Press.

Glassberg, S. and Sprinthall, N. (1980) 'Student Teaching: a developmental approach', Journal of Teacher Education, XXXI (2), 31-38.

Goldhammer, R. et al. (1980) Clinical Supervision: special methods for the supervision of teachers (second edition), New York: Holt, Rinehart and Winston.

Good, T. and Brophy, J. (1978) Looking in classrooms (second edition), New York: Harper and Row.

Gregory, A. and Allen, I. (1978) 'Some effects of the practicum on the professional self concept of student teachers', Canadian Journal of Education, 3 (2), 53-65.

Grimmett, P. (1981) Clinical Supervision and Teacher Thought Processes', Canadian Journal of Education, 6 (4), 23-39.

Hopkins, D. (1980) 'The role of the practicum in bridging the gap between school and university', ERIC document ED 202-821.

Hopkins, D. (1982) Enhancing the extended practicum, Research report prepared for Professional Programs, Faculty of Education, Simon Fraser University.

Hopkins, D. (1984) Doing Teacher Based Research, Milton Keynes: Open University Press, (in press).

Hopkins, D. and Norman, P. (1982) Professional Development: a self directed studies course, Vancouver: Challenge Education Associates.

Joyce, B. et al (1981) Flexibility in Teaching, New York: Longmans.

Joyce, B. and Showers, B. (1980) 'Improving Inservice Training: the Messages of Research', Educational Leadership, Feb., 379-385.

Joyce, B. and Showers, B. (1984) 'Transfer of Training: the contribution of coaching' in Hopkins, D. and Wideen, M. Alternative Perspectives on School Improvement, London: Falmer.

Joyce, B. and Weil, M. (1980) Models of Teaching (second edition), Englewood Cliffs, New Jersey: Prentice Hall.

Kaufman, D. and Shapman, S. (1977) Evaluation of the teacher education program at Simon Fraser University, Paper presented at CSSE.

Kinard, C. (1968) 'A study of changes in openness of student teachers during the student teaching experience', Dissertation Abstracts, 28: 1466A Oct.

Kropp, R. and Anderson, J. (1963) 'Teacher roles before and after internship', Journal of Educational Research, 56 (7).

Marble, W. (1982) Development of Student Teacher Effectiveness over an Extended Practicum, Unpublished Ph.D. thesis, Simon Fraser University.

Rudduck, J. and Sigsworth, A. (1983) Partnership: an exploration of the student-tutor relationship in teaching practice, Norwich: University of East Anglia School of Education.

Sarason, S. (1982) The Culture of the School and the Problem of Change (second edition), Boston: Allyn and Bacon.

Seperson, M. and Joyce, B. (1981) 'The relationship between the styles of student teachers and those of co-operating teachers', in Joyce, B. et al Flexibility in Teaching, New York: Longmans.

Sergiovanni, T. (ed.) (1982) Supervision of Teaching, Alexandria, Virginia: A.S.C.D.

Stenhouse, L. (1975) An Introduction to Curriculum Research and Development, London: Heinemann.

Stones, E. (1984) Supervision in Teacher Education, London: Methuen.

Sullivan, C. (1980) Clinical Supervision: a State of the Art Review, Alexandria, Virginia: A.S.C.D.

Tattersall, R. (1979) Patterns of Change in Teaching Anxiety, Professional Self-concept and Self-concept during an extended practicum, Unpublished M.A. thesis, Simon Fraser University.

Terry, B. (1980) Summary of Interviews with School Associates, Simon Fraser University, unpublished paper.

Walberg, H. (1967) 'Effects of tutoring and practice teaching on self concept and attitudes in education students', ERIC document Ed 015-155.

Watson, C. (1964) A study of the effects of student teaching upon the attitudes of prospective teachers and interns, Unpublished Ph.D. thesis, Northwestern University.

Wideen, M. and Holborn, P. (1983) 'Research in Canadian Teacher Training: a review', The Management of Change in Teacher Education - 3, Ottawa: Social Sciences and Humanities Research Council of Canada.

Wideen, M. and Hopkins, D. (1978) Professional Renewal Through Teacher Education, Oslo: IMTEC (IMTEC case study No 8).

Wideen, M. and Hopkins, D. (1984) 'Supervising Student Teachers: a means of professional renewal?', The Alberta Journal of Educational Research, XXX (1), 26-37.

Chapter Nine

PARTNERSHIP SUPERVISION (OR GOLDHAMMER REVISITED)

Jean Ruddick and Alan Sigsworth

INTRODUCTION

'Practice teaching has the texture of reality because it gives
the student the distinct sense of movement towards the goal –
teaching' (Lortie, 1975). No-one in initial teacher education
would seriously dissent from Lortie's assertion. Moreover, his
subsequent statement, supported by research studies, that in
the main students value practice teaching more than any taught
education course, squares with the experience of those engaged
in teacher education. Experience in schools represents for
students the peaks of their training. Such episodes are also
important to teacher tutors and college tutors, for it is only
when their students are loosed on a diversity of classrooms
that they can see how effectively seminar and classroom
activity interweave
        There is, of course, a great deal of stress involved in
undertaking a teaching practice, for the experience is not
only to do with learning by practice – it is also concerned
with demonstrating competence to be licensed. This is where
the difficulties begin and where the students' perceptions of
the twin supervisory functions of aid and judgement can result
in student energies being directed more towards the
construction of a facade of competence than to achieving
competence itself.
        It was dissatisfaction with the general ideology of
teaching practice supervision, and our own performance within
it, which provided the motivation to engage in the small scale
experiment which we describe in subsequent pages (Rudduck and
Sigsworth, 1983). We wanted to see teaching practice as an
occasion for laying the foundations of professionalism. By
this we mean the readiness of teachers to study the events and
interactions of their own classrooms and to use reflection as
a basis for problem-solving and the improvement of practice.
Our concern was to establish a habit of self-monitoring via
classroom study in initial teacher education and, equally
importantly, to establish open, practice-orientated dialogue

as part of the natural order of professional events. What follows is an account of our attempt to implement a form of supervision sympathetic to such an end.

THE EXPERIMENT

> He holds all the cards and if I had a complaint about the course it would be that — but I wouldn't make it because there's no-one else (but him) to make it to, because he has somehow managed to hold every card. He is my tutor — looks after my personal problems, TP adviser, course assessor; he marks all our essays, decides what final grades we're going to get and marks our teaching practice. He writes out references and he is in charge of our references until we get a first teaching post. And he lectures us on some of the courses (comment by a student, 1979).

Our main concern was to develop a relationship for the supervision of teaching practice in which the negative impact of the tutor's cumulative power would be contained so that his/her experience and expertise could be positively used by the student. (The nature of the problem that power represents may of course be different when the classroom teacher acts as tutor.)

To help us redefine the relationship, we relied on a formal contract derived from the work of Goldhammer (1969), which has been widely used in Australia, Canada and the USA (Cogan, 1973; Sullivan, 1980). Goldhammer called the approach 'clinical supervision'; we have changed the title to 'partnership supervision'. The terms of our contract were drawn up specifically to contain the authority of the tutor and to provide conditions which would promote colleague-like dialogue grounded in evidence of events in the student teacher's classroom. The most distinctive item in the contract is that the focus for the tutor's observation is defined by the student and not by the tutor:

1. The student proposes a focus for observation by nominating one or more topics or problems which he/she would like to have feedback on. The focus is discussed and clarified until student and tutor feel that they have arrived at a shared understanding.
2. Tutor and student discuss what kind of evidence would illuminate the agreed focus and, given the constraints of the situation, agree how best the evidence might be gathered.
3. The tutor shapes his/her observation according to the agreed focus.
4. The tutor disciplines the content of his/her

post-observation feedback by accepting a strict principle of relevance as defined by the focus.

In addition, the tutor agrees not to discuss the student's chosen focus or the content of their discussions with anyone but the student unless the student accepts that such a move would be helpful.

In practice, partnership supervision falls into three stages of activity:

1. Pre-observation discussion, where the student proposes a focus for the tutor's observation and where the proposal is discussed and clarified.
2. The observation itself.
3. A post-observation discussion where the tutor's field notes are discussed in relation to the agreed focus.

Ideally, the post-observation discussion would follow close on the heels of the observation. There would then be a gap before the second supervision cycle began so that the student could reflect on what he/she had learned from the post-observation discussion and consider what topic to propose for the next observation. In practice, however, circumstances sometimes require the ideal time-span to be compressed so that all three activities take place on one day rather than on different occasions.

Three of us took part in the study, Alan, Jim (who acted as tutors) and Jean. We decided to try the partnership approach with postgraduate certificate of education (PGCE) students and we planned three cycles of supervision with each student. We wanted to involve students who were not considered by their regular teaching practice tutors as either well above average or well below average in terms of practical classroom competence. We thought it important to avoid having two students from the same school lest their discussion of the approach make it difficult for us to assess its impact on individual students. The tutors who were in charge of the regular teaching practice arrangements agreed that the approach was worth trying, and they discussed it with students whom they thought might be interested in working with us and who fitted the criteria. Four students volunteered: Pat, Sally, Kate and Tom. They were all postgraduates in their early 20s and all were undertaking the final practice of their PGCE year. Pat worked with Alan (his other commitments prevented him from taking on more than one student at this time); Sally, Kate and Tom worked with Jim who was on study leave from an Australian college and was prepared to take a larger load.

Meetings were held with the students individually, in order to ensure that they understood the nature of the activity and the terms of the contract and were clear that involvement in the study would in no way affect their regular teaching practice assessment. Since we had to conduct our experiment within the normal framework of teaching practice supervision, the students who took part experienced both the form of supervision to which a previous teaching practice had accustomed them and the partnership approach with which we were experimenting. The tutors taking part in the experiment ensured that their visits did not take place on the same day as the visits from the normal teaching practice tutors. The heads of the schools involved were all contacted and all agreed to co-operate.

For the purposes of the study, all the pre-observation and post-observation discussions were tape-recorded and then transcribed, and field notes of observations were kept. At the end of the study the four students and the tutors met to consider what had been learned and to assess the strength and weaknesses of the approach. Discussion with colleagues began on 20th March and the final review meeting took place on 20th June.

THE POTENTIAL OF PARTNERSHIP SUPERVISION

Identifying a focus for the tutor's observation - an educative process

'Normally if you enter a student's classroom you sit down and you define what the situation is. You look at it through your own eyes - the eyes of somebody who has been in a lot of classrooms' (interview with Alan).

We would question whether a higher education tutor, who sees only isolated episodes in the continuum of a student's experience on teaching practice, can be sensitive to the 'fine grain' of a particular student's development in a particular context. There is inevitably a tendency for tutors to rely on their own 'travelling kit' of standard diagnoses - which they can mentally 'flick through' until they find some that match the performance they are observing - as Alan recalled: 'Eventually you say: "Ah, Yes. It's this kind of situation." And you run through your checklist: "Was her preparation good? Is she well organised? Does she relate the lesson to what she was doing before?" These are common and significant issues, but they are general. What was striking in the experiment with partnership supervision was the fact that the issues that students identified were highly personalised and, on the whole, unpredictable - many of them did not feature in the tutor's pack of teaching practice 'problem cards'. One student, for example, told Alan that the difficulties she was experiencing in the classroom might be the result of the fact that she looked young; she asked Alan to observe her interaction with her class, taking her appearance as a

starting point. Alan commented: 'Now this was a unique problem
to deal with. You are not relying on the theory of what it's
all about but actually engaging with the action of the
classroom.' Students may, of course, nominate conventional
problems - it would be surprising if they did not - but given
the time that is allowed in partnership supervision for pre-
observation and post-observation discussion, a conventional
problem can be atomised so that it becomes individualised.
Kate, for example, proposed 'classroom control' as a focus for
Jim's observation, but before the observation started, Jim
encouraged Kate to try to 'get behind the label'. This she was
able to do - and the experience of trying to do so was itself
productive:

> Kate:
> Perhaps I should be more specific then. I suppose the
> whole thing centres around the very beginning of the
> lesson - how you start it off can determine the way the
> whole lesson goes, so perhaps if you see how I introduce
> the lesson ... as I do feel, thinking about it, that
> perhaps I am particularly weak at introducing the lesson
> and settling the children down quickly and explaining it.
> Perhaps this is more my problem.

Thus, in partnership supervision, students are learning
not to depend on others for a diagnosis of their classroom
problems but are instead developing the capacity and
confidence to make their own diagnoses. This, in our view, is
an important professional quality.
It is not surprising if students find it difficult at
first to frame a worthwhile focus for observation. Classrooms
are, after all, highly complex social arenas which frequently
challenge the analytical powers of even experienced observers.
Moreover, the academic biographies of students tend to have
been dominated in successive phases of education by the habit
of responding to the teacher's or the tutor's agenda - they
are not used to building and valuing their own agenda. Our
fear was not that students would not be capable, in time, of
diagnosing their own problems; it was, instead, that the
students - despite our reassurances - might be cautious about
drawing attention to real problems that in a normal assessment
situation they would be at pains to disguise lest they were
interpreted as evidence of ineptness. Not so. Once trust had
been established - largely through the tutors' obvious respect
for the contract and their self-critical monitoring of their
own role in the partnership - students began to explore, in a
very open fashion, issues that had become problematic for them
during their sustained contact with a particular group of
pupils. Alan, for example, was taken aback by Pat's directness
when she said that she suspected that the children in her
maths lesson (6-7 year olds) were getting the right answers

without actually engaging in any mathematical thinking. She asked him to gather evidence, through observation, that would help her to see whether or not her fears were grounded. They were. Alan said that in a decade of teaching practice supervision he had never known a student invite a tutor to make a close analysis of something that could expose his/her failure to achieve a fundamental goal of teaching.

By the third pre-observation session, three of the four students were quite at ease with the supervisory relationship and excited by the opportunity to identify topics for observation - as this comment suggests:

Sally:
It's funny. I was only thinking to myself this morning: 'Ah, I think I'll also get Jim to look at so-and-so'. And then, it's funny - I had this thought. It's a shame you're not coming more often, because I'm developing a sort of thing - 'Oh, I'll get Jim to look at so-and-so now.' It's been building up. But at the first session we did I thought: 'Oh goodness! What on earth can I get him to look at!' And now it's changed to: 'Ah, I'll get him to look at so-and-so.'

Tom, however, did not make the transition. Circumstances did not permit more than two cycles of supervision and so we cannot tell whether he would have felt more comfortable as time went on. Tom was the most dependent of the four students. In the evaluation that concluded the experiment he declared that he found the conventional supervisory relationship more useful - the criticisms and proposals that his regular teaching practice tutor offered gave him clear targets to work towards. Tom's reaction is cautionary. It suggests that for some students the partnership approach may be too disconcerting. At the same time, one might argue that it is just such students who most need a structure in which to develop self-reliance and professional judgment.

The other students were gradually learning that to reflect on experience analytically is a route to professional understanding and confidence. One can see something of this in the way that Sally initiates a critique of her failure, in a geography lesson, to ensure that the pupils grasped the logic of its structure.

Sally:
I was going to teach them all about rivers and the geography of rivers, and first of all I got them to do some mini-experiments on how stones wear away, and water wears away the ground, and how rivers start. Then I thought I should connect that up with the life-story of a river. They didn't make the connection at all, whereas

having such an analytical mind, I was able to make the connection. It was perfectly logical to me.

The development of a capacity for balanced and reasoned self-criticism (not the mortifying self-flagellation that students sometimes indulge in in post-observation sessions with their supervisors) is something that the procedures of partnership supervision are capable of supporting. Another achievement seems to be the capacity to develop an eye for significant detail. This is encouraged in two ways: first, by the documentary field notes that the tutor gathers to feed the student/tutor discussion (see later); second, by the need for vivid recall (by the student) of critical classroom incidents, as a basis for identifying and refining a focus for observation. During the relentless busyness of teaching, a student cannot consciously analyse such incidents at any depth, even though there may be some implicit theorising about them that determines his/her response to them. These incidents, retrieved in good time from the back of the mind, where they lodge, yield data that can be effectively worked on. Here, for example, is one of Sally's seemingly ordinary recollections.

Sally:
At the front of the class on the left hand side from my view there is a little group of girls who are very good workers. Now I've noticed that I'm tending to be nice to them because they are nice to me. If they're noisy then I tend to tell them off in a lot nicer manner than I do those two girls at the back who are continually noisy.

Out of this modest anecdote some important questions emerged: Sally asked herself: 'Am I consistently nicer to some children than to others? If so, what do those I favour have in common? What form does my niceness take? And what are the observable effects? What do I really mean by "nice"?'

Interestingly, Tom, who did not take to the partnership approach, had difficulty in reassembling critical incidents or vivid sequences of interaction. It may have been a weakness in visualisation that prevented him from being able to identify a focus for observation that had meaning for him and that would give a clear directive to his tutor.

Tom:
I think it's probably organisation ... I think it's probably coping with the materials, coping with the workbooks and any other non-workbook activity that I want to introduce. It's probably coping and organising that and being on top of the materials that are in the classroom ... Does that give you enough of a brief? ...

> The focus is that there is ... the focus, um ... is that
> I'm unhappy with the ... maths.

There was little here that Jim could help Tom to work on,
and so arrive at a better understanding of the dimensions of
the problem. Consequently, Jim was disabled, and it was
tempting to revert to a conventional supervisory relationship
in which he could 'tell' Tom what his problems were.

The relationship between theory and practice

In traditional supervision, the student's lesson plan and the
lesson itself are subject to critical scrutiny. It is not
uncommon for a tutor at the end of an observation to comment
on several aspects of the student's behaviour. In relation to
classroom management, for example, comments might be made on
voice production, timing of delivery, vocabulary, questioning
behaviour, the use of silence, movement about the room and
strategies for writing on the blackboard. The tutor might also
go on to comment on the structure of the lesson, pupil
motivation, materials used, and so on. The comments do not
necessarily cohere in terms of helping the student to theorise
about a particular fragment of classroom life. One advantage
of the partnership approach is that the single focus serves to
unify the tutor's observation in such a way that the
relationship between theory and practice is explored as a
dynamic reality. In Alan's encounter with Pat (which was
mentioned earlier), for example, the evidence that Alan
gathered in response to Pat's asking whether her pupils were
arriving at the right answers as a result of mathematical
thinking, raised and related interesting issues about
classroom management; about the process of learning; and about
socialisation. Because the teacher was under pressure at her
desk to respond to completed work which pupils wanted marking,
she could not engage in observation of other pupils at work,
nor enter into dialogue about the work in ways which might
expose the process of learning. Moreover, the evidence showed
that even young pupils had acquired a 'right answer'
mentality: for example, when asked to guess the length or
width of an object and then check their estimates against the
measurement, the pupils, obviously uneasy about a guess being
wrong, tended to complete the measurement first and then fill
in the answer box for the guess so that both estimate and
measurement were the same.

In time, the sharing of vivid evidence of classroom
events and interactions helped the students to appreciate the
complexity of problems encountered in particular settings. In
this way they began to see problems in terms of the phenomena
of classroom life, rather than as an index of their own
deficiencies as student teachers. This realisation contributed

to their confidence and to their readiness to engage in what
amounted to a form of grounded theorising.

PROBLEMS IN ADJUSTING TO THE PRINCIPLES OF PARTNERSHIP SUPERVISION

In trying to develop the partnership approach, the tutors had
to face, and come to terms with, the habits and assumptions of
their professional past as teaching practice tutors - and this
was not easy.

The discipline of respecting the focus for observation nominated by the student

Both tutors working in our small scale experiment acknowledged
an initial tendency to underrate the significance of the
problems that the students identified as a focus for
observation. Instead of 'unpacking' the problem so that an
appropriate design for observation could be planned, tutors
were tempted to 'improve' on the problem selected, thereby
running the risk of making it theirs rather than the
student's. We were reminded here of King's work (1978). He
notes how the infants' teachers he studied claimed to work
from infants' interests but, in fact, created the curriculum
they wished to teach by re-shaping the pupils' predilections
so that they more closely matched their own.

Another temptation that must be strongly resisted by the
tutor who is still feeling his/her way into the unfamiliar
role of a 'partner' in supervision is to 'improve on' the
student's lesson plan just before a lesson is due to begin. It
may, of course, be legitimate for a tutor to look at the
student's lesson plan in advance of the lesson itself, even in
partnership supervision. In trying to clarify the focus that
the student has nominated for observation and consider how
best to respond, the tutor will probably need to know what is
likely to happen during the lesson. A brief example shows how
Jim, instead of being content with briefing himself by
listening to how Sally proposed to handle the lesson, begins
to ask questions that sap her confidence:

> Sally: Um ... well, there (referring to her lesson
> plan) I've written - 'I don't want to produce a
> complete story' because that is the standard idea
> in their heads and I want them to get away from
> that because they all think that they've got to
> produce a complete story because that's all
> they've been used to, so far.

> Jim: I see ... and this can be in the form of a poem.
> Do they have a concept of 'poem' or do you have a
> concept there?

Sally: Oh, that's a thing I hadn't thought about.

Jim: The concept of poem - can be rhyming doggerel, which is even more of a tie than conventional sentences.

Sally: Yea, ah ... no, no. They don't have that idea of poem.

Jim: It might be worth considering the word 'poem' and thinking of another way of putting it, for them.

Sally: I see, yeah.

Jim: Do they know what words are? That's a silly question. Do they know the difference between phrases and sentences?

Sally: I don't think so ... I really don't think so.

Jim: So if they're used to writing only conventional sentences there could be a new concept involved here?

Sally: Mm ...

This seems to be the kind of reaction that Goldhammer observed in his original development work on clinical supervision:

> The worst mistake that could occur during pre-observation, happens, curiously, to be the most common ... [to] unnerve the teacher so badly, just before his class, that his adequacy becomes impaired and his lesson is weakened. Of all the things that supervisors do to undermine confidence and equanimity before class, the most common I have observed, is to introduce new elements into the teaching plan that are unassimilable in the remaining time, or raise questions about the plan - that is, to attack it when too little time remains for the teacher to take corrective measures (Goldhammer, 1969).

There may be more at stake here than just unnerving the student before he/she begins to teach. The tutor, in anticipating problems, is making a powerful claim about his/her powers of professional prediction. It may well be more productive for the student to learn from experience, rather than from the tutor, what will work and what will not work in the particular conditions of a particular classroom. Moreover, there may be times when, despite his/her experience, the tutor could be wrong in forecasting the outcome of moves proposed by the student.

If the temptation to tamper with the focus in the pre-observation session is great, that of widening the focus in the post-observation session is even greater. Such temptation is not surprising, for within the conventional supervisory relationship any aspect of the student's preparation or performance is a fit target for tutor comment. In partnership supervision, the principle of concentrating upon the student's chosen focus 'flies in the face' of the tutor's freedom. If we dip into a post-observation session Jim held with Sally, an extract will show how easily the tutor's discipline can slip. Sally had nominated the structure of the lesson as the focus for observation. In the exchange reproduced below, Jim begins to shift the spotlight away from structure towards an embryonic consideration of the pupil's view of classroom life.

> Jim:
> Down here I've got something, and I am not sure if it comes into 'structure', about giving instructions or control but at the risk of getting outside my brief I'll mention it ... If you're sitting there – you're not clear about what you have to do, and the teacher says 'Is everybody clear about what you have to do?' Would you put your hand and say, 'No, I'm not clear, you haven't explained it', or 'I'm dumb; I don't know.' – How would you respond?

Moving into prescriptivism

Hogmo and Solstad (1977), in recording the failure of an integrated curriculum to 'take' in a Lofoten Island school, report teachers as saying: 'We failed because we had the ghost of a compulsory curriculum hanging over us.' In a not dissimilar way, the tutors in this experiment recognised that they had the ghost of traditional practice hanging over them. It was all too easy for prescriptivism to surface in the relationship – particularly when a student became despondent about a lesson that the tutor had observed. Although the tutor was prepared to regard a lesson which had gone 'off course' as a resource which they both could work on, the student was less likely to see it dispassionately. Sensitive to the student's preoccupation with his/her own performance, and to the accompanying sense of defeat, the tutor can easily forsake the principles of partnership supervision, abandon the exploration of problems, and provide 'ready-made' solutions as a temporary life-line. By so doing, the balance of the relationship is altered, and the familiar pattern of tutor dominance and student dependency is re-instated. Kate in her first pre-observation discussion, for example, had nominated as her focus, 'classroom control, particularly at the start of the lesson'. The lesson did not go well as a whole and Kate was

depressed when she met Jim for the post-observation
discussion. During their rather diffuse discussion - it was
the student this time who had difficulty in maintaining
concentration on the agreed focus - Jim turned his attention
to a familiar problem which had in fact been manifest in the
lesson - that of the 'fast finishers who, once disengaged from
their assigned task, feel free to create havoc in the
classroom at large'. This was a problem rich in potential for
understanding. Instead of exploring the problem in the spirit
of partnership supervision, though, Jim offered teaching tips
- and in so doing created the very dependency which he was
trying to avoid:

Jim: Yes - I remember once, many years ago, worrying
about this problem when I was due for inspection.
I got over it at that time by making some
interesting work stencils and giving them to all
the children and -

Kate: What - a whole sort of package for each child?

Jim: Yes, and saying 'Is there anybody who hasn't got
something to do if they run out of work while our
visitor is here?' and that was a simple way of
getting out if the problem.

Kate: Oh yes - that's a good idea! - full of maths and
english and all sorts of things.

Jim: This was how I got over that particular problem
- I don't know that you can keep them going
indefinitely.

Kate: Oh, yes - I want to go and do that now.

Jim: I don't know that you can keep that going
indefinitely, through a whole ... but it served my
purpose at that time.

Kate: For seven weeks that I'm here it might just do
the job ... yes.

Although Jim recognised the strategic error that he had
made, and acknowledged it to Kate before their next
discussion, the dependency which his prescriptivism had
generated was difficult to dispel, as the following selection
of Kate's contributions to the next discussion indicates:

Kate:
Perhaps I could go in and say ... sounds a bit corny but
... um ... 'Did everyone have a nice holiday?' I'll say:

'well good because I want you to tell me something about what you did.' Is that too ... would that work?

What about what I did? If I say something about what I did on my holiday um ... do you think that might motivate them?

Well, is that a good idea, then? Could you suggest something else that I might be able to think about?

I just hope I'm not besieged by 'how do you spell this' again ... at the very beginning. Um ... OK, then, well do you think that I should give out the paper at the beginning or wait?

That Kate and Jim did break through to a genuine partnership before the end of the experiment is a tribute both to Jim's and Kate's determination to try to adhere to the terms of the contract and to Jim's readiness to reflect upon his approach and, in discussion with Kate, to acknowledge any wrong moves.

The need to develop new skills in making and using observational fieldnotes

Comments written by the tutor after observing a student on traditional supervision tend mainly to consist of the tutor's views of the strength and weaknesses of the student's handling of the lesson. It is likely that there will be some advice about ways of improving particular techniques, and it is also likely that an aspect of the student's performance will be singled out for praise - as the following comment, from Alan's files, indicates:

Your preparation indicates some sound and imaginative thinking. Additionally, your lesson evaluation has a good deal of perceptive reflection in it.

You have a good working relationship with the group and your supervision during the time that I was present was quiet and unobtrusive.

One or two quick comments:

1. When you are operating on a group-based activity and are moving from group to group, work out the position at each group location that will give you maximum possibility for surveying the rest of the class. This enables you by the usual non-verbal means to deal with the odd child, e.g. eye control, or to

give a swift verbal comment. This helps to reduce the number of disengaged characters.

2. Lesson evaluations. Your lesson evaluations (which are sound as they are) can be varied. At present they tend to focus on general class response to a lesson. Try, for example, reflection on the contribution, or otherwise, of an individual or a very small group. Occasionally widen your focus to reflect on a period longer than a lesson, e.g. what were the rhythms of activity; when did the flashpoints of trouble occur; why, and so on.

Written comments may be passed on to the student to guide the student's subsequent practice; they may constitute an agenda for a follow-up tutorial. They may also constitute an agenda for the tutor's observation on the next visit: 'I noticed that you haven't done much to improve your non-verbal strategies for classroom control - which I pointed out to you last time!'

The small group of students with whom we worked reacted to written supervisory comments in a uniformly critical manner. They saw them less as an aid to the improvement of their practice than as negative documentary evidence which they had no power to modify. These two comments sum up the feelings of frustration and unfairness which all the students expressed:

I don't mind criticism as long as it's fair. It's when it's unfair and when it's written down. There's nothing you can do about it. Then that's when you start to feel bad and that's when your relationship starts to deteriorate.

When I had my first lesson supervised there were some comments written down which I explained afterwards but nevertheless they are still on that bit of paper which will go back to college and they'll read that. Then they'll forget about the conversation we had afterwards.

It is rare for lesson comments in traditional supervision to contain closely detailed observation of the field note type, unless the tutor utilises this technique as a means of providing evidence to 'bring home' to a student an aspect of the reality of his/her classroom performance which, in the tutor's eyes, he/she obstinately refuses to recognise. Partnership supervision, however, requires a considerable shift of perspective in relation to what is written down during the tutor's observation; in relation to the status of what is written down; and in relation to how what is written down is used. Tutor judgement now shifts from how competent

the student is to what counts as appropriate evidence, given
the nature of the student's chosen focus for observation. In
partnership supervision the tutor will tend to write
intensively. Ordinarily, furious scribbling by the tutor can
be distracting, for a student will tend to see the notes as a
judgemental record, and suspect that more writing means more
criticism. In partnership supervision, field notes come to be
accepted as a resource for the student, and the student is
less likely to be disturbed by his/her awareness of the
activity of note-taking. As Sally remarked to Jim at the
crossroads of one of their discussions: 'Well, you should know
what happened next, you've got the script.'

The taking of good field notes in relation to an agreed
focus is a demanding research task requiring vigilance and
discipline. Both Alan and Jim, with years of teaching practice
behind them, still found it difficult, as Alan explained:

> The kind of written notes that you produce for
> partnership supervision are very, very different from the
> ones that you would produce under traditional supervision
> because what you are trying to get down is some kind of
> picture of what was happening ... so that it's there,
> it's recorded, it's concrete. You can present it to the
> student as your version of what was going on. In a way
> you write it in neutral language as far as you can be
> neutral – a fairly cool look at what is happening. It's
> simply trying to record what was happening.

A sample of Alan's notes is reproduced below. They come
from the observation in which Pat was curious about her
children's learning in mathematics. Alan decided that the
pupils might respond well to being interviewed by a stranger
and he decided, therefore, to work entirely through
observation of a small number of individual children. In a
first school classroom, a stranger sitting down will tend to
draw interested enquiry from the children or calls for help. A
stanger standing up and doing nothing more alarming than
scribbling into a pad on top of the cupboard is, though,
possibly by virtue of his height, soon disregarded. In his
note-taking Alan tried to identify the pupils under
observation and then to record as closely as possible what he
saw them do or heard them say:

> Boy in red and blue. Obs. begins. Has written: 'The black
> domino box is'. Goes off to T's desk. Returns and passes
> out of range of observer. Observer wanders about. Boy not
> to be seen. (Toilet?) Returns after interval of six
> minutes. Observer asks what are you doing? Child: 'I
> can't think of word.' Silence. Writes '6' in box. Did he
> measure the box? Converses with a girl. Returns to paper.
> Child says: 'Now I got it' (girl has shown him 'black

dominoes long' on reverse of sheet). Completes 'The black domino box is 6 black dominoes long.' Goes off with paper. Returns and announces: 'I'm going to do a puzzle now.' Goes to puzzle cupboard. Selects puzzle. Settles on carpeted area.

The temptation to go beyond recording what one sees and hears and to record interpretations and judgements was, at first, strong. To have surrendered to it, though, as both tutors recognised, would have limited the potential of the field notes – for it is the shared examination and interpretation of classroom data that lies at the heart of partnership supervision. The extract below shows how useful field notes are as a way of reconstructing a chain of events which the teacher does not have easy access to during his/her teaching, and how they can support explanation-seeking reflection:

Alan: I don't know whether we can ... I got the names of one or two but I don't know whether we can identify –

Pat: Yeah, this one's Laura's.

Alan: Is it? I didn't watch her for very long. She was engaged with task 'My tray is ... wide.' She copied it for a while but I think she was distracted by my presence, and then she intervened with a child measuring table lengths in milk mats. Then it all became highly baffling. She picked up the box of rods and went to the wall unit, and she took out the tray, and then she went across to you, and then took the tray back to the –

Pat: Oh, yes, she came and asked me which way was 'wide'.

Alan: And then she sat on the floor ... I didn't see her measure and then she –

Pat: Was that because you weren't watching, or she just did not measure?

Alan: I was watching but I didn't see her measure, and then she reboxed the Cuisennaire rods and took them back to the table. But she'd got a number (i.e. the answer) by then, so I was quite surprised. I didn't know how she'd, how she'd got it. No, quite mystified.

Pat, intrigued by the evidence that Alan had produced, asked him to return and continue observation for an additional session. Had Alan defined his task in terms of judging Pat's 'on-the-spot' effectiveness as a teacher, then the observations from both sessions would have been bad news indeed for Pat – none of the eight pupils that Alan observed had achieved their answers by teacher-approved means. What the discussion did provoke in Pat, more perhaps than any lecture on pupil strategies, was an active interest in how pupils understand and learn to cope with teacher demands.

COMMENTS

A student's time in school is the occasion in his/her training which offers experience of the world in which adult working life will be spent and in which professional identity will be shaped (q.v. Nias, 1984). The development of a 'teacher' self-image is obviously important to students, and anything which inhibits such development will, understandably, be resented be them. For example, the exclusion of students on teaching practice from administrative and supervisory routines (such as registration and playground duty) bothers them because such things are seen as integral components of a teacher's professsional responsibility:

> I'm supposed to be a teacher and the only thing I can't touch is the register. Fair enough, I don't touch the register ... but I'm not getting trained in those things ... the little messages that come round ... my name is never on the list. (When it's a film to be shown) they don't (inform me), they inform the class teacher ... but I'm the one who ... and they've never asked me to do playground duty.

Similarly, the visits of tutors to the classroom – whether teachers or college tutors – mark students off as different from the rest of the school staff. More significant, perhaps, than the tutor's physical presence, is his/her role as judge and critic – the tutor's right to require students to account for their activity underlines their lack of autonomy, which is an important element in the identity which they are seeking to develop. The frequent references made by students to conscious changes in their behaviour on the entry of their tutor to their classrooms is evidence of the tension which is caused by the conventional reminders of the student's novitiate and non-professional status.
Partnership supervision, while it does not dispense with the physical presence of the tutor in the classroom, is at least constructive – it offers the student an opportunity to employ a human resource to work on aspects of practice that

the student considers important. One hallmark of the competent
professional is, after all, the capacity (within his/her
professional mandate) to attend to the identification,
analysis and solution of classroom problems. Moreover, by
fostering dialogue in a situation which minimises the tutor's
institutional power and, instead, emphasises a colleague-like
relationship, the student's developing sense of 'self as
teacher' is nurtured.

We would claim, from our limited experiment with
partnership supervision, that its main strength is its
potential for laying the foundation of a proper
professionalism - i.e. the capacity of a teacher to remain
curious about the classroom; to identify significant concerns
in the teaching-learning process; to refine his/her
understanding of the structure of those concerns through
empirical study; to value and seek dialogue with experienced
colleagues as support in the analysis of classroom data; and
to adjust patterns of classroom action in the light of new
understanding. This is surely what Stenhouse (1984) meant when
he wrote about classroom research by teachers as the basis of
the art of teaching and, thereby, of the improvement of
schooling:

> To say that teaching is an art does not imply that
> teachers are born, not made, on the contrary artists
> learn and work extraordinarily hard at it. But they learn
> through the critical practice of their art ...
> exploration and interpretation lead to revision and
> adjustment of idea and practice. If my words are
> inadequate, look at the sketch book of a good artist, a
> play in rehearsal, a jazz quintet working together. That,
> I am arguing, is what good teaching is like. It is not
> like routine enquiry or routine management.

Teacher training is in a state of flux; current
experiments with approaches that support greater partnership
between training institutions and schools offer new
possibilities - but also new problems. The new possibilities
include extended time in classrooms for students, and a
greater contribution to the students' professional development
for classroom teachers. A major problem will be how university
or college based tutors and teacher tutors in schools can
develop shared roles and responsibilities in relation to their
students' realisation of the classroom as a professional
knowledge base. All aspects of teaching are much influenced by
tradition and prescriptivism. The danger, in the present
context, is that resort will be made to conventional forms of
supervision as a safe means of coping with a novel situation.
This, we think, would represent a sad loss of opportunity.
Conventional supervision is predicated on an assumption that
students should 'take' the problems and prescriptions which

supervisors offer and should work upon them in order to improve. While this may be one component of professional preparation, it is important that teacher education offers enough freedom so that student teachers can identify aspects of their teaching and classroom interaction which are of personal and professional interest. If such a position is accepted, then a form of supervision close to our partnership model would be useful. Some tutors and some students will, of course, feel more comfortable with more traditional conceptions of what a tutor is, of what a student teacher is, and of what teaching practice is. What we have tried to do is document the potential of an alternative approach for those who may be interested in developing something different.

Note
We should like to acknowledge the contribution that Jim Chivas made to the study on which this paper is based.

REFERENCES

Cogan, M.L.(1973) Clinical Supervision, Boston: Houghton and Mifflin.

Goldhammer, R.(1969) Clinical Supervision, New York: Holt Reinhart and Winston.

Hogmo, A and Solstad, K.J. (1977) 'Towards a Relevant Education', in Sigsworth, A.(ed.) Innovation and Rural Education, Tenth Interskola Report, ERIC.

King, R.(1978) All Things Bright and Beautiful? A Sociological Study of Infants' Classrooms, London: Wiley.

Lortie, D.C. (1975) Schoolteacher, Chicago: University of Chicago Press.

Nias, J.(1984) A More Distant Drummer: Teacher Development as the Development of Self, Unpublished paper, Cambridge: Cambridge Institute of Education.

Rudduck, J. and Sigsworth, A. (1983) Partnership: an Exploration of the Student-Tutorial Relationship in Teaching Practice, Norwich: University of East Anglia School of Education.

Stenhouse, L. (1980) 'Curriculum Research and the Art of the Teacher', Curriculum, 1 (1), 40-44.

Sullivan, C. (1980) Clinical Supervision: a State of the Art Review, Alexandria, Virginia: ASCD.

SECTION FIVE — CURRENT ISSUES

Chapter Ten

SUBJECT CENTRED AND SCHOOL BASED TEACHER TRAINING
IN THE POSTGRADUATE CERTIFICATE OF EDUCATION (PGCE)

Jim Eggleston

CONTEMPORARY INFLUENCES ON THE CURRENT PGCE DEBATE

The succesful design and implementation of courses for the
professional preparation of teachers requires that the
following dilemmas are resolved. First, the relationship
between teaching practices and those theoretical constructs
which inform our knowledge of how pupils learn, and of the
conditions propitious for their educational growth, must be
understood and used as principles of design. Second, the
relationships between, and division of labour among, those who
contribute to the professional education of teachers, must
grow out of a shared perception of the nature of this process
and its goals. Third, those features of knowledge upon which
professional practice is based, and which are generalisable,
must be separated from those which are subject or context
specific. Fourth, the means by which student teachers learn to
cope with the demands of teaching in the short term must not
limit or distort their later professional growth. This chapter
deals with those issues in the context of experience of recent
changes in PGCE courses, and in the light of empirical
enquiries.

When most PGCE students were destined to teach in the
grammar schools (in which they themselves had spent seven
formative years) these schools were, in terms of their
administrative arrangements, curricula, goals and
expectations, as similar as clones. This similarity was
reflected in the professional preparation these students
enjoyed. Until recently (and in some cases, still), PGCE
courses typically consisted of a teaching methods component
narrowly focused on the discipline with which each student was
associated by virtue of his/her degree, and which he/she would
teach. Such teaching 'methods' were rarely if ever presented
as a generalisable pedagogy (the study of teaching methods).
The theoretical part of the course usually consisted of
sociological, psychological and philosophical considerations
of schools, their inhabitants and their raison d'etre. These

aspects of the PGCE course tended to have a life somewhat detached from the 'methods' component. The making of connections between the practice of teaching, the profession of teacher, life in schools, and the theoretical constructs of supporting disciplines, was striven for but rarely achieved - few would claim to have achieved a productive symbiosis between theory and practice. Two conflicts resisted resolution. The first was the dilemma faced by the lecturer in a discipline. Should he/she, in the limited time available, attempt to induct students into its form of disciplined enquiry, or should his/her contribution be limited to describing those theoretical constructs which relate particularly to the students' experience of schools, teachers and children which they will have during the course and their first year in the teaching profession? The second is the partly logistical problem of giving the students time to reflect on their school experiences in a way which facilitiates the use of disciplined theory to give meaning to these experiences.

Such issues as these were perennial problems before the coming of comprehensive secondary education. Now the PGCE student will typically, during the practical part of the course and later in his/her first post, be faced with a potentially bewildering diversity of schools which vary in their administrative arrangements, curricular provision, teaching systems, the kind and amount of pastoral provision, and in the methods used to assess and communicate pupils' progress. This increase in the complexity of the professional responsibilities and tasks of teachers is one of the factors which has led to widespread agreement that the PGCE course should henceforward focus sharply, perhaps even exclusively, on the professional preparation of students for their first teaching appointments. As Professor Hirst (the author of the Universities Council for the Education of Teachers [UCET] working party document, 1979) emphasises, professional preparation is not meant to convey 'training of a narrow, routine, mechanical kind'. Quite the reverse is indicated by his description of the 'mark of a professional', which is:

> to have a sound knowledge of the circumstances in which he or she is called to operate; the ability to judge responsibly the appropriateness of various possible lines of action; the skills and dispositions to act effectively; the ability to assess the outcome of actions; and the capacity intelligently to adapt future practice accordingly.

In order to achieve these professional competences Hirst points to the requirements of 'serious study of what is currently known about the many factors that affect teachers' professional concerns especially those of teaching and learning, and by careful training in the skills and personal qualities involved in the application of this knowledge'. If the PGCE courses are to prepare students for the duties and responsibilities of class teacher; member of a schools' staff; and member of the teaching profession; then, according to the working party, four 'still very generally expressed goals' must, among others, be achieved. These are:

1. An understanding of the subject taught and of its place in the secondary school curriculum.
2. An understanding of the learning of the subject by secondary school pupils.
3. The understanding, skills and personal qualities necessary to teach the subject to secondary school pupils.
4. The understanding, skills and personal qualities necessary to exercise the forms of classroom discipline and control appropriate for the teaching of the subject in secondary schools.

Despite the facts that these goals are limited to teaching the subject, they lack the specificity necessary to generate strategies for their achievement. They do, however, indicate two important features of professional preparation courses. The first is the diversity of knowledge and understanding required; the second the variety of intellectual and social skills (which can only be acquired by practice in real teaching environments) required in order that students become progressively disposed to act appropriately.

Under what conditions can students acquire the knowledge, understanding, intellectual and social skills necessary to effectively pursue a career in teaching? What experiences will equip them to develop the dispositions and personal qualities which will enable them to apply this understanding and these skills so as to teach their pupils with increasingly beneficial effects? These are the central questions raised by the UCET working party. Activities prescribed exclusively by training institutions (e.g. listening to lectures, reading appropriate literature, tutorial discussion, undertaking written assignments) and teaching practice(s) conducted largely independent of the institution are, by implication, rejected as a potentially effective set of procedures. This is not to deny that each of these elements can make a useful contribution to professional training, but it is to deny that these elements individually or collectively are sufficient to achieve the elaborate model of the functioning professional teacher which is set out in the document. As the author states: 'if the study of educational theory is left dissociated from the development of practice judgements, skills, and personal qualities it cannot be expected to contribute significantly to professional preparation'.

It would seem that the kind of teaching strategy nearest to the vision of the working party is one in which the central feature consists of experience in schools, initially limited, possibly including some teaching, but under controlled and carefully monitored conditions. This would be followed by reflection and analysis. Whatever theory is necessary to give meaning to this experience would be introduced when it was required. Progress through the course would be marked by an increase in the extent and diversity of tasks undertaken by students in schools; by the development of a coherent body of practical knowledge with an increasing willingness to use this knowledge to define and solve pedagogical problems; and the growth of cohesive bodies of theoretical constructs which give form to educational knowledge and facilitate tests for both the truth and usefulness of such knowledge. The orientation of students will thus be empirical: their tasks will be to define problems; to acquire data (especially of their own performance and dispositions); to speculate; to theorise; to subject ideas to 'field' testing.

Problems for course designers and tutors include: how to select and sequence the kinds of experiences which facilitate both developments; how to divide the labour between school teachers and training tutors; and how to select schools and tutors who are willing to engage in this form of professional training. Whatever arrangements might be made to use 'second hand' evidence of classroom behaviour (e.g. videotape), nothing can replace 'first hand' experience as a means of developing those skills, dispositions and personal qualities which are the goals of professional training described by the working party.

New relationships with schools and a collaborative exploration of ends, means, forms of practical training and pedagogically relevant theories will be essential if those tentative steps towards new methods of professional training are to be sustained and developed.

The block teaching practice with its demand for 'whole class – whole lesson' teaching almost from the start is perceived by students to be 'part training – part assessment', but mainly a test of their ability to 'survive'. Models of teaching, half remembered from their own schooldays or acquired by unsystematic observation of their qualified colleagues, may serve as 'survival tactics'. Organised critical reflection on teaching strategies and tactics, and the evaluation of alternative procedures, can only be undertaken under conditions which guarantee some measure of security – and then only after appropriate training. These conditions do not exist on a typical teaching practice which is often sandwiched between 'theory' terms. Hence, many departments are experimenting with various forms of school attachment over a time scale longer than a term; others are collaborating with their schoolteacher colleagues and using the school as a 'laboratory' in which to explore pedagogical problems, or are conducting some of their method-work sessions in schools with selected classes. There seems to be an increasing awareness of the problems of how to build in to a professional training regime: gradualness of exposure; systematic observation; controlled experience; critical reflection; investigation and evaluation; and the means for relating practical experience to theory.

The UCET report rightly considered that 'a one year course cannot possibly hope to deal at all adequately with the knowledge, skills and qualities that professional preparation ... involves' and that 'courses are at present forced to be selective even among ... obviously necessary topics'. Although these statements were made with reference to a particular list of topics with which not everyone might agree, the important point is that the time required is less a function of which topics to include than it is a function of the methods of professional preparation chosen. Teacher training is about the development of professional knowledge and understanding in a way which facilitates the concomitant growth of effective backing skills and dispositions and, ultimately, the achievement of a professional autonomy to implement methods which are theoretically, defensibly and demonstrably effective. Consequently, more time is essential. Furthermore, the structure of courses and the roles of tutors and school teachers need also to be critically examined.

ASPECTS OF SUBJECT CENTERED OR METHODS TRAINING

One of the tasks facing those involved in teacher training may be illustrated by reference to an investigation of the teaching behaviour of student teachers undertaken at Nottingham (Dreyfus and Eggleston, 1980). The incidence of certain kinds of 'intellectual' transactions between student teachers (of physics, chemistry and biology) and their pupils were monitored on six occasions during the spring term teaching practice. These transactions included different kinds of teachers' questions (classified in seven categories including those demanding recall of information, speculation, observation, and experimental design). Similarly, the kinds of statements the student teachers made and the directives they gave were recorded. In addition, pupil-initiated transactions, such as pupil consultations and pupils' questions, were recorded. In a previous study (Eggleston, Galton and Jones, 1976) similar data had been obtained for experienced teachers, thus facilitating a comparison. The rather surprising result was that early in their teaching practice student teachers of science (especially of the physical sciences) behaved, as far as the instruments we used could detect, in ways very similar to experienced teachers. Moreover, differences in style between student teachers of all three sciences were not significant. As the teaching practice proceeded, however, the student teachers behaved increasingly less like experienced teachers. The differences progressively made manifest were increases in 'factual transactions', i.e. more questions requiring recall, more factual statements, more directives to find facts. Of the pupil-initiated transactions, more consultations and questions were directed to the acquisition of information. There was conspicuously less activity in the speculative and experimental design categories. The impression created was that as the teaching practice advanced, student teachers increasingly engaged in 'safe' transactions, i.e. those least likely to precipitate problems of management and control of classroom relationships.

These findings could be accounted for if one supposed that the teaching behaviour of student teachers was the result of a modelling process. Students may bring to their training a model of teacher behaviour based on their own experience of teaching when they were pupils. Thirteen years of exposure to teaching, seven of them in secondary schools, had equipped them with models of teaching which provided them with a set of teacher behaviours for emulation, and which they supposed represented the key to successful performance.

The observed regression to transactions increasingly dominated by fact acquisitions, may be due to the risks evidently involved in the transfer of initiative into the hands of pupils when they are involved in speculation, experimental design, or any open-ended activity for which the student teacher may feel unprepared, and in which engagement might risk a loss of what they construe as authority or control.

Another interesting finding of this enquiry is the progressive emergence of a distinctive style of teaching for physical sciences (chemistry and physics) which is different from that adopted for teaching biology. The former style (both with experienced teachers and student teachers) has a problem solving but essentially convergent character, the latter style is much more dominated by 'factual' transactions. Other evidence suggests that this phenomenon is constant across cultures. Studies in both Canada (Hacker et al, 1979) and Australia (Hacker, 1978) have demonstrated similar differences between the styles of teaching associated with physical and life sciences.

If there is substance in these speculations, there are serious implications for the initial training of teachers. Students entering professional training may enter their course with a model or stereotype of how teachers behave. During their course they may attend selectively to those experiences which are consistent with this model and which reinforce aspects of it. Their commitment to teaching methods to which they were exposed as pupils (perhaps ineffective or including features which cannot be defended by psychological or pedagogical theory) may result in their rejection of critical theory so as to leave their model intact. It might be that the common phenomenon that students perceive teaching practice to be the most valuable part of the PGCE course has precisely these origins.

The difference between the teaching behaviours of physical sciences and biology teachers might be explained in terms of differences between the two disciplines - the former having a convergent problem solving character related to the rich array of algorithms available; the latter having a more descriptive character, being less well endowed with explanatory theories. Alternatively, it may be that the cultural traditions of teaching these disciplines determine how teachers behave. It has been argued that these differences may relate to the nature of demands made in 'CSE' and 'O' level examinations. If this is the case then it would provide a powerful homeostatic influence on teaching methods.

Given some measurable success in terms of goals such as success in public examinations, considerable professional courage would be required to test whether alternative methods might be more effective. The resistance of the teaching profession to change has been well documented by those who have studied the dissemination data on curriculum development projects.

These models, transmitted by a sort of 'cultural imprinting', may have been effective with the pupil groups in which potential graduates found themselves, but less successful with other pupil groups. Those same teachers may have varied their teaching strategies and tactics according, for example, to the achievement level of pupils. The likelihood is that potential graduates would be denied the opportunity of experiencing adaptive variations of their model's style of interaction.

However this may be, there seems little to commend a process of transmission which does not incorporate critical reflection on professional practice, systematic variation of practice in response to different demands, and a rationale which provides both theoretical and empirical grounds for professional decisions.

If the findings of this enquiry and the interpretation placed upon them are true and are generalisable across school subjects, then it is possible to attempt to account for the attitudes of PGCE students to existing courses, and to speculate about the effects of evident trends in the evolution of PGCE courses.

It is interesting to speculate whether the new and evolving structures of PGCE courses for secondary school teachers are providing for this rational/critical approach to teaching, and to try to identify those elements which may still subscribe to, or even reinforce, the cultural imprinting mechanism. According to Reid and Patrick (1980), Taylor (1969) raised what seems to be essentially the same question much earlier when he stated that: 'there was very little research evidence concerning the effects of [PGCE] course training methods upon trainee styles' and that 'it remained unknown whether trainees acquire or use the teaching styles which they themselves experienced ... in their formative or training years.'

These authors also point out that in the time which has followed there has been both a growth of public knowledge about the contents of PGCE courses and of research into various aspects of these courses (q.v. chapters 4 and 5 of this book).

This increase in knowledge has been accompanied by fairly widespread (and sometimes fundamental) changes in the intentions, content, organisation, and process of PGCE courses.

The dimensions along which change has occurred seem to be the theory-practice relationship axis, and the training institution-school axis.

It would appear nowadays that the disciplines which purport to explain the phenomena of institutionalised education are less likely to be given separate consideration. This might, however, be given if the intention was to induct students into the concepts and methods of the disciplines. Instead, each discipline may be asked to examine a series of practical issues in education from its unique perspective, to show students how through its concepts it can inform judgements on these issues and, by reference to its methods of enquiry, establish claims to validity.

One can also detect the emergence of another species of theory which is more closely related to practice. This might properly be described as 'pedagogical' theory, examples of which might emerge from Bruner's ideas about theories of instruction, from Gagne's learning hierarchies, from studies of concept formation, from classroom interaction studies, or from Wragg et al's work on classroom management. I believe that many enquiries conducted during recent years contribute to pedagogical theory — no matter under what 'flags of convenience' they originally 'set sail'.

The evidence from PGCE courses which I have examined, persuades me that the adaptability of tutors in the contributory disciplines of education has yielded approaches which are both academically respectable and professionally relevant.

There is less evidence that PGCE subject methods tutors are able or willing to recognise the emergence of pedagogical principles and practices which transcend their subject-bound concerns. My experience, limited to the two universities in which I have worked and the half dozen or so institutions in which I have served as external examiner, leaves me fairly confident that assignments/essays/dissertations, orthodox products of scholarly endeavour, provide evidence of systematic study which has bases in theory and application in practice. This is less true of either method work or teaching practice. I accept that it is easier to make judgements about work grounded in something like orthodox scholarship, but I still wonder why the outputs from method work as presented for examination often seem unsystematic and lacking an explicit rationale. If enquiries have been undertaken in order to examine the effectiveness of teaching strategies or tactics, why are accounts of these investigations so rarely included in examined method work? If such enquiries have not been undertaken, are methods' tutors either reinforcing the cultural imprinting to which I referred earlier or simply trying to replace this with an alternative model?

Another puzzling feature of method work is the apparent failure to recognise generalisable features of pedagogical theory, strategies and tactics. The management and control of a class, the handling of mixed ability groups, matching task demand to cognitive developmental state, assessing the readability of textual materials, establishing a congenial affective climate in a classroom, assessing and reporting achievement, and other pedagogical problems, are not subject specific. Arguably, there would be an advantage in identifying and systematising such generalisable pedagogical principles, and engaging the collaboration of consultants from appropriate disciplines where necessary, rather than each method tutor being expected to be au fait with current developments in all aspects of pedagogy. Current practice may waste precious resources.

SCHOOL BASED TRAINING

Equally worthy of critical investigation is the trend towards greater school based training. Some problems associated with block teaching practice have been referred to earlier, but equally critical is the extension of school based experience which may be increasingly under the influence of practising teachers.

A review of 38 PGCE courses validated by the Council for National Academic Awards (CNAA) (Smith, 1982), showed that out of a total possible number of 175 course days (35 weeks x 5), courses varied in their provision of school based experience from 60 (the CNAA minimum) to 90 days; the mean was 78.15 days. We know from a collection of descriptions of both CNAA and university courses included in the Society for Research into Higher Education (SRHE) publication Developments in PGCE courses (Alexander & Whittaker, 1980), how varied school based experience can be. The nature of the link established between work undertaken in schools and that undertaken in colleges or universities, depends critically on the nature of the tasks undertaken by students in both, and on the congruence achieved between the perceptions of tutors and teachers of the purposes and nature of the training processes. The definition and allocation of tutors' and teachers' roles in the training process requires thoughtful and sensitive negotiation. When Smith allocated the 38 courses which he studied to positions on a responsive—reflexive continuum, he was able to point to features of the college—school relationship which appeared discrepant. On a scale represented as:

A. Total tutor directed.
B. Student responsive.
C. Student reflexive.
D. Totally student directed.

he defined A as 'highly structured and content orientated with the theoretical input being determined by the institution, with at best the practical experience of the student in school being illustrative of theoretical and pedagogic proposition being made by tutors in very general terms'. D was defined 'not in terms of content but in terms of process, since such content would change from year to year and from individual student to individual student'. He claimed that no PGCE course validated by the CNAA fell into either of these categories. These courses, according to Smith, could be classified in terms of B, 'always purporting to be in some sense responsive whilst being predominantly structured and college—directed' or C, 'always conveying some degree of imposed structure but stressing the reflexive student role as content initiator'.

When Smith examined the contingency between responsive—reflexive course intentions and the commitment to school based training (indicated by time spent in schools) he found the following distribution:

	Responsive	Reflexive
Degree school based		
High	School located 18.5%	School located 26%
Low	College located 55.5%	College located 0%

Smith points to the apparently incongruous finding that 18.5% of courses are apparently committed to 'responsive' tutoring and to more than average school based work: 'These colleges purport to provide the major input yet reduce substantially the opportunity for this, without claiming anything special for the school experience element over (the other responsive group)'. As Cortis (1979) has pointed out: 'it should not be accepted as a new conventional wisdom that more school based work necessarily leads to a better prepared student'.

Among the necessary conditions for effective collaborative tutelage are:

- The division of labour between college tutors and school teachers must be made explicit.
- Tutors must understand their own role and that of teachers and vice versa.
- There must be a large measure of agreement about intentions.
- Co-ordination of engagement with students on professional tasks must be secured.
- Students should be made aware of the hoped-for professional outcomes of tasks undertaken in school (as well as at college), the means by which these may be achieved and the kind of support available from school teachers and tutors.

The strengths and weaknesses of different degrees and kinds of collaboration between training institutions and schools may be explored by reference to three examples taken from the SRHE review quoted earlier.

The University College of Cardiff reported a series of pilot schemes in which the 'idea of enlisting external aid in the supervision of PGCE students during their teaching practice' was translated into action by 'asking practising teachers to participate' (Ashton and Yochney, 1980). Since 1968 when six schools participated, the scheme has grown so that 75 schools were involved in 1979.

The duties of heads of schools and numbers of staff selected to act as the school based tutors include:

- The representation to the students of a proper sense of professional responsibility both inside and outside the classroom.
- Arranging of teaching timetables.
- The supervision of lesson preparation.
- Liaison with school subject teachers.
- Observation of students' teaching wherever practicable.
- Collation of reports on students' development as teachers.
- Recommend grading from students.
- Provide material to be included in testimonials.

Head teachers from participating schools and their nominated school based tutors were invited each year to 'initial meetings held well before the teaching practice began in the spring term'. The purpose of these meetings was 'to agree upon a consistent procedure regarding, for example, form of lesson preparation, number of lessons students were expected to teach, and method of assessment'.

We are also informed that most schools arranged weekly meetings 'where the school based tutor discussed with the students in his school, as a group, the art of teaching in general and their performances in particular and in turn received the students' views'. Also, 'talks on school administration, finance, timetabling and pastoral care were arranged. ... To these meetings the department tutor concerned was usually invited and very good results were achieved as a consequence.'

During this teaching practice, students returned to the college each Friday for 'general' tutorials and 'specialised' lectures. The report explains that 'the students ... had an hour or more with their appropriate general tutor to discuss their teaching during the week ... this gave them a sense of belonging even if they were not visited in school by their internal tutor'.

This account is restricted to teaching practice arrangements and, therefore, it would be inappropriate to compare it with more sophisticated arrangements which often accompany other forms of school based work. With this in mind, however, the reader may be struck by the similarity between this scheme and traditional practice. Teachers, though, are given greater responsibilities for assessing students' performances which, as evaluations of other schemes have demonstrated, is for teachers (initially at least) a major cause for concern. Also, they are committed to a weekly meeting with their students.

From this description, the basis of the collaboration seems vague and bureaucratic. It sounds as though teachers had taken over part of the tutor's job, but that little attempt had been made to connect it with the residual tutorial functions with which it was formerly logically or empirically connected. It may be significant that 'a detailed evaluation' of the scheme in 1976 emphasised five points. The first two were concerned with the beneficial effects of allowing PGCE staff time to undertake other duties. The third was concerned with the value of 'giving schools a stake in the responsibility for preserving standards'.

It seems unlikely that in future evaluations of this scheme, teachers will report that 'the challenge of analysing students' teaching has caused me to re-examine some of my own assumptions about effective teaching'. In the Cardiff scheme, the growing knowledge which college based tutors ought to have from researches into teaching (or from, for example, cognitive psychology) have no apparently ready means of entry into student/tutor or tutor/tutor conversations.

The second example is one which I have selected partly on the grounds of its apparently 'full-blown' commitment to school based training and partly because of the kind of evaluation to which it has been subjected. It is the Sussex scheme, described by Burrell and Sexton (1980) as follows:

> The first intention was to associate a student over an extended period with an experienced teacher from whom, it was assumed initially, the student would receive all the professional instruction and support needed. The teacher was contracted to the University to act as teacher tutor to a pair of students in his or her care and was paid an honorarium for providing weekly tutorials out of school hours. A university tutor, called an 'E' tutor, acted as personal tutor for the students in a particular curriculum area and conducted a series of seminars concerned with general aspects of teaching in that curriculum area. The seminars were organised for the students, but the teacher-tutors attended half of them, held in the evening. It was intended that the university 'E' tutor should be responsible for selecting the teacher-tutors with whom he wished to work. Once selected, the teacher-tutors had responsibility for the supervision and assessment of the students in their charge.
>
> The second intention was that students should share in the life of a school over an extended period. Thus students were placed in one school for three days a week during school term from October to mid May and a general tutor was appointed in each school to be responsible for the oversight of the more general aspects of the work of all the students in that school. They too were paid an honorarium to provide fortnightly seminars for the students out of school hours. This aspect of the course has been further strengthened, we believe, by transferring the responsibility for personal tutoring from the 'E' tutor, who was responsible for a number of students in one curriculum area in several schools, to a university tutor appointed to act as personal tutor to all the students in one school. These tutors also have the responsibility for the teaching of 'Education' in the university component of the course. This is part of a more general attempt to help students to relate the theory part of the course to their experience in schools. The structure of the school experience has been modified so that it finishes for most students with a full, three week block at the beginning of the summer term. This was introduced first for the primary students and subsequently for the secondary students so as to give students experience of a full week in the life of the school. During this three-week period some students may

be offered alternative experience in a sixth form college, a further education college, or at the Urban Studies Centre in Bethnal Green.

A third intention, lying behind the school experience aspect of the course but also related to a second proposition that theory should feed off practice, is that students should collect information and ideas about teaching and the organisation of the school which can be used in the theory seminars in the University. Thus, most of the content of the University discussions grows out of the students' experience in the schools. It is hoped that the initial impetus for this dialogue emanates from the student's experience in the school rather than from early inputs of theory.

Here, in Smith's terms, is a reflexive, highly school based course. It is explicitly based on the belief that 'students learn the craft of teaching best by working alongside experienced colleagues and sharing the life of a school over an extended period.' The danger of this approach is that it may either reinforce the modelling process or precipitate model conflict which will require sensitivity and detachment to resolve. Moreover, this system may not readily accommodate empirical enquiries undertaken by students into curricular or pedagogical problems. The student's role is close to that of apprentice. Given a careful selection of teachers and schools, however, many of the criteria mentioned earlier might be met, even though the effectiveness of the system will be limited by the extent to which its 'articles of faith' are true.

The scheme has faced difficulties. Selection of 'ideal' teacher tutors proved to be a problem as local education authorities' and universities' financial positions deteriorated, forcing 'students to be more concentrated in schools'. Teachers found it increasingly difficult to carry out the major task of supervision 'in the extensive way envisaged', and also discharge their normal professional duties. As teaching posts became more difficult to obtain, the assessment of students' performance became increasingly critical, and teacher tutors sought help and advice in this aspect of their work. Also, the honorarium paid to teacher tutors lost value as a result of inflation.

Lacey et al (1973), in an account of an evaluation of the Sussex scheme, pointed out some of the problems associated with it, particularly the danger of the 'craft apprenticeship' model and doubts about the school as a place to train teachers:

it is clear that schools are not ideally suited to the training of teachers. Examples of this are conflicts between the needs of students and the time-table of the

school, or problems of the amount of time school-based
tutors can actually spend with students during the school
day.

Another problem identified by Lacey et al is that of
selecting appropriate schoolteachers as tutors. Initially,
when the scheme involved a relatively small number of pupils,
it was possible to 'hand pick' the tutors required. These
teachers, presumeably, would be on professionally open terms
with the university tutors with whom they were to work. Later,
for a variety of reasons, other schoolteachers became involved
who were not all suited to the task. Placing students in
schools depended 'more on negotiation and agreement than upon
the selection of the ideal teacher tutor in the ideal school'.
To be a good teacher trainer required security and confidence
about one's own teaching; the ability to explain it in terms
meaningful to very inexperienced students; and, I would add,
to allow aspects of it to be observed, questioned and
investigated.

The third example I have selected is one where the
commitment to school based work is far less than at Sussex. It
is notable, however, for the attempts made not only to relate
experience in schools to other aspects of teacher training in
the PGCE year, but also to map out professional (including
pedagogical) principles and use this map as an instrument of
course planning (Carter and Steele, 1980).

North Staffordshire Polytechnic Education Department's
PGCE Division works closely with eight schools (five
secondary, three primary). The professional studies (general)
course which occupies nine hours per week in the autumn term
was 'planned by teachers in the schools concerned, education
tutors and method tutors'. Explicitly, the rationale for joint
planning was 'to ensure the students will be engaged in
relevant and practical activities'; to enable students to
perform classroom based tasks which provide opportunities to
bring the educational disciplines to bear on problems of
immediate relevance to the student; and '[to] enable method
tutors to design their courses in relation to the core themes
and activities'.

Groups of twelve students work with a 'core' tutor for
their professional studies, and divide their time between
college and their 'attachment' school. Teachers are appointed
as professional tutors; professional studies tutors are
associated with particular schools. Students, therefore,
operate in a close working relationship with a tutor and a
teacher. The core professional studies, with its four themes
(the school, the child, the teacher, classroom organisation)
reflects joint planning with teachers, and is designed to
influence other college based work. The method work in the
secondary school programme (e.g. geography method) will take
up the same themes in the same order as the professional

studies general course, but will translate the general principles into subject specific applications.

This is a genuine attempt to identify general education/pedagogical principles and to use these in a way which may give the course a degree of cohesion which would be otherwise difficult to achieve. As the author of the account states, though: 'problems arise in ensuring that all contributors have a common understanding of the rationale and structure of the course'.

One might not be surprised to learn that teachers' heavy commitments in school prevent them 'attending meetings regularly' and thus being au fait with the programme. The author's main complaint is, however, directed at methods tutors. Apparently, methods tutors are sometimes unable or unwilling to harmonise their contributions with the themes in the professional core. As the author rather nicely expresses the related problem of trying to encourage tutors to use curriculum theory as a basis for method work: 'various subject tutors view the rational planning model in different ways, particularly with regard to the use of objectives and "assessment"'.

These three examples indicate clearly that there is some way to go before we can achieve the ideal relationship between teacher training institutions and schools, between tutors and teachers, and between students and teachers (or tutors) in school settings.

COMMENTARY

At the beginning of this chapter I tried to sketch, in very broad terms, the evolution of PGCE courses. The old pattern of disciplines associated with education (e.g. psychology, sociology and philosophy) and methods leading separate existences, seems to have given way to a new pattern in which knowledge obtained from disciplined enquiry is brought to bear on thematic studies of pupils and schools. This evolutionary drift has to some extent contributed to a climate in which the professional components of teacher training courses have been increasingly under critical scrutiny. The UCET report reflected this in its proposed rationale for courses of 'professional preparation'. Hirst's professional was to be able to 'assess the outcome of actions and the capacity intelligently to adapt future practice accordingly'. This is a consideration for professional autonomy. How best to achieve this was the quest of the three schemes outlined. A study of them indicates some of the barriers which lie in the path of developments in the teaching methods component of courses of professional preparation. These barriers might demand that the role of the methods tutor changes as radically as his/her colleagues' roles have already done. Traditionally, the methods tutors have enjoyed a quite remarkable degree of autonomy. Appointed, presumably because they had demonstrated their skills as practitioners, they represented to their students the nearest thing to a 'real' teacher which they were likely to encounter in their training before or after teaching practice. Their students, with whom they have contact throughout the course, come to rely on them for moral support in what (for some) are threatening circumstances, as well as for professional and intellectual guidance. The conditions in which method groups have thrived in teacher training institutions encouraged the development of close and mutually supportive bonds between tutor and students.

With the exception of primary training, tutor and students belong to the same sub-culture - physics or history or whatever. The tutor, with his/her local knowledge of schools and teachers, is the link between the institution and the real world of schools and teaching, and a buffer between the student and the school (where their interests might conflict). Because the student meets the methods tutor more often than his/her colleagues, and in many cases socially as well as professionally, relationships are forged in trust. The student, after a miserable day in school, can 'open up' to his/her tutor. This counselling relationship is believed to be of paramount importance by many methods tutors. The fervour with which the cause of a weak student is advocated in examiners meetings is a testimony to the feelings of responsibility of tutors for their students. Some of my own colleagues have resisted changes in the arrangements for the supervision of students on a three week block of primary school experience in the third to the fifth weeks of the first term of the PGCE course, on the grounds that if the early development of this close relationship did not occur then it might be in some way impaired. The supervision of 'their' students by other tutors, even for experiencing life in primary schools, was not acceptable.

The Sussex scheme is particularly interesting in this respect, in that it has attempted to dissociate 'personal tutoring' from 'teaching methods'. The 'E' tutor works with a number of students in different schools, evidently on problems of teaching methodology in a 'particular curriculum area'. The student receives 'professional instruction and support' from a teacher in the school in which he/she spends three days a week for two and a half terms. A further dichotomy is imposed - tutors being appointed in each school to be 'responsible for oversight of the more general aspects of the work of all the students in that school', who also give fortnightly seminars and, working in conjunction with a university tutor, are responsible for the same mixed subjects group of students. It would appear that the methods tutor's work is divided into 'professional/personal' support to students (which is provided by schoolteachers) and the study of teaching methods (which is managed by the 'E' tutor). Similarly, the 'general oversight' of students' work in schools is under dual control, but the division of labour between the school based 'general' tutor and the university tutor is less clear. We may note that the word 'personal' is also applied to the latter's tutorial responsibilities. The factors which contribute to a student's ability or inability to teach may be personal (they may have in abundance, or lack, those personal qualities which may predispose them to become potentially effective teachers); contextual (the conditions under which they are required to practise may be so good as to facilitate rapid development and the growth of confidence or so poor that even experienced teachers are relatively ineffective); or fundamental (students simply lack knowledge of subject matter and/or the ways in which it is learnt and might be taught).

An attractive feature of the Sussex scheme is that the 'E' tutor is freed to keep up-to-date with the literature, and may be disposed towards pedagogical enquiry. To be effective, however, this scheme does require teachers with the energy, commitment and time to do the job and with sensitivity in handling relationships. It also requires 'E' tutors who are willing to devote time to the study of pedagogy and to those aspects of psychology which sustain it.

Again, the Sussex scheme is interesting in the shared function of the school general (across subjects) tutor and his/her university general (non-'E') tutor. This arrangement is described as 'part of a more general attempt to help students to relate the theory part of their course to their experience in schools'. Hence, it is assumed that whatever discipline the university tutor 'owns' will be brought to bear on school related issues. One can see value in this, but there may be a danger that the student's selection of issues will be biased by the tutor's expertise. How to teach and pedagogy are central to the student's immediate concerns. Some pedagogical questions are subject specific, others are general. Are the general pedagogical issues picked up by the general tutors?

In currently typical PGCE courses, the methods tutor seems to be mainly responsible for the achievement of all four of the goals listed by the UCET working party (quoted earlier) as well as for the counselling of students before, during and after teaching practice. He/she may be helped in these tasks by teachers in schools who may enjoy special, even contractual, arrangements with the training institution. More rarely, I suspect, is help sought from colleagues within the institution whose expertise could help in the definition of pedagogical problems, and facilitate the formulation of teaching strategies. I conclude that methods tutors have too much responsibility and too many functions. I find it difficult to understand the reluctance they sometimes express to divide their labour with other colleagues. While methods tutors seem to cling to their special relationship with their students, even in the face of publicly expressed and usually ill-founded criticisms that they have lost touch with schools, they try to immerse themselves by spending more time in schools - on their own, in front of, or alongside their students.

Pedagogical enquiries may be narrowly (and quite properly) subject focused. The conceptual analysis of a topic in a subject, and the investigation of the status of this concept in the minds of pupils and conditions propitious for its growth, require a knowledge of psychology and subject matter. Many pedagogical problems, however, especially those which my methods colleagues tell me are particular causes for anxiety in trainee teachers, are sufficiently general to benefit from consideration by methods tutors who have acquired a knowledge of general pedagogical principles which is unrelated to particular subjects. The last 30 years has witnessed a resurgence of the study of teaching. Descriptions of teaching processes, initially informed by implicit or 'grounded' theories, have given way to more explicit (though still descriptive) theories, and correlational studies are providing data from which explanatory theories and hypotheses will grow.

There is now a substantial literature on many aspects of teaching to which British authors have made a useful contribution. No methods tutor can be expected to be sufficiently familiar with all of this, so as to be able to guide his/her students in the kinds of explorations and enquiries which he/she must make in order to teach effectively. Students model their teaching behaviour on what they believe to be effective procedures. These could be the way they were taught or the apparent preferences of tutors. If we do not provide students with the means to try out in a systematic way alternative procedures, and means for enquiry and reflection informed by theory and the reported experience of others, we will not produce the adaptable teachers the UCET working party have in mind. If students of mathematics or biology were to share, along with their english or history colleagues, enquiries into problems (e.g. those associated with motivation, questioning, classroom grouping, task analysis, readability of text, disruptive behaviour) under the guidance of tutors familiar with the literature and practitioners experienced in practical enquiries into these matters, I am convinced that all would benefit. Specialised subject tutelage could then concentrate on the task of conducting analysis of, and enquiries into, those subject-specific pedagogical factors which relate to the conceptual structure and investigative practices of their subjects.

Some tasks may be learnt by watching an expert and copying his/her actions. Teaching is not such a task: even if it were there are few experts. Teaching is an activity about which it is possible to theorise, but one cannot learn how to do it by reading theories. How to teach can, however, under certain conditions, be learnt by doing. It will be learnt more effectively if actions are systematically undertaken and the results of actions observed. Learning to teach requires the growth of empirical knowledge. For such knowledge to grow and be a guide to action it is necessary that schools and teachers collaborate with training institutions, not only to provide students with appropriate opportunities to practise, but also to provide articulate feedback when engaged in a programme of activities to which both teachers and tutors are committed. Alexander and Whittaker (1980) give descriptions of practice in which schools are significantly involved in teacher initial PGCE training. Of these, very few give a sufficient description of the nature of the tutor/teacher/student relationship. Many imply that by 'doing it' (not always specified) in school with tutors and teachers, theory (again unspecified) and practice are consummated in a fruitful union. This leaves too much to chance.

It is significant that, when research and development have been undertaken in professional training (e.g. Wragg, 1984), research has involved the investigation of particular problems in classroom settings (e.g. the teaching of mixed ability groups, questioning, management and control). The step from craft knowledge (which tends to be specific and non-adaptive) to knowledge informed by organising principles which facilitate appropriate action according to circumstances, requires research. By a similar process students may learn how to teach effectively.

Note
This chapter is a revised and expanded version of a paper that previously appeared under the title, 'Evolutionary trends in postgraduate initial teacher training', in Galton, M. and Moar, B. (1983) Changing Schools ... Changing Curriculum, London: Harper and Row. Permission to print here is gratefully acknowledged.

REFERENCES

Alexander, R. and Whittaker, J. (1980) Developments in PGCE courses, Guilford, Surrey: Society for Research into Higher Education.

Ashton, B. and Yochney, J. (1980) 'A School-based Tutor Scheme', in Alexander, R. and Whittaker, J. Developments in PGCE Courses, Guilford, Surrey: Society for Research into Higher Education.

Burrell, D. and Sexton, T. (1980) 'School Experience and the

Role of Practicing Teachers', in Alexander, R. and
Whittaker, J. Developments in PGCE Courses, Guilford,
Surrey: Society for Research into Higher Education.

Carter, R. and Steele, J. (1980) 'Course Coherence through
School Attachment', in Alexander, R. and Whittaker, J.
Developments in PGCE Courses, Guilford, Surrey: Society
for Research into Higher Education.

Cortis, G. (1979) 'An Evaluation of School-Based Training
within a PGCE Course, British Journal of Teacher
Education, 5 (2).

Dreyfus, A. and Eggleston, J. (1980) 'Classroom Transactions
of Student Teachers of Sciences', European Journal of
Science Education, 3.

Eggleston, J.F., Galton, M.J. and Jones, M. (1976) Processes
and Products of Science Teaching, Schools Council
Research Studies, London: Macmillan.

Hacker, R.G., Hawkes, R.C., Hefferman, M.K. (1979) 'A
Cross-Cultural Study of Science Classroom Interaction',
British Journal of Educational Psychology, 49, 51-59.

Hacker, R.G. (1978) Cognitive Development in Science
Classroom Practices: Prescriptions of Theories of
Learning, unpublished paper, University of Western
Australia.

Lacey, C., Hoad, P. and Horton, M. (1973) The Tutorial
Schools Research Project 1964-73, Social Science Research
Council.

Reid, K. and Patrick, H. (1980) 'The Structure and Process
of Initial Teacher Education within Universities in
England and Wales', in Alexander, R. and Whittaker, J.
(eds) Developments in PGCE Courses, Guilford, Surrey:
Society for Research into Higher Education.

Smith, R.N. (1982) 'Towards an Analysis of PGCE Courses',
Journal of Further and Higher Education, 6 (3).

Taylor, W. (1969) 'Towards a Policy for the Education of
Teachers', Colston papers, No 20, Butterworths.

UCET. (1979) The PGCE Course and the Training of Specialist
Teachers for Secondary Schools, London: Her Majesty's
Stationery Office.

Wragg E.C. (ed.) (1984) Classroom Teaching Skills, London:
Croom Helm.

Chapter Eleven

INTEGRATING THEORY AND PRACTICE

Michael Fullan

We have learned virtually nothing about how to integrate
theory and practice in teacher education in the 80 years since
Dewey's (1904) article on the relation of theory to practice
was published. In the area of in-service education and school
improvement, however, we have, in recent years, begun to
obtain glimpses of how successful processes might be working.
The understanding of these processes is still at a very
preliminary stage, but it is a start. In this paper I present
some of this knowledge and develop some of its implications
for teacher education.

The paper is divided into two main sections. In the first
section, examples of successful school improvement projects
are presented that illustrate the relationship between theory
and practice. Conclusions are formulated which are intended to
depict how and under what conditions changes in theory and
practice occur. While the first section of the paper focuses
on in-service education, the second section takes up the
question of theory and practice in pre-service programmes.
This section is shorter than section one, because the record
of theory/practice integration in pre-service teacher
education programmes is dismal. I present some data from a
national study conducted in Canada (Fullan et al, 1983), and
refer to other studies that have focused on the problem. These
studies tend to demonstrate what the problems are rather than
what solutions might be developed. In the conclusion of the
paper some implications are derived for addressing the problem
in which the critical importance of theory in teacher
education is stressed.

CHANGES IN THEORY AND PRACTICE

Theory concerns the beliefs, philosophical basis, pedagogical
assumptions, conceptual understanding, and rationale related
to such questions as what should be taught, why teach it, and
how to teach it effectively. Bussis et al's, (1976)

distinction between 'surface structure' and 'deep structure'
in their study of 'open education' teachers captures the
nature and importance of theory. They found that open
education teachers differed fundamentally in their approach to
open education. Some teachers operated at the level of surface
curriculum, focusing on materials and seeing that students
were 'busy'. They tried to address open education goals
literally, but they did not comprehend the underlying purpose.
They wanted, for example, to ensure that children were
'learning to share materials, to take turns, to respect the
properties of others, and so on – with the focus of concern
being the manifestation of these behaviors rather than
concomitant attitudes and understanding' (Bussis et al). It
was these teachers who reacted to the problem of ambiguity by
requesting further guidance on 'what exactly has to be
covered'. Other teachers had developed a basic understanding
of the principles of open education and concrete activities
which reflected them. They were 'able to move back and forth
between classroom activities and organizing priorities, using
a specific encounter to illustrate a broader concern and
relating broader priorities back to specific instances'.
Reflexivity, purposefulness, and awareness characterized these
teachers, but not in a linear way. They would, for example, do
something out of intuition and then reflect upon its meaning
in relation to overall purpose. Assumptions about and
orientations to children varied similarly. Teachers ranged
from those who felt that children's ability to choose was
unreliable and idiosyncratic (some could, others couldn't) to
those who assumed that all children have interests and were
thereby able to relate individualised interests to common
educational goals across the curriculum.
    In the pages of quotations from teachers, and in their
own analysis, Bussis et al clearly demonstrate (although not
using the same words) the relationship between theory and
practice. Some examples: teachers who saw open education as
literally covering subject content but who had no underlying
rationale; those 'who were reasonably articulate in indicating
priorities for children [but] were more vague in describing
concrete connections between these priorities and classroom
activities'; still others who 'may provide the classroom with
rich materials on the faith that they will promote certain
learning priorities'.
    Bussis et al (1976) were, of course, describing teachers
according to whether or not they possessed understanding of
what they were doing, not the much more difficult question of
how or whether one could set out to develop this deeper
relationship between theory and practice. The following case
studies do provide ideas on the process of changing and the
relationship between theory and practice in the classroom.
They do not raise macro theoretical questions about the
relationship between theory and society (which are outside the

terms of reference of this paper), but they do indicate the role of conceptual or theoretical change in reference to particular programmes. The findings from three studies are described: Huberman's (1981) case study of a reading programme, Showers (1983a,b) work on coaching and Little's (1984) examination of staff development.

Huberman (1981) conducted a case study of the implementation of a new reading programme (called ECRI) in the classrooms. Two of the explanatory factors singled out were 'the quality and amount of technical assistance' and 'sustained central office and building level support'. The district arranged for certain principals and teachers to receive training at the developer's centre. All teacher users received training and follow-up assistance from the principal and other helping teachers who had received the initial training. Huberman (1981) comments:

> It was also decided that ongoing assistance should be provided, hence the idea of a 'helping teacher' who would give workshops, demonstrate the ECRI techniques, provide supplies and materialsm chair a monthly in-service meeting between users, provide ongoing consultancy.

The developmental nature of learning how to do something new was recognized by a policy of easing teachers into ECRI rather than expecting comprehensive implementation at once. Moreover, Huberman found that early difficulties were typical: 'teachers, trainers and administrators all talk of a "difficult", "overwhelming", sometimes "humiliating" experience during the first six months, and for some during the initial two years'. He noted that almost every respondent attributed the survival of ECRI during this period to the strong administrative support and the helping teacher. Activities mentioned as valuable included frequent in-service meetings 'during which teachers exchange tips, war stories, encouragements, complaints and formulated requests to the helping teacher'.

As Huberman describes it, the initial six months is a period of high anxiety and confusion. After some 'settling down', there still remains a significant period of relating the specific behaviours to the underlying rationale of the new programme. After six months:

> there is cognitive mastering over the individual pieces of ECRI, but little sense of the integration of the separate parts or, more globally, why certain skills or exercises are related to specific outcomes. Concern for understanding the structure and rationale of the program grows as behavioral mastery over its parts is achieved.

This study and, especially, the latter quote is one of the few examples in the literature which alludes to the processes of alterations in conceptual or theoretical understanding on the part of teachers. It appears that changes (increased understanding) at the belief and conceptual level are fundamental to successful implementation, changes in beliefs follow changes in behaviour rather than vice versa, and changes take many months during which the initial states are characterized by anxiety and uncertainty.

Showers (1983a,b) designed a training programme based on work developed by Joyce and Showers (1980) in which they suggested that effective in-service programmes consisted of five components – theory, demonstrations, practice, feedback and coaching. (Joyce and Showers did not discuss the ordering, mix and sequence of the five components.) In the training programme, Showers (1983a) approached the problem from the perspective that mastering a new teaching approach requires teachers 'to think differently and organize instruction in fresh ways'. In the experiment reported, 17 junior high school language, arts and social studies teachers were trained in three models of teaching during a seven week period totalling 21 hours of training (Showers, 1983a,b). Following initial training, the sample was randomly assigned to a coaching treatment group (n=9) and a control group (n=8). Coaching is conceived by Showers to comprise three elements: provision of companionship, the giving of technical feedback, and the analysis of application. Coached teachers 'were observed once a week for five weeks and after each observation, met with a consultant for a coaching conference.' One session provided oportunities for teachers to share specific lessons. All teachers were asked to 'transfer' their learning by preparing and teaching a lesson using the same set of materials, but receiving no assistance with respect to instructional strategies. Transfer scores were derived through observation with respect to teachers' technical competence in the use of the models, ratings of the appropriateness of the model used given the objectives, and ratings of the teachers' ability to teach the model to students as indicated by student response (Showers 1983a,b). Transfer of training scores for the coached teachers showed a mean of 11.67 compared to 5.75 for uncoached teachers. Showers makes several interesting observations:

> During teaching of the final unit, coached teachers spent approximately twice as much instructional time at the conceptual and theoretical levels of information processing as did uncoached teachers (recall that uncoached teachers received the same initial training as coached teachers). Factors that contributed to success included 'practice with new models of teaching, successsful experiences with the trained strategies, and understanding the requirements of transfer'.

She corroborates one of Huberman's main findings that all teachers were initially 'stymied by the discomfort of using a strategy awkwardly and unskillfully' (1983b), and that most of the uncoached teachers did not get beyond this 'difficulty of fit' stage.

Showers also notes that the design was individualistic rather than organisational in focus and that, for the most part, little support existed in the schools for the development of new teaching behaviours. She concludes that in order for coaching to occur on a broad scale, peer coaches will have to be trained and that:

> Peer coaching will necessitate some organizational changes for most schools, if time for observation and conferencing of teachers by teachers is to be possible. Furthermore, the establishment of conditions for peer coaching will necessitate the building of school norms which encourage and legitimize ongoing collegial attention to curriculum and instruction (Showers, 1983a).

Little (1984) reports similar findings in her case studies of staff development activities in three elementary and three secondary schools attempting to implement a mastery learning programme. In the more successful schools, teachers and principals participated in a staff development programme (including training and implementation) as a group (rather than as a series of individuals). Little reports that new material was gradually introduced to groups of teachers, consultants and the principal over a period of two years. Each set of ideas was discussed, applied and discussed again. As with the previous two examples, 'the first six months, according to teachers, were slow and clumsy on all sides. Teachers were uncertain how to make sense of what they were hearing'. Also, the 'extended duration provided for gradual and incremental command over a set of ideas and cumulative discovery of the ways they could be applied in the classrooms' (Little, 1984). Stated another way, the theory and ideas did not make sense until they could be applied, discussed, and re-applied over periods of months. There was constant simultaneous preoccupation by the group with both theory and its application.

Several conclusions can be drawn from these three studies and other more comprehensive research literature on school improvement (q.v. Crandall et al, 1984; Fullan, 1982). We might best summarise the conclusions by responding to three questions: When we talk about changes in theory and practice in schools what are we referring to? What can we say about the process of changes in practice? Under what conditions do changes in theory and practice occur?

WHAT IS CHANGE IN THEORY AND PRACTICE?

In previous work it has been suggested that change in practice
in the classroom involves at least three dimensions: new
materials, new teaching practices, and new beliefs (Fullan and
Park, 1981). Alterations in theory and practice can be seen as
the interplay between a set of specific practices (activities,
methods, teaching behaviour etc.) and its underlying belief
and conceptual structure. Materials (learning resources)
represent the medium in which this interplay is carried out.
In most instances, of course, the problem is that no such
interplay occurs because the dimensions are considered in
isolation. For example, a new curriculum is produced as a set
of learning resources with little clarity of its theoretical
and practical usage; a workshop is conducted expounding the
theoretical rationale of a new programme with no connection to
its use; or practical activities are presented with no
attention or formulation of the underlying rationale. Whatever
the case, in referring to changes in theory and practice in
the classroom, it is the relationship of materials, practices
and beliefs that are at stake.

WHAT ARE THE PROCESSES OF CHANGE?

While the first question addresses the elements of the
problem, the second question is much more complex because it
concerns the relationship among the elements over a period of
time. The three studies mentioned earlier provide some
evidence about how theories and practices change in the the
use of new programmes which suggest that:

1. Changes in theory and practice take place over
    time (some two years for significant changes).
2. The initial stages of any significant changes are
    always characterized by anxiety and uncertainty.
3. Change involves learning new skills through
    practice and feedback - it is incremental and
    developmental.
4. The most fundamental breakthrough occurs when
    people can cognitively understand the underlying
    conception and rationale with repect to 'why this way
    works better'.

Research is not precise about the specific dynamics of
theory and practice but some interesting inferences can be
derived from this work. First, it is likely that some
behaviour change must precede changes in attitudes, beliefs
and conceptions. People apparently understand new conceptions
by first trying out practices and then reflecting on and
discussing the underlying assumptions. If this is true, it

helps explain why most workshops which introduce a new programme by dwelling on objectives, theory and rationale fail to have an impact.

Second, the solution is not to emphasize only practical activities. As Bussis et al (1976) and others (e.g. Joyce and Showers, 1980) have shown, it is possible to change 'on the surface' by endorsing certain goals, using specific materials, and even employing the new practices mechanically without understanding the principles and rationale of the change.

Third, it is necessary to examine the role of conceptual understanding in relation to beliefs. Beliefs and understanding may or may not go together. The case studies describe processes of change in which new beliefs were acquired based on understanding and mastering new skills. Two examples can be used to demonstrate the role of beliefs without understanding: one can firmly endorse a new change and believe in it without really knowing what it is. Bussis et al (1976) refer to such an example in reference to certain teachers highly committed to open education as a matter of faith:

> action based on valuing and faith is not very likely to lead to an enlargement or strengthening of the teacher's own understanding. The potential informational support available in feedback to the teacher is not received because it is not recognized

This phenomenon accounts for the frequent finding in the implementation literature that people who sincerely claim to be using a new practice turn out not to be using it in any recognizable form (numerous studies have documented this, starting with Goodlad et al, 1970). Laing captures this aspect in his phrase 'if I don't know I don't know, I think I know' (in Watzlawick et al, 1974). The other, and somewhat opposite, example occurs when people reject a change, vociferously disbelieving its worth. They may or may not be right in a given instance, but it is certainly the case that people sometimes reject changes which they do not understand. Huberman's (1981) case study refers to this type of situation, in that teachers had grave misgivings about the the new reading programme during initial implementation, but eventually came to believe in it firmly. This raises ethical and strategic dilemmas in the planning of change (e.g. how much participation in decision making to allow, how to get started, etc.) which I do not have the space to discuss, but should be carefully considered. In any event, understanding is a basic component of theory.

INTERGRATING THEORY AND PRACTICE

UNDER WHAT CONDITIONS DO CHANGES IN THEORY AND PRACTICE OCCUR?

It is not my intention to provide a list of factors related to a successful change in theory and practice. The answer at the most general level is that the conditions necessary are ones that support the four aspects of the process cited above (i.e. change takes place over time, involves anxiety, is incremental in skill development, and is cumulative in developing cognitive understanding). At a more particular level, the research literature has found the following to be important: the instructional leadership role of the principal; in-service or professional development activities that are ongoing, programme related, and involve a variety of formats and resource people; collegial norms within the school fostering frequent peer interaction; and external facilitation, direction and support from district authorities or other agencies external to the school (for further elaboration and evidence see Crandall et al, 1984; Fullan, 1982, forthcoming). The conditions amount to ongoing, intense forms of support and pressure through interaction on the part of those involved in programme changes. There are examples of such schools (see Little, 1984) but they are clearly in the minority. These conditions do in fact call for changes in the culture of the school, i.e. changes in the values, norms, organisational conditions and patterns of interactions in schools, and in the external agencies supporting schools (Joyce et al, 1984).

In summary, recent research on school improvement and associated change processes provides some information on how changes in theory and practice (and their relationship) occur at the school level. This research represents very modest progress since Dewey's writings at the beginning of the century, but some sense of the nature of the problem and the direction of the solution is emerging.

THEORY AND PRACTICE IN PRE-SERVICE TEACHER EDUCATION

Given the conditions necessary for integrating theory and practice described in the previous section, it is not surprising that teacher education institutions have been unable to produce teachers capable of integration. What is surprising, is that unrealistic expectations continue to be pursued and that so little progress has been made in defining the problem. Half the critics claim that there is too much irrelevant theory, while the others argue that there is too much mindless practice. Most seem to agree that the integration of theory and practice is a desireable if elusive goal. In a Canadian survey of faculty members and students in ten english-speaking faculties of education we asked a sample of 1400 students and 500 faculty members for their assessment of how much importance was attached to certain goals in their institutions and how much importance they thought should be attached to them. One of these goals was 'to prepare teachers who can integrate theory and practice'. Students and faculty members had essentially the same views: while about 30% of each group thought that their institution actually attached a strong emphasis to this goal (calculated by those who responded 'great' or 'very great' on a five point scale), about 90% thought that this goal should receive a strong emphasis (Fullan et al, 1983). This discrepancy between the real and the ideal was one of the largest among the nine goal areas we asked about. Approximately 40% of all faculty members and students thought that the problem of integrating theory and practice was a serious or very serious one in their institution.

Three aspects of the problem are worth considering: the relationship of practice to theory in existing pre-service programmes, some questions about the role of theory in pre-service programmes, and the absence and emergent role of induction programmes in the first years of teaching. I examine each of these aspects in the following paragraphs in terms of what is currently happening in teacher education, not what should ideally happen.

Many institutions have adapted to the problem of the irrelevance of theory by increasing the practice teaching or other field aspects of the programme. Student teachers have responded favourably; indeed it is almost a truism that practice teaching, internship or other forms of being in the school, are cited by students as by far the most valuable part of their programme. Serious problems have, however, been identified by several researchers. We do not, in fact, know much about the nature of the practicum as experienced by student teachers. Tabachnik et al (1979) in the United States conducted one of the few intensive studies of a field component in examining twelve students in a four semester programme. They note:

> Student teaching typically involved a very limited range of classroon activities. When student teachers were observed, they were most often engaged in the rather routine and mechanical teaching of precise and short-term skills, in testing and grading children, or in 'management procedures' ... Typically, the students tended to follow the lessons contained in ... materials somewhat rigidly rather than using them as guides.

Goodman (1983) makes a similar observation:

> when asked why they were teaching what they were teaching, students rarely mentioned educational principles or intellectual interest in subject matter. Instead, the most common answers were: (1) the

cooperating teacher told them what to teach (2) the
lesson was next in line in the textbook ...

Dewey (1904) forecast this problem (in an increasingly
quoted passage in the literature of the 1980s):

Practical work should be pursued primarily with reference
to its reactions upon the professional pupil in making
him a thoughtful and alert student of education, rather
than to help him to get immediate proficiency. For
immediate proficiency may be got at the cost of power to
go on growing.

The vast majority of programmes in teacher education do
not attempt to explicity relate theory and practice. By
extending the field component they add opportunities for
students to adjust to the routines of teaching without any
advance in the underlying knowledge base (and possibly some
loss). What is perhaps more revealing in light of the previous
section, is the hypothesis that even if pre-service programmes
were designed to strengthen the integration of theory and
practice (as a few have [e.g. Gitlin, 1982]), the conditions
and experience would be too weak by themselves to accomplish
any significant integration.

The second aspect I would like to mention briefly is the
role of theory in pre-service education programmes. The
research literature is much more precise in defining and
studying practice components than it is relative to theory.
Faculty members and student teachers alike have vague and/or
different notions when they refer to theory (Fullan et al,
1983). Judging from how most current programmes are organised,
one can speculate that there are two theory problems: one
concerns the foundation disciplines of philosophy, psychology
and sociology; the other involves subject or methods courses.
Focusing on the way things are (rather than how they might be)
foundations courses (and those who teach them) in most
institutions are totally removed from the rest of the
curriculum and from student teaching. Potentially relevant
ideas (e.g. related to educational philosophies, child
psychology and learning theories, social development and the
impact of community and society on the school) are treated in
the abstract. Again, given what we know from the previous
section, there is no way that this arrangement could possibly
lead to applying or otherwise integrating theory and practice.
The subject or methods courses raise another issue. Here, the
course is directly relevant to what has to be taught. The
problem, as we have seen, is that the nature of the experience
of student teachers provides little opportunity for moving
back and forth from application to underlying rationale.

The third aspect - the first years of teaching or the
induction period - compounds the problem. Even if there were

some initial beginnings in taking up the theory/practice relationship in the pre-service programme they would be quickly lost in the beginning year or two. It is a fact that for the vast majority of new teachers in North America nothing particular is done to support the first year teacher. The effects of this on beginning teachers have been amply documented by McDonald and Elias (1980), Ryan et al (1980) and Griffin and Hukill (1983). It is a period of anxiety, fear and isolation. The most prevalent feeling reported by teachers is one of being totally 'on your own' with little or no help. It is obvious that little integration of theory and practice will occur under these conditions. In the last few years some school districts have established supportive induction programmes. McDonald and Elias, 1980, identify 24 exemplary programmes, Griffin et al 1983 conducted case studies of three sites which had mandatory induction programmes. These examples provide some direction for the implications section, but the point here is that most first year teachers receive no support. The pressure is to adjust to and keep a job, not to integrate theory and practice.

CONCLUSIONS

The general idea for reforming teacher education in the direction of integrating theory and practice involves internal restructuring and continuity within and between pre-service, induction and continuous professional development for teachers (and for administrators and other staff positions). It entails changes in the curriculum or learning experiences and in the conditions (i.e. structures and norms) under which learning occurs at each of the three levels. The main theme of these revisions is best captured in Schon's (1982) concept of the 'reflective practitioner'. What he said about managers applies equally well to teachers:

> Managers do reflect-in-action, but they seldom reflect on their reflection-in-action. Hence this crucially important dimension of their art tends to remain private and inaccessible to others. Moreover, because awareness of one's intuitive thinking usually grows out of practice in articulating it to others, managers often have little access to their own reflection-in-action.

Stimulating individual reflection in relation to action, and collective (two or more people) sharing of an analysis of this practice based reflection is at the heart of reforms in teacher education at all three levels. In this concluding section I will consider the following aspects of reforming teacher education: the limitations of concentrating on any one of the three aspects in isolation from the other two;

illustrations of the kinds of changes that will be required within and between the three levels; strengths and weaknesses in our knowledge base; and the very difficult strategic problem of where and how to start.

Limitations of a Segmented Approach

Initial pre-service teacher education, no matter how effective the programmes are in addressing the relationship between theory and practice, are severely limited in what they can do to prepare teachers. There are two serious constraints. First, a matter internal to the programme: we know the kind of intensive, continuing interactions necessary for developing new theory based practices. Pre-service programmes by themselves are not intensive enough, long enough or real enough to result in substantial benefits. Second, an external factor: the first years of full-time teaching (under existing conditions) will negate the best beginnings because schools pay little attention to the first year teacher, and are not set up to support the 'reflection-in-action' which is required for the continual interaction and integration between theory and practice. Put differently, 'real life/on-the-job' learning is essential to address the problem and schools are not conducive to effective follow-through in this regard even if the pre-service programme was ideally designed.

Induction programmes to support beginning teachers have appeared in a small number of states and districts recently and are psychologically and practically helpful. They face, though, similar limitations in developing integration between reflection and action. Several such problems are mentioned in Griffin and Hukill (1983) about one such programme:

(1) difficulties inherent in translating research vocabulary into meaningful terms for principals and peer teachers; (2) the attitude of some principals that the beginning teacher program is only one more responsibility involving paperwork; (3) the minimal emphasis placed on training in supervision given the peer teachers; (4) lack of understanding of evaluation procedures; (5) the small number of university personnel used by districts for the support team; and (6) the focus on technical teaching skills competencies at the expense of beginning teachers' concerns as individuals.

The few induction programmes in existence are, on balance, successful because they meet such a desperate need. The real issue is that problems related to teaching effectiveness, teacher morale, longevity, etc., are probably more closely related to the conditions of schools affecting development of all teachers than they are to problems specific to the induction period (Griffin and Hukill, 1983).

Staying with the theme of limitations in focusing in isolation on any one of the three components, it is likely that changes in the conditions of schools that support continuous professional development of teachers and other staff would have the greatest 'payoff' of the three (and would be the most difficult to accomplish). Work at this level would obviously benefit if it were co-ordinated with pre-service and induction programmes, a topic to which I now turn.

Illustrations of Needed Reforms

It is not my intention to present a comprehensive set of recommendations. Joyce and Clift (1984) have already provided a systematic and impressive reform agenda organised into five structural propositions, nine curricular propositions, and three change propositions. I would, however, like to indicate several illustrations within and between the three components that are especially relevant to the question of integration between theory and practice. In general, it will be necessary for teacher education institutions to join with school districts in designing programmes that comprise aspects of all three components - pre-service, induction, and in-service (see Goodlad, 1984; Joyce and Clift, 1984).

At the pre-service level, three interrelated changes might be envisaged. First, revise the impossible expectation that initial teacher education will be adequate to produce qualified teachers and correspondingly expect most training to occur after employment begins (Joyce and Clift, 1984). This will relieve the pressure on teacher education institutions and student teachers, and allow them to concentrate on more feasible goals which can initiate and emphasize the process of reflection-in-action. Second, set up 'clinical opportunities' for student teachers in methods or subject courses to work collaboratively with both university and school personnel - courses or programmes which incorporate what we know about effective theory/practice learning, i.e. including integrated elements of theory, demonstration, practice, feedback and coaching. This is 'easier said than done', but there are already programmes organised in this direction (see Joyce and Clift, 1984; Gitlin, 1982). Such clinical work should not be noted for its immediate practical benefit but for the opportunity it provides for action and reflection (Dewey, 1904). There are certainly major barriers to futher developments along these lines, not the least of which are the need for staff development programmes for college professors to enable them to work in a clinical, reflection-in-action mode. Third, eliminate foundation courses in their current form and reintroduce these disciplines by incorporating them within a clinical focus. Sociology, psychology and philosophy could be related to methods courses (as mentioned above) and/or new clinical foci could be established (as recommended by Joyce and Clift) around areas such as: the design of curriculum, the design of teaching, the nature of students, and the design of schools and their relationship to committees and society. These programmes could examine both the content of each area and the processes of change, in terms of the barriers and strategies for bringing about changes. Since the programme would not attempt to produce the complete teacher, it would be possible to organise clinical activities based on their 'learning power'.

The major change at the beginning teacher level is to establish as a matter of practice a gradual induction period into full-time teaching (Joyce and Clift, 1984). There are programmes already in existence, albeit at early stages, which might form the basis for further development (Defino and Hoffman, 1984). Provision for gradual induction would not work unless accompanied by changes in pre-service and continuous professional development.

Continuous professional development for all teachers depends on changes in the organisation and culture of the school. There are some clear proposals for making improvements relative to the instructional leadership of principals, effective collegiality and professional development among small groups of teachers, linkage to external resources etc., and even some successes (Hersh and McKibbin, 1983). One of the encouraging signs is that approaches which have stressed field based reflection among groups of teachers have had very positive effects on teacher thinking and the relationship of theory and practice (Bolster, 1983; Clark and Yinger, 1977). In effect, these proposals call for integrating professional development or in-service education with programme implementation and the kinds of organisational changes necessary to support this integration (Fullan, forthcoming).

Strengths and Weaknesses of the Knowledge Base

For the first time we have a reasonably strong knowledge base in certain areas: classroom effectiveness (Brophy, 1983), school effectiveness (Purkey and Smith, 1983; Good and Brophy, forthcoming), staff development (Joyce et al, 1983), leadership of principals (Leithwood and Montgomery, 1982), and planned change (Fullan, 1982, forthcoming). In addition to further developments needed in these areas, there are some glaring weaknesses in our knowledge base in teacher education. We actually know very little about how to integrate theory and practice. For one thing, the real issue is how to integrate theories and practices, since teachers at any stage will be faced with a variety of teaching models, subjects, theories and the like. We have not (nor have I done so in this paper) carefully defined the epistemology of theory and practice. Are there differences between practical reasoning, theoretical reasoning, procedural knowledge, etc. (Robinson, 1984)? What we need is not an abstract typology of knowledge, but a programme and field based analysis of theory and practice components of existing curriculum and teaching activities. We also need case studies of clinical attempts to integrate theory and practice, especially at the pre-service and induction levels. The underlying point of all these suggestions is that reform should be based on further development of the knowledge base of teacher education.

Where and How to Start

The problem with recommendations for reform in teacher education is that they often neglect the issue of 'how to implement the implementation plan' (even if recommendations are incorporated into a plan for implementing them). The educational innovation field is filled with unimplemented change proposals (Sarason, 1982). We should be cautious about proposing 'the grand plan', and take seriously the lessons from the planned change and implementation literature (Crandall et al, 1984; Fullan, 1982). Even these lessons are deceptive, because what has succeeded in one setting may not be easily transferable to other settings. The suggestion, then, is to 'start small', with experimental programmes attempting to integrate pre-service, induction and continuous in-service with small numbers of people in schools, and teacher education institutions taking care to document both the nature of the educational changes (particularly as they relate to attempts to integrate theory and practice) and the processes of change occurring in those situations.

80 years seems like a long time to get started on a problem so central to education. I would not call it momentum, but there is some movement in some quarters in doing something about the integration of theory and practice in teacher education. We do not know whether the goal is achievable.

REFERENCES

Bolster, A. (1983) 'Towards a more effective model of research on teaching', Harvard Educational Review, 53, N.S, 1983, 294–308.
Brophy, J. (1983) 'Classroom organization and management', The Elementary School Journal, 83, 265–286.
Bussis, A., Chittenden, E. and Amarel, M. (1976) Beyond surface curriculum. Boulder, Colo.: Westview Press.
Clark, C. and Yinger, R. (1977) 'Research on teacher thinking', Curriculum Inquiry, 7 (4), 279–304.
Crandall, D. and associates (1984) People, Policies, and Practices: Examining the Chain of School Improvement, Vols.I-X, A Study of Dissemination Efforts Supporting School Improvement, The Network, Andover, Mass.

Defino, M. and Hoffman, J. (1984) A status report and content analysis of state mandated teacher induction programs, Research & Development Center for Teacher Education, University of Texas at Austin.

Dewey, J. (1904) 'The relation of Theory to Practice in Education', in C. McMurray (ed.) The Third Yearbook, National Society for the Scientific Study of Education, Part I, Chicago: University of Chicago Press.

Fullan, M. (1982) The Meaning of Educational Change. New York: Teachers College Press.

Fullan, M. (forthcoming) 'Change Processes and strategies for change at the local level', Elementary School Journal.

Fullan, M. and Park, P. (1981) Curriculum Implementation: A resource booklet. Toronto, Ontario, Ministry of Education.

Fullan, M., Wideen, M. and Eastabrook, G. (1983) A Study of Teacher Training Institutions in Anglophone Canada, Vol. I: Current Perspectives on Teacher Training in Canada: An Overview of Faculty and Student Perceptions, Ottawa: Social Science and Humanities Research Council.

Gitlin, A. (1982) Reflection and action in teacher education programs. Paper presented at American Educational Research Association annual meeting.

Good, T. and Brophy, J. (forthcoming) 'School Effects', Third Handbook of Research on Teaching.

Goodlad, J. (1984) A Place Called School. New York: McGraw-Hill.

Goodlad, J., Klein, M. and associates. (1970) Behind the classroom door. Worthington, Ohio: Charles A. Jones.

Goodman, J. (1983) 'An analysis of the relationship between university and field-based experience', Paper presented at the American Educational Research Association annual meeting.

Griffin, G. and Hukill, H. (1983) First Years of Teaching: What are the Pertinent Issues. Research & Development Center for Teacher Education, University of Texas at Austin.

Huberman, M. (1981) Exemplary center for reading instruction (ECRI) Masepa, North Plains: A Case Study. Andover, Mass: The Network.

Joyce, B. and Clift, R. (1984) The Phoenix Agenda: Essential Reform in Teacher Education. Educational Researcher. May. 5-19.

Joyce, B., Hersh, R. and McKibbon, M. (1983) The Structure of School Improvement, New York: Longman.

Joyce, B. and Showers, B. (1980) 'Improving inservice training: The messages of research', Educational Leadership, 37 (5), 379-85.

Leithwood, K. and Montgomery, D. (1982) 'The role of the

Little, J. (1984) Designs, contexts and consequences in the real world of staff development. Paper presented at the American Educational Research Association, annual meeting.

McDonald, J. and Elias, P. (1980) Study of Induction Programs for Beginning Teachers, Vols I-IV, Final Report to National Institute of Education, Princeton, N.J.: Educational Testing Service.

Purkey, S. and Smith, M. (1983) 'Effective schools: a review', The Elementary School Journal, 83, 427-452.

Robinson, F. (1984) Developing procedural knowledge, Paper presented at Canadian Society for Studies in Education, Annual Meeting.

Ryan, et al. (1980) Biting The Apple: Accounts of First Year Teachers. New York: Longman.

Sarason, S. (1982) The Culture of the School and the Problem of Change. Boston: Allyn & Bacon 2nd edition.

Schon, Donald A. (1982) The Reflective Practitioner: How Professionals Think in Action. New York: Basic Books.

Showers, B. (1983a) Coaching: a training component for facilitating transfer of training. Paper presented at the American Educational Research Association.

Showers, B. (1983b) Transfer of training, Paper presented at the American Educational Research Association.

Tabachnik, R., Popkewitz, T. and Zeichner, K. (1979) 'Teacher education and the professional perspectives of student teachers', Interchange, 10 (4), 12-29.

Watzlawick, P., Weakland, J. and Fisch, R. (1974) Change, New York: W.W. Norton.

Chapter Twelve

INITIAL TRAINING NEEDS OF SPECIAL EDUCATION TEACHERS

David Thomas

FIRST STEPS

Much of the content and orientation of initial teacher
training is based on the assumption that what is taught,
learned and experienced during this period is the first of
many steps which the teacher will take on the journey to
becoming an effective practitioner. Initial training has
something of the characteristics of early socialisation; an
induction into basic skills and attitudes rather than a
programme which produces a final and finished product. The
material is selected and rough-cut, but awaits faceting and
polishing. The assumed continuous nature of professional
development by teachers is structured by one year and one term
courses, Department of Education and Science (DES) regional
and other courses, local education authority (LEA) workshops,
induction schemes, higher degree opportunities, and Open
University offerings. In spite of these, initial training
provides for many teachers the longest continuous exposure to
calculated attempts to impart pedagogic skills, affect
attitudes, and to provide a philosophic basis for professional
behaviour. Although initial training is the beginning of a
career-long process, it assumes a particular significance
because of its primacy in that process. It can be argued that
the experience gained in initial training provides a
fundamental work and value format which must sustain
professional activity. To this, of course, must be added the
impact upon practice and beliefs resulting from the neophyte
teachers' personal experience and daily contact with fellow
professionals. The tension that can be generated between ideas
developed during training and 'on-the-job' socialisation has
received attention (Lacey, 1979). It has been suggested that
the impact of practical experience leads to initial training
being discounted as the teacher absorbs the values of his/her
school and colleagues. Clearly, those involved in initial
training hope that their contribution is not so negligible or
ephemeral, and that their products are not so susceptible as

to indulge in mindless institutional docility and thereby become incapable of affecting change or resisting attacks upon newly acquired values. Neither do trainers of teachers believe that their ideas are so divorced from practice, reality and rationality as to be operationally and idealogically vulnerable to the first 'whiff of grapeshot' from staffroom reactionaries.

Teacher trainers have the difficult tasks of effectively preparing student teachers for immediate roles and of implanting ideas and values which will assist the process of change. This has a marked significance for special needs courses since they are concerned with participating in and extending current trends, and not simply reproducing the patterns of the past.

The concept of 'initial' training suggests a position which is modest ('we can not do it all in nine months/three years') and also provides an escape clause ('this is why we leave "x" out'). The concept of partial or incomplete training is exacerbated by the multiple pressures on training institutions ('every teacher a teacher of english, language across the curriculum, multi-cultural education, competencies in mathematics and computing, etc.') and the time scale of the training programme (most sharply felt in the postgraduate certificate of education [PGCE]) so that, inevitably, initial training must be concerned with establishing rational priorities - what to include, what to leave out, what to treat thoroughly, what to mention en passant, the balance between theory and practice and between academic and professional development.

CONTINUOUS ASSESSMENT

What has happened to the PGCE in the last decade suggests that judgements over priorities are being constantly re-appraised. The swing from the earlier dominance of the foundation disciplines (history, philosophy, psychology and sociology), with the concomitant low status of subject specialisms, to the present pre-eminence of classroom and curriculum skills, indicates how views on priorities can fluctuate radically. Indeed, so marked has been the drift into the area of 'professional' competencies, that anxieties have been expressed lest the present generation of teachers will emerge under-equipped to play an informal part in the major educational debates of our time (Hartnett and Naish, 1981).

The continuous re-appraisal of initial teacher training suggests that there is no consensual prescription. Instead, we have a continuing debate (and a process of constant re-negotiation) not only in response to fundamental changes in assumptions as to the nature and purpose of initial training, but also in response to changes in the child population, altering social patterns, and the re-structuring of the educational system. The place of 'special needs' courses cannot be easily identified within this changing perspective. A further complexity occurs when we reflect on the major changes that have taken place, and are taking place, within the special education field itself. Views and opinions are, therefore, statements about current beliefs, and are subject to amendments and revisions in the light of constantly changing parameters (Hegarty, Pocklington and Lucas, 1982).

If, as has been suggested, initial training is an area where there are a variety of perspectives and ever-present pressures to select priorities, where do special needs courses fit into these priorities, and where shall we look for even a temporary consensus on content and approach? In one sense, the argument concerning priorities has been conceded – it has become almost morally indefensible to deny a place for special needs courses in initial training. This rhetorical support for special needs courses is considerable but (rather like Scheffler's idea of educational slogans) although supporters may congregate under the same banner, each may have a different interpretation of the 'cause' and each may assume that the others support his/her personal interpretation. Once again we may see unwillingness to thoroughly debate an educational issue being celebrated as an example of self-congratulatory approval of diversity – with differences and inconsistencies masquerading as a vigorous opposition to centralism (Scheffler, 1960).

THE NEED FOR SPECIAL NEEDS

The rhetorical support for special needs courses derives from the priority given to teacher training by the Warnock Report (1978) with its recommendation that an 'element' of special education be included in initial training. The 1981 Government White Paper Special Needs in Education gave this idea further impetus when it noted that special education required teachers to be especially sensitive to children's needs, and to recognise each child's individual pattern of abilities and disabilities. These skills, it suggested, need to be 'progressively' reflected in training. While efforts have been made to make the element of initial training compulsory, the responsibility for the content of training remains with the training institutions. With the Education Act 1981 and Circular I/83 Assessment and Statements of Special Needs, further emphasis was given to the skills of the teacher and, by implication, to the importance of special education in initial training and in-service education.

A survey carried out by the Royal Association for Disability and Rehabilitation (RADAR, 1983) asked 130 training institutions (universities, polytechnics, and colleges of

higher education) about the extent of special needs courses in
B.Ed. and PGCE programmes. The report is encouraging, showing
significant development in provision, but also points to
shortcomings and inadequacies in that provision. One of the
difficulties in assessing the survey, however, is that no
definition of special needs courses was applied and, as the
report notes, it was not possible to 'determine a substantial
impression of the standard or quality of courses'. The titles
of the courses on offer indicate something of the diversity of
interpretations of special needs employed in training
institutions (the report abbreviates special educational needs
to SEN). Among the titles are: 'The identification of SEN',
'Assessment and diagnosis', 'Aetiology of handicap',
'Curriculum for children with SEN', 'Support services',
'Language problems', 'Behaviour problems', and 'Slow
learners'. We can presume that the diversity of titles also
reflects a diversity of content.

80% of training institutions had specific SEN courses,
and 52% offered at least one compulsory course. These courses
varied in length (10-40 hours) and in the numbers of students
on the course (20-80). The dates when these courses were first
offered show two peaks (1975 and 1980), suggesting the impact
of the Warnock Report and subsequent legislation. As far as
the PGCE is concerned, 62 of 83 institutions offered SEN
courses. The duration of courses varied between 5 and 30
hours. These courses are typically led by one or two tutors,
although there was an example of one involving 15 tutors. The
RADAR report notes that during a period of diminishing
resources, training institutions have made a notable attempt
to start and maintain SEN courses and that, in spite of
considerable diversity of formats, these courses appear to
have two inter-related aims: to give a basic minimum grounding
to all students ... in the education of children with SEN, and
to provide opportunities for those students with particular
interests to develop their knowledge of children with SEN to a
much greater extent.

While the picture of provision in B.Ed. courses was
encouraging, it was less so in PGCE courses. Another positive
feature noted by the report was the widespread use of outside
speakers, giving students a chance to meet practitioners from
a variety of disciplines associated with SEN. On the negative
side, it appears that at least half of the students currently
in training receive no specific instruction on children with
special needs, and only a third of PGCE students take an
option in this area, although there is evidence of student
demand exceeding available places (e.g. Reid, Patrick and
Bernbaum, 1981).

While the argument for SEN courses has been conceded, it
can be suggested that the overt or covert rationale may
substantially influence the nature of syllabuses. Where the
institutional reaction to SEN is a symbolic response to

external pressures, or is a calculated obeisance to current fashion, its response may be minimal and ritualistic. A brief but prestigiously packaged input which is encapsulated and divorced from the rest of the training programme may satisfy minimalist cosmetic requirements. In contrast, there are SEN courses which aim to inculcate particular ideological premises. Almost everywhere there are resource problems which limit what can be offered.

ASSUMPTIONS

The case for SEN courses may be suggested to rest upon a number of assumptions or beliefs such as:

Evangelical
Promoting the cause of special education.

Political
Supportive of institutional image.

Professional
The majority of students will encounter pupils with SEN and need suitable preparation.

Ideological
Meeting SEN in mainstream schooling is essential on moral, social and political grounds.

Affective appeal
Handicaps are 'interesting' and draws upon student motivation.

Practical
Some background of SEN will help in a difficult job market.

Pragmatic
The need to find a role for special education tutors.

It is likely that the rationale and motivation for running SEN courses will be a mixture of the above and others. Given the current climate, the case against such courses is difficult to sustain, but this still leaves open the issue as to the priority that should be assigned to these courses and their content. These are related problems.
As suggested earlier, initial training implicates the selection of appropriate experiences. Consequently, if SEN is regarded as having a legitimate place within these formative experiences, then is it's place on that agenda as a main item or under 'any other business'? On what basis could the

relative importance of SEN and, for example, multi-cultural education, the problems of urban deprivation, and the education of travellers' children be decided? An equally difficult problem is which topics to include in SEN courses. Tutors will have differing views on this in the context of their general position on SEN courses. Consider, for example, the following list of possible SEN topics, select the ones you would include and then justify your selection:

> Dyslexia, autism, slow-learning pupils, stammering, mental retardation, cerebral palsy, spina bifida, left-handedness, diabetes, asthma, nail-biting, phonic skills, brain damage, Down's syndrome, school psychological service, adapted curriculum, micro-electronics, school phobia, assessment and diagnosis, anorexia, disruptive pupils, muscular dystrophy.

It would be possible to advance a plausible argument for all these and many more, so there is little difficulty in filling a SEN course with 'interesting' topics. The real issue is, however, how to make the appropriate selection. What selection criteria should be adopted?

INTEREST AND RELEVANCE

The RADAR report identifies that training institutions select topics for SEN courses on different bases. The identification of a rationale based on an appreciation of the nature of such differences would be time-consuming. The following, however, could serve as preliminary criteria:

Immediacy
SEN courses should include topics which experience suggests are likely to have an immediate impact upon teaching practice and the early years of teaching.

Incidence
SEN courses should include topics which address major issues and problems in the child population (e.g. behavioural problems before autism, the retarded reader before dyslexia, curriculm issues before recondite diagnosis of learning difficulties).

Contextual relevance
SEN courses should include topics which are anticipated to be relevant to the ordinary teacher (e.g. mixed ability teaching rather than conductive education in a special school).

When the rationale for SEN courses has been developed and the content parameters subjected to criterion analysis, the next issue which will arise is the manner or style of the course. Here, important decisions as to the length of the course, it's timing within the training programme, and the number of students that can be accommodated, will have to be taken. Related to these matters (and in some sense prior) are views concerning the 'ideal' allocation between knowledge, skill and awareness, given the probability that many students will lack a rich background of relevant experience. Tactical decisions will have to be made on which of the selected topics the student will need a thorough grounding and on which the student need only be acquainted. It might be argued that all students need to be familiar with the range of supportive services, but not with psychological assesment, speech therapy or physiotherapy. Intimately connected with these questions is one relating to the primary objective of the course - whether to concentrate on producing a narrow range of classroom skills or on a broadly based informative input which will enable teachers to acquire such skills at a later date and thereby place them within an informed context. Courses of both kinds exist - those where the intention is to overtly influence observation, assessment, management and curriculum practice, and those which are largely directed towards attitudes and information. Putting it crudely, there seems to be a distinction between those who want to help students to be able to help a child with a reading problem, and those who feel that they should provide a booklist.

Decisions on these matters have important consequences for the organisation of courses, particularly the allocation of time between lectures and field work and between theory and practice. Equally important is the 'ideal' allocation between relevant school based experience and opportunities to engage (under informed guidance) in discussion on wider issues (e.g. the social experience of handicapped children, community reactions to impairment, integration and equal opportunities), in which the students' own values can be explored (Thomas, 1978; Thomas, 1982).

Perhaps most crucially, we need to consider the relationship between SEN courses and the training programme as a whole. Self-contained offerings may be functionally necessary but, unless they are planned as extensions of the main course, they are likely to be perceived as disjunctive. The observation that encapsulated SEN courses often preach integration is a social message unlikely to be missed by students.

SUMMARY OF ISSUES

- What is the rationale for including SEN courses in

initial training?
- What priority is given to such courses?
- How do we define and delimit SEN courses?
- What are the criteria for the curriculum of such courses?
- What is the balance between skill and information?
- What is the relationship between SEN courses and the training programme?

To most of these questions a bewildering array of answers are possible, depending upon differing political, professional and educational perspectives.

PERSPECTIVES

As noted earlier, Scheffler (1960) described education as an area of practical activity and reflection in which, through an absence of a direct link between soundly based theories and their supportive empirical data (as, for example, between mathematics and engineering), there is a tendency to offer slogans and metaphors as a surrogate ('we teach children not subjects', 'the child as a growing plant, the teacher as potter'). Equally, it can be claimed that there is no unambiguous body of knowledge which can be unequivocally determined as 'special education'. It, too, has developed it's share of slogans ('all children have special needs', 'one child in six has special needs', 'recognizing individual strengths and weaknesses', 'individualising instruction', 'prescriptive teaching', etc.). Even where slogans are shared, there is no certainty that similar meanings are implied. One of the tasks for the future is to explore the value assumptions that underpin SEN courses.

Since most courses are not based on theory and empirical data but are derived from value positions, one that would receive personal support would be an SEN course engaging in what Geene (1977) called 'the process of de-mystification'. One of the functions of SEN courses is to systematically unshroud special education of the cloak of mystery which special educators have endeavoured to place over their activities. Here, the past is not so easily shaken off. Since its inception, special education has claimed (partly as a defensive ploy) a particular set of credentials for dealing with pupils with exceptional learning difficulties. This expertise is seen as residing within sub-divisions (e.g. concerned with blindness, deafness, etc.), where there is an implicit assumption of expertise, insight and understanding, not easily available outside special education. While special schools continue to operate this self-constructed definition, it is sustained by the complicity of ordinary schools because they have a vested interest in special schools as legitimate locations for the 'unmanageable' and the 'hard to teach' (Tomlinson, 1982). Research has been devoted over the past five years to demolishing the mythology of expertise, establishing the capacity of the ordinary school to meet special needs.

That great movement which had its roots in civil liberties, equal rights and equal opportunities, broadened its concern to incorporate the education of the children of minority groups and special educational placement practices. This led the way to a re-appraisal of the concept of segregated provision, and threw a revealing light upon the achievements of special education (Hegarty, Pocklington and Lucas, 1982). This is not the place to review the comparative achievements of pupils in mainstream and special education, but the general conclusion is that placement in special schools does not of itself ensure effective learning. What has come to be realised is that their claims of expertise are essentially the positive utilisation by committed teachers of additional resources, access to multi-disciplinary teams, and more favourable teacher/pupil ratios. The ability to meet special needs does not reside mainly in the possession of distinctive techniques or technologies.

The dual argument that it is both morally correct and educationally possible (given comparable resources) for a significant portion of handicapped pupils to receive their education in ordinary schools, convinces many SEN tutors that their courses should materially assist this process. From this perspective, SEN courses should consciously strive to develop in students a belief in the social and moral correctness of integration - their role is not the identification of children for removal. It is natural that the ordinary school and it's staff should assume responsibility for the effective education of children with a wider diversity of abilities than was, until recently, thought appropriate. In terms of motivation and professional commitment, the potential for every teacher to help meet special needs is great. Identifying and meeting special needs need not be conveyed as the prerogative of the expert, but part of the expectation for all teachers. Equally, one needs to emphasise that such a view pertains within a school as well as within external agencies and institutions.

INTEGRATING TRAINING

If this view prevails (the normalisation of special needs), it gives us an indication of how SEN courses can be located within the total training programme. The recent Her Majesty's Inspectorate discussion document, Teaching in Schools (DES, 1983) in its summary of main recommendations stated:

All courses of training should include practical experience and knowledge of class management and control; knowledge of the variety that constitutes the full range of pupils in terms of ability, behaviour, social background and culture; experience and knowledge of the level of performance appropriate for differing ages, abilities and backgrounds.

There is no specific recommendation in the document relating to SEN, but there is a recommendation that students should be familiar with 'the practice of assessment; individual differences in the way in which children learn [and] with understanding of some of the more common learning difficulties'. In other words, initial training should, as part of its general preparation, incorporate the study of individual differences - the concepts of individual diversity in styles of learning, special needs and developmental level are an integral part of the preparation of all teachers. While it may be organisationally necessary to label a course as a SEN course, its content and approach should clearly reflect and draw upon other continuing areas of academic and professional study.

Such a synthesis is made somewhat harder by at least two factors:

1. Many of those centrally involved in planning training programmes, while supportive of SEN courses, were socialised in a professional context in which the range of normality considered appropriate for schools was narrowly defined.
2. Those institutional experts in special education who are likely to be given responsibility for SEN courses have had their formative experiences in segregated settings. There may be an experiential gap in the resources of training institutions with little direct and relevant experience of the most recent developments in integration, mainstreaming and resource centres (Jones, 1981).

The dangers of offering courses that are either nostalgic recapitulations of times past or enthusiastic proselyting by recent converts to de-segregation are obvious. Perhaps the greatest disservice which the 'capsule' course can do is to encourage other specialists in the training programme to omit a consideration of individual differences and special needs from their offerings, on the assumption that this is being dealt with on the SEN course. If the SEN course is to be valid, it must deal with contemporary issues. This is why it must include the contributions of practitioners who are dealing with new organisational structures, new forms of teaching and new materials, and who are active in re-shaping teacher and teaching values.

The major consequence of the HMI recommendations would be to circumscribe the SEN course into those areas which have a high degree of relevance to classroom practice. This is an obvious necessity, but a limiting one. In addition to these immediate topics, a place should be found for making clear the principles which inform current beliefs, so that students in their turn will have sufficient background against which to present a case for change. The vagueness of the concept of special needs, and the issues of who has the power to decide on needs and whose needs are to be met, for example, are worthy of debate (Aspin, 1982). Other examples include the role of educational psychology in maintaining a segregated system of schooling (Sutton, 1981), the unmasking of special education's rhetoric (Tomlinson, 1982), the structuring of attitudes to disabled people (Finkelstein, 1980) and, at another level, the views of parents (Hannan, 1980). Starting from the assumption that SEN courses are from the outset conceived as integral to the training programme, and that formal and informal links are established between SEN courses and academic and practical courses, we can describe four types of courses.

Level I

Designed for all students. A short, concentrated course, introductory and general in nature. The aims of this course are:

1. Providing an awareness of children with special needs; major typologies, classifications (and weaknesses), characteristics; frequency, incidence, causation; major patterns of support and provision.
2. Exemplification of aspects of aim 1. (above) through case studies and contact with teachers, psychologists, etc. with emphasis on intervention.
3. Presenting examples of effective integration and mainstreaming.
4. Stressing the role of all teachers in meeting special needs.
5. Knowledge of roles of the supportive services.
6. To provide resources for students; selected readings, curriculum materials, remedial programmes; suitable tests and diagnostic measures.

A course of this kind could well be organised around input from practitioners, and include case studies (of schools as well as individual children), film and video and, ideally, some opportunities for visits and observation. As indicated above, the main objective of such a course would be to create a sense of awareness of children with special needs and the positive role which teachers can play, and to supply background resources and relevant materials which students can draw upon selectively. It must be stressed that one feature of courses using a number of speakers from differing disciplines is the need for someone to act as a co-ordinator and link.

Level II

These courses, while drawing upon some of the content of Level I courses, are different in two main ways: they are more classroom orientated and they have a specific organisational context. The nature of the Level II courses implies smaller and more cohesive groups of students than can be accommodated in the Level I course. Smaller groups also enable more opportunities to employ school based learning strategies. A Level II course for students specialising in the primary age range could include some of the following:

Early identification of learning and behaviour diffficulties; individual and group assessment; diagnosis of reading and language problems; remedial programmes in mathematics, language, reading; diagnostic programmes for visual and auditory perceptual skills; child study of pupils with a learning problem with emphasis on intervention; working with small groups of slow learners; classroom management; adapting curriculum materials for pupils of differing conceptual levels.

Level II courses for students specialising in the secondary age range might have a differing emphasis, such as:

The problems of transfer and adjustment at 11+; communication and contact with primary schools; group and individual assessment; assessing text books for readability and interest; curriculum modification for slower pupils; mixed ability teaching; classroom management; disruptive and dissaffected pupils; resource room learning systems; working with remedial specialists; curriculum needs of non-academic pupils; practical experiences with children with learning difficulties; co-operating with supportive services.

Both Level I and Level II courses exist in our training institutions. It can be argued that there is a place for both types (especially if the concept of 'progressive experience' is considered) and that the Level I course could act as a preliminary to the more specific and practical Level II. Level I courses are suitable for delivery to large groups and can be relatively autonomous, while the effective Level II course requires extensive co-operation between SEN tutors and others involved in the general training programme.

SPECIAL EDUCATION: INITIAL TRAINING NEEDS

In some colleges there is in existence a 'Level III' course where a SEN option is offered in an honours degree course. These courses seem to combine many of the elements of I and II, and are often attractive to students who have been exposed to a Level I course and who have an interest in following a course of academic and professional study which will lead them to an active role in meeting special needs when they are qualified.

Finally, there is the Level IV course, which is a preparation in initial training for work in special education. Most notably, this has expanded since 1970 with the specialised courses for intending teachers of the mentally handicapped. Quite recently, this form of training has come under review (Jackson, 1983) and resurrects a debate of considerable antiquity - whether students in initial training ought to be trained for special education or whether they should receive a conventional initial training and then have an additional (and highly specialised) course, after spending some time working with 'normal' children. This raises issues such as the wisdom of too early specialisation and the possible loss to special education of a small group of highly motivated students.

CONFLICTS AND CONSENSUS

Perhaps one of the most interesting issues which arises from considering the role and nature of SEN courses in initial training is what might be called 'the secure knowledge base'. What aspects of special educational needs can legitimately be regarded as confirmed, consensual or verified unambiguously by empirical research? What constitutes the bedrock of theory and practice which we can put before students? What can be regarded as the unimpeachable core?

As might have been anticipated from debates in other areas of initial training (Hartnett and Naish, 1981), no clear answers emerge. The Open University course 'Special needs in education' (E 241) demonstrates that there is little consensus about provision or approaches to special needs. Considerable discrepancies exist between local education authorities in their attitudes to special needs, their miscellaneous provision, and their confusions over philosophies. Further, the variety of approaches within and between schools makes a convincing rational picture difficult to draw. In addition, many sources of debate exist within special education (e.g. the debate on oral and signing methods for the hearing impaired; the conflict between psycho-dynamically orientated teachers of maladjusted children and those committed to a behaviourist approach - and those who have heard of neither; conflicts about reading methods; curriculum for the slow learner; special classes in ordinary schools; mixed ability teaching; etc.). It must therefore be a matter of concern whether initial training students are exposed to or shielded from the 'fallout' from such controversies.

The Times Educational Supplement recently carried a correspondence on initial training courses in special needs (ITSE) in which polarised views have been expressed. Part of the debate concerns the place within ITSE of a rigorous critique of segregated special schools and the place of a cadre of 'elite' specialists to meet the learning needs of handicapped pupils. Central to the argument is the issue of exposing initial training students to 'problematic' areas such as the effects of curricula, school organisation and social values. The debate has widened to include discussion of the relationship between integration policy and practice, and resources (Is integration being backed by 'skinflint' authorities anxious to reduce expenditure while claiming to be leaders in the area of mainstreaming?). On similar lines, we can wonder about the presence or absence of the powerful but controversial sociological perspective of Tomlinson (1982), or of the committed integrationist views of Booth and Potts (1983).

These are matters on which we should not take 'a low profile'. It seems to me that SEN courses are vigorous and stimulating precisely to the degree that they lay before students these controversial matters. Nothing could be potentially more fruitful for the generation of intellectually and professionally exciting courses, than the sense of being part of an engaging debate where there are strongly held beliefs on both sides. Awareness of SEN often evokes in students a strong sense of wishing to play an active part in meeting special needs. Such a part will be that much greater if, in addition to necessary classroom skills, the students possess the vocabulary of the current debates on which they can then arrive at a personal, rather than a prescribed, perspective. In part, this requires tutors to set before students the range of alternative positions, and to make explicit their own value beliefs.

Like most training institutions we, at Liverpool, have been reflecting upon our SEN provision for PGCE students at the primary and secondary level. We have, so far, made provision for all primary students and, initially, for a proportion of secondary students. The latter option (originally designed as a Level II course with a heavy emphasis on school based practice) has generated a demand beyond our expectations, so that the original option group has expanded to form an informal additional option. This has made us realize that such experiences can have major influence upon many aspects of the whole course, and has considerable significance for all teachers – irrespective of their subject specialism. If we are to achieve a 'whole school' approach to meeting special needs, we may reach this goal faster if our students are exposed to praxis which is illuminated by familiarity with broader and problematic issues, and which takes the integration of special needs training as seriously as it does the integration of children with special needs.

REFERENCES

Aspin, D.N. (1982) 'Towards a concept of human being as a basis for a philosophy of special education', Educational Review, 34 (2), 113-123.

Booth, T. and Potts, P. (eds) (1983) Integrating Special Education, Oxford: Basil Blackwood.

DES (1983) Teaching in Schools, London: Department of Education and Science.

Finkelstein, V. (1980) Attitudes and Disabled People: Issues for Discussion, New York: World Rehabilitation Fund.

Greene, M. (1977) 'The Matter of Mystification: Teacher Education in Unquiet Times' in Gleeson, D. (ed.) Identity and Structure, Nafferton: Nafferton Books.

Hannan, C. (1980) Parents and Mentally Handicapped Children, Harmondsworth: Penguin Books.

Hartnett, A. and Naish, M. (1981) 'The PGCE as an educational priority area', Journal of Further and Higher Education, 5 (3), 88-102.

Hegarty, S., Pocklington, K. and Lucas, D. (1982) Integration in Action, Windsor:NFER-Nelson.

Jackson, R. (1983) 'Will INSET ever be something special?', Times Education Supplement, Sept. 2.

Jones, E. (1981) 'A resource approach to meeting special needs in a secondary school' in Barton, L. and Tomlinson, S. (eds), Special Education: Policy, Practice and Social Issues, Chichester: Harper and Row.

Lacey, C. (1979) 'Choice and constraint and the possibilities of autonomous behaviour in Barton, L. and Meighan, R. (eds) Schools Pupils and Deviance. Nafferton: Nafferton Books.

Open University (1982) Special Needs in Education (E241) Milton Keynes: The Open University Press.

RADAR (1983) Teacher Training with Regard to Children with Special Educational Needs, London: Royal Association for Disability and Rehabilitation.

Reid, K., Patrick, H and Bernbaum, G (1981) On Course: Students and the PGCE. Unnpublished paper presented at UCET conference, Oxford, October.

Scheffler, I. (1960) The Language of Education, Springfield, Illinois: C.C. Thomas.

Sutton, A. (1981) 'The social role of educational psychology

in defining educational subnormality' in Barton, L. and
Tomlinson, S., (eds) Special Education: Policy, Practice
and Social Issues. Chichester: Harper and Row.

Thomas, D. (1978) The Social Psychology of Childhood
Disability, London: Methuen.

Thomas, D. (1982) The Experience of Handicap, London:
Methuen.

Tomlinson, S. (1982) A Sociology of Special Education,
London: Routledge and Kegan Paul.

Warnock Report (1978) Special Educational Needs, Cmnd
7996, London: Her Majesty's Stationery Office.

SECTION SIX – FUTURE PERSPECTIVES

Chapter Thirteen

THE FUTURE FOR TEACHER EDUCATION

William Taylor

TEN YEARS OF CHANGE

'Give them a number, or give them a date, but never give them
a number and a date together'. So runs the old saw about
forecasting. To predict what teacher education in England and
Wales will look like in the 1990s is a hazardous business. In
respect of one of the key factors shaping its future, we do at
least know how many students will be starting secondary school
up to 1995, for they are already born. Future birth rates that
will determine the overall size of the school population are
harder to forecast. Even more so are the political, economic,
social and educational developments that will shape the
organisation, content, and control of teacher education.

    Who, at the beginning of the 1970s, studying the
Government White Paper Education, a Framework for Expansion,
would have guessed that ten years later the colleges of
education (that alongside the universities and polytechnics
formed a 'third sector' of post-secondary education) would, as
a consequence of merger, diversification and closure, have
ceased to exist?

    In the light of what the 1972 James Report (DES 1972) had
to say about the role of the universities in teacher
education, would it have seemed sensible to predict that the
proportion of newly qualified teachers who were university
trained would be substantially increased, and that several
university departments would be embarking upon the development
or expansion of primary postgraduate certificate of education
(PGCE) courses?

    For any one familiar with the growth of performance based
and competency based teacher education in the United States,
might it not have been plausible to suggest that within ten
years the professional curriculum of colleges and departments
in this country would be much more systematic, modularised,
research based, and task oriented?

    Could it reasonably have been assumed that the Schools
Council (only half a decade old, but already responsible for

about 100 curriculum projects) would, within ten years, have ceased to exist as a representative body, and that there would be separate organisations for curriculum and examinations, with directly appointed membership?

Given estimates of increasing demand for higher education (with some organisations urging provision for a million students by 1980, with as many as 450,000 in universities), would anyone who talked about 20% cuts in resources, cash limits, and departmental closures have been listened to?

Also, given the firmness with which officials and politicians were re-stating the binary principles enunciated by Crosland in the mid 1960s, and the lack of encouragement in the 1972 White Paper for any trans-binary arrangements, could the possibility of 'polyversities' have been foreseen?

The educational history of this period has yet to be written. When it is, the extent to which educational seers of the early 1970s had 'egg on their face' by 1984 will become even more clear. The examples already given are enough to induce caution. Consequently, before launching into specific predictions, it may be prudent to identify as many as possible of the conditions and events that might plausibly affect the way in which we educate and train those who are to work in the classrooms and schools of the future.

1. Teacher Demand

Pride of place must go to demographic trends, although the demand for, and supply of, teachers does not depend completely upon pupil numbers. The priorities that Governments attach to improvements in pupil teacher ratios and in-service study opportunities for teachers, the extension of educational provision at the pre and post compulsory stages, and higher rates of participation by under-represented social groups, can all affect the number of teachers required to meet system 'needs'.

Although there are still plenty of uncertainties, the forecasting of teacher demand is now much more sophisticated than even a decade ago. Differential fertility rates between social classes, wastage from a teaching force of changing age and sex composition, and demand generated by particular patterns of curricular organisation, all play a part in the sums. Many of the assumptions on which any model of teacher demand is based are influenced by events outside the control of those who wrestle with the figures. Forecasting such demand requires the skills of not just the demographer, but of the economist, the manpower planner, the policy pundit and the psephologist. The overall size of each birth cohort remains, though, of central importance. More than any other single consideration, it is the prospect of larger or smaller numbers of children coming through the gates at the beginning of each school year that stimulates planners to action.

THE FUTURE FOR TEACHER EDUCATION

Summarizing, the employment prospects of teachers depend on birth projections, teacher wastage (including early retirement), the possibility of improved staffing standards in the schools, increased participation in education at pre compulsory and post compulsory ages, the level of in-service provision and release, the decisions of governing bodies and local authorities in respect of appointing new entrants to the profession as against applicants from the so-called 'pool of inactive teachers' (the unglamorous PIT) and, finally, the spending plans of Government.

If we aggregate the reasonable assumptions that can be made in respect of each of these factors, then how many vacancies will there be for primary and secondary school teachers between 1982 and the mid 1990s? Table 1 (based on data from the Department of Education and Science [DES] Report on Education, 1983) gives some illustrative figures.

Table 1

PROJECTED VACANCIES FOR FULL TIME TEACHERS IN ENGLAND AND WALES (Thousands)

	Nursery and infant	Junior	All primary	Secondary	All primary and secondary
1982/83	4.0	2.5	6.5	17.5	24.0
1983/84	4.5	2.0	6.5	13.0	19.5
1984/85	7.5	2.5	10.0	11.0	21.0
1985/86	8.0	4.0	12.0	10.0	22.0
1986/87	5.0	6.5	11.5	8.0	19.5
1987/88	4.0	8.0	12.5	5.5	18.0
1988/89	4.5	9.0	13.5	5.5	19.0
1989/90	6.0	8.0	14.0	7.5	21.5
1990/91	7.5	6.5	14.0	10.5	24.5
1991/92	7.0	6.0	13.0	11.5	24.5
1992/93	7.5	7.0	14.5	13.5	28.0
1993/94	7.0	9.0	16.0	14.0	30.0
1994/95	7.0	9.5	16.5	14.5	31.0

From this table it can be seen that vacancies for primary school teachers increase quite sharply until 1989/90, and are then maintained until 1994/5. Vacancies for secondary school teachers, however, fall substantially until 1989/90, and then rise sharply until 1994/5.

On the assumption that 60 out of every 100 teachers filling primary school vacancies are newly qualified (the remainder come from the PIT), the 1983 forecasts suggested that effective output from colleges and universities after 1984/5 would, on the basis of existing intakes, not be adequate to meet demand.

As far as vacancies for secondary schools are concerned, even if three quarters go to the newly qualified (a quarter to re-entrants from the PIT), the effective output is higher than likely demand for the next few years, and remains so until the end of the decade. In summary: there will be too few primary school teachers and too many secondary.

If reducing public expenditure was the only criterion, and a teacher could be regarded as qualified for any kind of classroom work, anywhere, it would be possible to argue for a sharp cut back in secondary training, and for the pool of inactive teachers to be drawn upon to compensate for reduced numbers of the newly qualified. Numbers are not, however, the only consideration. However highly they may rate the control of public expenditure, Governments also have other commitments, one of which is to improve the quality of schooling. Quality is not improved by transferring large numbers of teachers trained and experienced in secondary schools to primary teaching. Neither is it improved by drawing extensively and haphazardly from a PIT that, if it holds many dedicated professionals keen to return to the classroom, also contains some recruited when entry qualifications and courses were less exacting than they are today, and when shortages sometimes necessitated the sacrifice of selectivity.

Colleges, polytechnics and university departments of education cannot be opened or closed at a moment's notice. Many fulfill important roles additional to initial teacher training. They supply most longer course in-service education for teachers (INSET), nearly all the specialised advanced work with teachers, and also undertake educational research. To weaken the institutional base of teacher training by tracking closely down the demand curve would entail heavy, medium and long term costs, for which short term financial benefits are poor compensation. That further rationalisation, including institutional closures, will take place seems certain. That it will be on a scale 'justified' by current birth trends seems unlikely.

It follows that ways will need to be found to increase the number of primary schoolteachers, to minimise unemployment among secondary schoolteachers, to make best use of those already in schools who are willing and able to retrain, and to maintain a wide range of institutions.

2.   The Supply of Candidates

Demand for teachers is one important consideration. Supply is another. Candidates for teaching form part of the total number of those qualifying for all kinds of higher education. In 1983, demand for teachers amounted to about 8% of the total qualifying group. The number of such qualifiers will soon begin to fall. In 1983 the DES estimated that by 1987/88 teaching will need half as many again - 12% of the total. By the middle of the 1990s, the proportion might be as high as 20%, and rising, although not to the proportion of 28% that represented the peak in the early 1970s.

These figures are sensitive to a number of contested assumptions. Some calculations suggest the number of candidates for all forms of higher education could fall by as much as 16% by the mid 1990s. Others disagree. They argue that such calculations take insufficient account of birth rates among the social classes from which most higher education candidates come. These are unlikely to fall as steeply as those for other groups. It is argued that the effect of increasing participation by women has not fully been taken into account. It is also maintained that age participation ratios - the proportion of each age group who qualify for and seek places in higher education - can and should rise, and improved opportunities for adult and continuing education will create new sources of supply from among mature candidates.

A third important consideration related to supply is the academic quality of those who train for teaching. In the United States, Vance and Schlechty (1982) have shown (on the basis of an analysis of scholastic aptitude test [SAT] scores) that teaching attracts a higher proportion of those in the lower bands of measured ability, and a markedly lower proportion from the higher bands. Furthermore, 'those with high ability who enter teaching are more likely to leave than those with low ability' (p.24). They go on to say:

> Whether the public schools will do well or poorly (in the status hierarchy) depends in large measure on their success in attracting and retaining as teachers those individuals with demonstrated ability for academic tasks. Whether research firmly links academic ability to teaching effectiveness or not, public perceptions of teachers' academic competence will strongly influence the future of the teaching profession and of education in general (p26).

There is a parallel between the position in the United States and that in many developed countries, including England and Wales. The teacher shortages of the 1950s and 1960s made rigorous selection for teaching very difficult. Modest salaries and historically low status, coupled with good career opportunities elsewhere, did little to encourage able and well-motivated individuals to look for careers in the classroom. Almost anyone who possessed the necessary entrance requirements and satisfied at interview could obtain entry to a professional course. Colleges and universities still managed to produce substantial numbers of competent teachers (even some of outstanding quality), but recruitment conditions outside their own control, and the priority that had to be given to supply as distinct from quality considerations, inevitably had their effects.

THE FUTURE FOR TEACHER EDUCATION

Hopes that a tighter job market in the 1970s would make
it easier to select in accordance with stringent criteria, and
to 'weed out' the unsuitable during training, have not been
fulfilled. Despite lack of employment opportunities elsewhere,
the ablest school leavers did not demonstrate a markedly
increased willingness to train for an occupation offering
unsure prospects of employment and promotion, qualifications
which lack broad currency, and only modest immediate and
prospective reward.

Past inability to recruit to teaching from the more able
and successful strata of school leavers and mature entrants
has often been ingeniously rationalised by reference to the
supposed antipathy between academic orientations and a genuine
interest in children and young people. Comforting as this may
be for all concerned, it is unsupported by evidence. Teaching,
like all other occupations, must compete in the marketplace
for talent. Its capacity to do so is limited by its sheer size
(teachers' salaries account for a high proportion of the total
education budget, which in turn constitutes the largest part
of local authority expenditure) and by the lack of success of
those who have sought to persuade governments, teachers'
organisations and employing authorities to retain maximum
flexibility in the deployment of their labour, with a minimum
of phase and subject specific certification.

During the 1970s, undergraduate courses for teaching did
not attract more than a small proportion of the most able
school leavers. Consequently, efforts were made to shift the
balance of training away from the three and four year B.Ed.
towards the one year PGCE, there being no lack of good quality
applicants for the latter award. Patrick, Bernbaum and Reid
(1982) found that of their sample of 4,300 students entering
PGCE courses in 1979, fewer had first class degrees than the
total graduating population, but there were also
proportionately fewer poor degrees.

DES figures show that in 1978 just under 3% of PGCE
admissions to university departments of education (UDEs) had
first class honours degrees, nearly three quarters had second
class honours degrees, and only 15% third class or other
ordinary or pass degrees. In the largest of the PGCE
departments, the University of London Institute of Education,
the percentage of first class honours degrees rose from 4.23%
in 1974 to 5.67% in 1982. The proportion of third class
honours and pass degrees fell over the same period from 17.22%
to 11.13%. It is likely that similar trends will have occured
in some other UDEs, and in those polytechnics and colleges and
institutes of higher education that offer postgraduate
training for teaching.

These trends all occurred in a context of diminishing
employment opportunities for graduates. Should the economy
become more buoyant by the early 1990s, and new technologies
enhance the demand for highly qualified labour, then teaching

will be in a weaker position to compete for a larger share of
a declining supply. In these circumstances, it might well be
that local education authorities (LEAs) and governments will
need to rethink the structure of teaching as an occupation,
taking steps to make the teaching of the subjects and age
groups on which shortages are likely to bear most severely
more attractive and better rewarded.

Particular attention is due to demand and supply
considerations because of the implications they have for
institutional changes, for techniques of training, for
patterns of course organisation, for in-service provision, for
advanced course opportunities, for accreditation procedures,
for the greater involvement of practitioners in the training
process, and for shifts in the balance of power exercised by
central government, LEAs, institutions and professional
bodies.

3.   Teacher Preparation and Educational Change
Primary and secondary schools are the only educational
institutions in which professional training is a condition of
employment. Such training is not required of those who
instruct youth trainees on Manpower Services Commission (MSC)
programmes, teach in further education colleges, lecture in
universities, or engage in a great variety of other
educational activities. The next few years will see a growth
of interest in, for example, training opportunities for
further education teachers and a continuing concern with
ensuring that university lecturers have a chance to improve
their lecturing and tutoring skills. It seems unlikely,
though, that formal certification requirements will be much
extended. Cost is a major consideration. It has so far not
been outweighed by belief in the value or necessity of
professional training at post compulsory levels. There may be
greater variety in the kinds of teacher education undertaken,
but its future is likely to be dominated by the requirements
of primary and secondary schools.

There is massive inertia in the patterns of teaching
organisation, curriculum and examinations in schools. The idea
of a single examination system at 16+, embracing both CSE and
GCE, is of long standing: there has been a measure of
agreement about its desirability for more than a decade.
Interest in reform of the sixth form curriculum in the
direction of less specialisation has recently revived, and
there are proposals to introduce 'A/S' (Advanced
Supplementary) subjects equal to half an existing 'A' level.
The absorption of energies in accommodating to falling rolls
and resource constraints has left limited opportunities for
organisational reform. The sixth form seems unlikely to be
replaced at an early date by tertiary colleges or other 16+
arrangements, other than where a commitment to such change has
already been made by the local authority concerned. The

existing variety among 104 LEAs in respect of age of transfer to secondary education, availability or otherwise of middle schools, and other organisational details, seems likely to persist.

It follows from all this that the changes to which teacher education will need to accommodate are more likely to be in the content of primary and secondary school curricula, rather than new organisational structures. Some new subjects, such as computing, may come to be seen more as techniques, applicable across a wide range of forms of knowledge. If youth unemployment persists (especially among the least able), more attention may have to be given to ways of achieving commitment (without the spur of economic necessity and the discipline of the workplace) to values such as tolerance, consideration, respect for privacy, honesty and conscientiousness. Efforts to break down present barriers between school education and youth training will persist. Given the historical and ideological roots and status associations of these barriers, progress is likely to be slow. In all these areas, though, changes will be taking place, and having their effects (often through indirect and unmarked channels) on the tasks that teachers confront.

4. Concurrent versus Consecutive Modes

Teacher education is presently undertaken in universities, polytechnics and colleges and institutes of higher education. Such plurality seems set to continue. If institutional closures are still to come in the face of declining numbers and resources, it remains to be seen whether these will fall evenly across the sectors, or whether student choice will be given full play in a single market for higher education.

The possibility of polytechnic and university mergers cannot be ruled out, but they are not likely to be numerous. At present, all universities (with the exception of the privately funded University of Buckingham and the Open University) are funded through the University Grants Committee (UGC). It is possible that within the next decade we shall see institutions resulting from mergers that are called universities, but which are not on the UGC list. The institutional pattern of teacher education is, though, unlikely to change as rapidly over the next ten years as it has over the last.

A number of universities, and many polytechnics and colleges, are currently increasing the numbers of students preparing for work in primary schools by means of PGCE courses. Opinion about the suitability of the PGCE for primary school training has been somewhat mixed. College and polytechnic staff tend to be critical of the merits of consecutive, 'three plus one' courses as a preparation for primary teaching. There has been much defensiveness in the face of anxieties expressed about shortfalls in B.Ed.

enrolments, exacerbated by the introduction at the end of the 1970s of 'O' level requirements in engish and mathematics. In response to headlines such as 'Is the B.Ed. doomed?', representatives of colleges and their associations were quick to point out some of the B.Ed's advantages, both as a professional qualification in comparison with the PGCE, and in terms of its general value in the employment market. It was claimed that B.Ed. graduates had entered such occupations as computer programming, retail management, the police force, planning, the probation service and librarianship, and that the range was as wide as for arts and social science graduates generally. However valuable the second of these arguments may be in relation to recruitment, it 'cuts little ice' as far as professional relevance is concerned.

Some members of the Council for National Academic Awards (CNAA) panels and boards urged the Council to consider the possibility of renaming the B.Ed. a 'B.A. in Educational Studies', in the hope that it might prove more attractive to students, and emphasise the broader scope of occupational possibility that such a qualification offers. Supporters of the B.Ed. continued to argue (e.g. Bruce, 1981) that:

> the B.Ed. graduate with demonstrable skills of communication, ability in personal relations and proven professional reliability at least comparable to those of any other graduate with a first degree, is gaining increasing acceptance in the field of graduate employment.

Against this, as already emphasised, it was claimed that consecutive courses possess not just administrative and logistical advantages, but attract better quality entrants and have a clearer professional focus than do longer programmes which combine both academic and professional elements. Defenders of the B.Ed. argued strongly for the value of a more gradual introduction into the responsibilities of the classroom; for the advantages of cross-fertilisation between academic and professional studies in the course of a four year programme; for the greater commitment to teaching in general, and a distinctive style of child-centredness in particular, that B.Ed. courses demand and generate; and for the gains from studying a wider range of subjects than in a typical one or two subject university or CNAA honours degree programme.

The shortness of the PGCE course attracted particular criticism. One year was widely recognised as being insufficient, yet to extend the course into a second academic session would be extremely expensive. This has been emphasised by those who defend the B.Ed. as a training for primary work. In the words of a group of staff from one college, 'The B.Ed. will afford far more scope for professional development than can possibly take place in the crash programme of the PGCE over the period of about eight months'.

Yet efforts to lengthen the PGCE course, based on ideas of 'clinical' or 'intern' years such as have long applied in medicine, have consistently run into financial, logistical and organisational difficulties. The idea of a two year, school based PGCE (talked about for the past 20 years at the very least!) has failed - mainly due to the cost and difficulty of administering such a plan at existing levels of resource. Repeated advocacy (by the Headmasters' Associations) of large comprehensive schools acting as 'teaching schools', analagous to the way teaching hospitals function, has so far not bourne fruit. Reduced resources, falling rolls, and teachers having little spare time to give sufficient attention to trainees, weaken an idea that in principle earns much support. 'Teaching schools' require a level of equipment and support at least equivalent to that of the training departments in which students would otherwise be spending their time. Such resources would necessarily be scattered among a large number of separate institutions, some of them quite small. Supervision, follow-up and explicit linkage between work done in school and that already completed or yet to be undertaken in college or university, would be difficult and costly.

The whole issue of 'consecutive versus concurrent' forms of course organisation is frequently discussed as if a clear distinction invariably exists between the two. The available evidence does not fully sustain this view. Some three and four year courses in colleges and institutes of higher education and polytechnics are effectively 'consecutive', subject work being grouped towards the beginning of the programme and professional studies towards the end. Three out of fifteen colleges studied in detail by Her Majesty's Inspectorate (HMI) in 1979 had concentrated academic and theoretical studies in the first, second and fourth years, with specific professional training taking place in the third. At another college, professional training (and hence any commitment to teaching) had been postponed until the second year.

Discussions about the relative merits of concurrent versus consecutive courses (which have been taking place for decades), are unlikely to be stilled in the 1980s. Those who support the continuation of B.Ed. programmes argue that students find it easier to see how their subject knowledge contributes to the aims of the school if they are able to pursue subject studies, to develop professional skills and to be introduced to educational theory in parallel rather than in sequence. The longer period available in which to evaluate one's practice also makes it easier to form sound judgments of what can and cannot be achieved with children of a given age and ability level. This can be of particular importance in respect of mixed ability classes. Earlier contact with pupils gives the student longer to judge whether his/her commitment to teaching is real. Finally, the longer course makes it possible for institutions to offer a wider range of options in both educational and professional studies.

Advocates of the consecutive mode point to the greater depth of subject study possible in a three year degree course uncluttered by the requirements of professional experience, the value of delaying commitment to teaching until a student's early 20s (often, as things are, until later still), the advantage of not exposing students to the problems of the classroom at an immature age and at too early a point in their higher education, and the fact that time devoted to professional studies in a 'three plus one' consecutive course need be no less than in some concurrent programmes.

Such advocacy has not only been based on educational principles, it has also been concerned with the viability of institutions and the availability of posts within them. Disagreements about the quality of teacher training courses validated by or taught within universities, and those that are the academic responsibility of the CNAA, together with arguments about the future of the B.Ed. in relation to the PGCE, are conducted against a background of institutional differences in status and prestige and anxieties about relative shares of what is seen as a declining market. All this gives a political edge to the academic, professional and logistical arguments involved, which is unlikely to disappear for so long as contraction and closure of courses remain issues.

That teacher trade unions have different viewpoints on these questions increases the probability that they will remain on the agenda. The National Union of Teachers, with a high proportion of non-graduate members who work in primary schools, has favoured the continuation of the B.Ed. The National Association of Schoolmasters and Union of Women Teachers, with substantial graduate membership, has backed the consecutive pattern. In the view of the National Association of Head Teachers, 'the B.Ed. qualification does not have the same standing as a B.A. or B.Sc. plus PGCE', and the Association recommends a four year course for all. The National Association of Teachers in Further and Higher Education, with many members in the former colleges of education and polytechnic education departments, is firmly in favour of the continuation of the B.Ed.

In a context of fluctuating demand, it is no bad thing that teaching qualifications have a currency beyond the profession. A proportion of both B.Ed. graduates and PGCE-holders do not remain in the classroom, but move on to other occupations. Many such leavers do, of course, return to teaching, for shorter or longer periods, from the PIT which supplies part of each year's requirements for new appointees. Rates of mobility in and out of occupations demanding high-level training vary a great deal. The MSC asked the National

Training Survey to undertake a review of inter-occupational movement, based upon a sample of 1 in 500 of the working population. It was not unusual to find half the men in the 16–24 age group having moved on to other occupations from those in which they were originally trained. This was true even in the case of craft jobs, in which there were shortages in the 1960s and 1970s. All those who had begun work as dentists had remained dentists. Only 70% who had started working life as accountants were still practising. Of the men initially employed in skilled mechanical and electrical occupations, no fewer than 72% had moved on elsewhere. Thus, teacher mobility is unsurprising in relation to that of other occupations, and even to be welcomed if it creates alternative employment opportunities.

5.   Professional Accreditation

In England and Wales, the status of qualified teacher is conferred automatically on students who successfully complete an approved course. Thus, the emphasis in professional recognition is upon the course, not the individual student. Over the past decade, a great deal of time and attention has been devoted to the design of B.Ed. programmes that are academically acceptable and professionally coherent. The task is not easy. When the former colleges of education began to diversify their work in the wake of the 1972 Government White Paper, many B.Ed. programmes were modularised. There were several motives for this. A modular structure enabled students on B.Ed., B.A., Bachelor of Humanities and B.Sc. courses to follow certain common course units, thus making it easier to form viable groups and to offer a wider choice of programme. Ability to respond to student choice and interest by offering a wider range of electives was highly valued. A programme made up of a large number of course units of equal value, not necessarily offered in a uniform sequence from year to year, enabled best use to be made of staff specialisms, and facilitated programme organisation. The Certificate in Education courses that the B.Ed. replaced had been validated by university based area training organisations (ATOs) with a generally 'light hand'. A great deal had been left to the college, department and individual member of staff. The ability to offer and obtain approval for one's own course units maintained important elements of such freedom.

Despite more rigorous validation procedures introduced after 1972 by universities and the CNAA which, sometimes for the first time, actively involved university and polytechnic staff from other faculties and departments than education, a great deal of programme variation between institutions still existed. Up until 1975, the ATOs (set up in the late 1940s and early 1950s on the recommendation of the wartime McNair report, based [with the single exception of Cambridge] on universities and funded through the UGC) had given practitioners and employers a chance to play a part in judging the professional content of PGCE and B.Ed. courses. The ATOs were abolished in 1975, due to the diversification of the former colleges of education and the introduction of revised further education regulations. This, plus the failure of efforts to create a 'General Teaching Council' which might eventually have played a major part in professional accreditation, created a vacuum which the setting up of local 'professional committees' (under the terms of Circular 5/75) went only part way to fill.

HMI surveys of the operation of professional committees revealed great variations in practice. Some had met infrequently and played no significant part in assessing the professional content of the courses offered by colleges and departments of education. Others had been more active, but spent a proportion of their time on matters beyond the issue of professional accreditation. Only a few had been undertaking professional accreditation activites directed to the provision of advice consistent with the Secretary of State's statutory responsibilities in this area. It became clear that the statement in Circular 5/75 that 'These committees will ... have a supervisory function over courses leading to qualified teacher status and over arrangements for recommending suitability for the teacher profession comparable with that exercised by the former Area Training Organisation' had, in the context of the development of more active validating procedures, failed to make a sufficiently clear distinction between validation and accreditation. The distinction is crucial. In its advice to the Secretary of State (August 1983) the Advisory Committee on the Supply and Education of Teachers (ACSET) included the following statement:

> We see validation as properly concerned with all those aspects of a course which bear on the decision by the validating university or the CNAA to award degrees on successful completion. Such consideration of 'degree worthiness' should entail assessment of the course as a whole - i.e. its professional aspects as well as its academic content and standard. Similarly, we would expect the Secretary of State to have a interest in all those aspects of the course which bear on the judgment about its suitability as a professional preparation for teaching. His consideration would not be limited to the 'professional' or practical teaching aspects, but would extend also to questions involving academic content and standard. We see validation and accreditation as complementary processes, each concerned properly with the whole course, but arising from quite separate sources of authority - university and CNAA charters as regards validation, the Secretary of State's formal approval powers as regards accreditation.

ACSET recommended the setting up of a new national accrediting body of about 15 to 20 persons, appointed after consultation by the Secretary of State, and operating through its own 'competent and properly staffed secretariat'. The future of teacher education in England and Wales could be significantly affected by the way in which this new body carries out its task. If able to establish itself in terms creditable both to Government and to the profession, it could play an important part in ensuring the maintenance of appropriate professional standards, suitable course content, and a desirable diversity and flexibility in provision.

6. Criteria for Course Approval

As well as recommending the establishment of a national body for the accreditation of teacher education, ACSET suggested criteria that should be applied to the recognition and approval of courses. HMI surveys had established the great diversity in content and organisation that existed in different institutions throughout the country. Their survey The New Teacher in School (DES, 1982) indicated, in addition to many positive features of the training new teachers had received, several deficiencies and mismatches between the content of training and the work beginners were attempting. Not all of these were the responsibility of training institutions. They nonetheless got headline treatment. The specialised education newspapers were more restrained. Even so, they managed to produce such headlines as '1 in 4 poorly equipped for job: HMI blames teacher trainers for not weeding out weak students' (Times Higher Education Supplement, 15th October 1982).

The combination of HMI surveys of teacher education provision, the review of professional committee arrangements, studies such as The New Teacher in School, and the Secretary of State's declared intention to exercise his statutory powers more stringently, lent a certain inevitability to ACSET's advice on criteria and mechanisms for course approval.

At the time of writing, the Council for the Accreditation of Teacher Education (CATE) has still to work out its procedures. It is clear that CATE and the Secretary of State will pay considerable attention to the reports made by HMI on the work of teacher education institutions. HMI presently have right of access to polytechnic and college departments of education, and reports on their work can subsequently be published. Agreement to setting up ATOs in the post-McNair era was delayed by disagreement about the role of HMI in evaluating university based courses. Representatives of the University of London were particularly involved in these disputes, finally resolved in a Senate minute of 1947 which, with modifications, formed the basis of the national 'concordat' which, since 1960, has governed relations between HMI and university based initial teacher training. The concordat has permitted HMI to visit university departments of education at the invitation of the university authorities concerned, but not to make judgements about any individual teacher. The issue of university autonomy is still a 'live' one. It has thus been necessary to seek means which enable the Secretary of State to receive HMI advice on the approval of university courses of professional training, but which do not confer automatic right of access to universities in order to obtain the information on which such judgements can be based.

The criteria suggested for approval of courses are, as might be expected, very general in character, and have more to do with course structure and organisation than with process and content. A minimum 36 week period for the PGCE course, or a certain number of weeks of practical experience in schools, are necessary minima which do not in themselves ensure improvement in the quality of what is taught and learned. Such improvement depends on the qualifications, experience and efforts of teacher educators; the abilities and motivations of students; the effective use of relevant research based knowledge, incorporated into carefully designed, competently communicated and well-evaluated programmes of study; and the commitment of students, as future teachers, to self-directed professional development, assisted by participation in courses, conferences and other in-service activities. All this is a 'tall order'. However clear and authoritative are the criteria and course specifications, and however rigorous is the evaluation of provision, progress is crucially dependent upon the existence of active networks of professional association, opportunities for staff to become aware of relevant new knowledge and to incorporate it into their courses, the sustenance of motivation, and the nurture of commitment. It also depends on professional leadership – a subject discussed less in this country than in the United States, but one to which the absorption of teacher education in large, multi-purpose institutions gives new prominence. Active knowledge networks, which encourage the generation and interchange of ideas, which effectively disseminate the fruits of research, challenge existing orthodoxies and maintain morale and direction, are essential features of a healthy profession.

The former ATOs, whatever their faults and flaws, did more than validate and accredit. Their specialised and generalised boards, committees and working parties encouraged active debate about content and methods of teacher education programmes, both by subject and by phase. Their demise has left a gap in these respects that neither ACSET, nor CATE, nor individual validating universities and the CNAA can fill. Valuable as the efforts of bodies like the Universities Council for the Education of Teachers (UCET) and the Standing Conference on the Education and Training of Teachers (SCETT) may be, along with the meetings and conferences of specialised groups such as the Standing Conference on Educational Studies and the Education sections of the British Psychological Society and the British Sociological Association, there is no single organisation which now brings together all those involved in the different aspects of teacher education for professional (as distinct from trade union) purposes. The issue was referred to briefly in a Government Green Paper on Education (DES, 1977), but so far no individual or group has been able to find the time and resources to mobilise interest and activity to repair the omission. Given the pressures under which teacher educators have been working, this is unsurprising. It remains to be seen if the conditions and available resources of the next few years allow teacher educators to re-assert their professional identity in organisational form.

7.   Developments in In-service Education

The complexity of the relationship between improvements in initial teacher education and learning outcomes in primary and secondary schools has long been recognised. Overall improvements in the quality of the teaching force take a long time to achieve. Insofar as the proportion of graduate teachers is an index of such quality, it took 30 years, from 1947 to 1977, to increase the percentage of graduates from 16.0% to 28.3%. The impact of 'new blood', presumably with fresh ideas and appraisals of modern teaching techniques, has been further reduced over the past decade by sharp cutbacks in the numbers in training – hence the attention given to increasing levels of participation in in-service activity of all kinds.

The aspirations of the James Committee (1972) that at any give time at least 3% of all teachers should be released for further study and training, rising as soon as possible to 5%, have yet to be fulfilled. The extent of the gap between aspiration and reality at the beginning of the 1980s will be clear from the outcome of the DES survey of in-service education for teachers provision undertaken in 1983. A study undertaken four years earlier, and published in 1980, showed that the full-time equivalent figure for release for in-service training was 1.07%. Only one or two authorities (notably the Inner London Education Authority) had done better than this.

Government has now found ways to fund direct support for specific in-service provision rather than relying wholly upon local education authorities, and has introduced a number of innovations (e.g. the establishment of a national centre for gathering and disseminating information on the training of heads and senior staff, located at the University of Bristol).

These moves, however welcome, are unlikely to bring the level of in-service release up to the level advocated by the James Report (widely accepted by the profession as a

worthwhile target in the early 1970s). Nor, during the last
decade, has there been much growth in the numbers of those
undertaking advanced work in education. In 1970, there were
4,114 men and 3,674 women registered on a full-time basis for
research degrees, taught higher degrees and other courses such
as advanced diplomas. By 1978, the number of men had increased
to 4,319, the number of women to 3,926. Five years later there
were a total of 7,848, made up of 3,033 men and 3,579 women of
UK domicile, and 1,236 from overseas. There were some 6,500
part-time postgraduate registrations in 1982. Full-time
registrations fell by 11.1% between 1981 and 1982.

With a teaching force in the order of 430,000, the fact
that only 2,395 doctorates and masters degrees were awarded in
education or combinations of subjects with education in 1983
(a substantial proportion of these to overseas students),
hardly suggests that teaching is becoming 'overcredentialled',
or that there is an excess of study opportunities at advanced
levels. Expenditure restrictions have made the secondment of
serving teachers to advanced study more difficult. Cutbacks in
universities and polytechnics, coupled with a less than
satisfactory basis for taking part-time numbers into account
in the calculation of institutional grants, have served to
limit part-time provision for advanced study.

A welcome outcome of the UGC's 1984 review of continuing
education could be an improved basis for funding short course
and part-time provision. Courses provided by universities for
updating commercial and industrial staff are meant to be self-
financing, with fees set at an appropriate level. No such
expectation exists, or could be sustained, in respect of those
employed in public service occupations, including teaching –
LEAs would be unwilling to pay economic fees. There is thus an
element of subsidy for such courses from the budgets of the
institutions that provide them.

Although levels of in-service provision are currently
well below those which employing bodies see as desirable,
there are already signs of possible saturation as far as
teachers' own expressions of need are concerned. Weindling,
Reid and Davis (1983) have shown, on the basis of a sample of
1,000 practitioners attending local teachers centres, that as
many as 44% could not identify any aspect of their job that
could currently be helped by in-service training. The
percentage so responding was as high as 51% among women
primary teachers. Earlier surveys (e.g. Cane, 1969) had
suggested a much higher level of demand. The 1983 Teachers
Centre survey also showed the wide variation in expenditure by
LEAs on teachers centres, some 485 of which still exist in
England and Wales and which meet many of the local in-service
study needs of staff. Average per capita expenditure was in
the order of £21, but one LEA spent as much as £40, and one in
five spent only between £9 and £12.

245

For some years, policy on in-service provision is likely
to be targeted more specifically towards identifiable needs,
to involve a substantial element of school based and/or school
focused activity, and to be linked to a greater extent than in
the past with 'national' strategies. In a paper discussed by
ACSET late in 1983, HMI identified a number of national
programmes, such as the implementation of the Cockcroft Report
on mathematics, applications of micro-processors and microelectronics, the requirements of the 1981 Act with respect to
children with special needs, and increased emphasis on
technical and pre-vocational skills - all of which demanded
concerted action. HMI also drew attention to the results of
their own surveys, which had shown that 'teachers' practice in
the classroom was most markedly affected when they themselves
had recognised the need for training and when it had been
possible for them to discuss alternative teaching strategies
with colleagues', and that the 'support of the head is
essential'. HMI were less happy about existing provision of
full and part-time courses leading to certificates and
diplomas, which they thought to be particularly in need of
'careful review'. They also felt that 'Some of these courses
may have outlived their usefulness'.

As part of its growing concern with the process and
content of teacher education courses (as against the
logistical and structural issues that had for so long headed
the agenda), ACSET decided late in 1983 to investigate such
matters as policies for INSET; co-ordination at local,
regional and national levels; the match between demand, need
and provision; the case for the creation of INSET 'centres of
excellence'; induction arrangements; and the funding of
teachers' release. A thorough examination of these issues will
take some time; recommendations acted upon will still be
working themselves out for some years to come.

All the evidence suggests that INSET provision in the
later 1980s and early 1990s will tend to be more specific in
relation to subject, phase and educational issues than in the
past; that the DES and, particularly, HMI will play a larger
part in shaping what should be provided; that clearer
statements of objectives will be sought; and that provision
will be targeted more closely to existing and putative need.

8.   The Technology of Teacher Education

From time to time hopes are expressed that a breakthrough
in the methods and techniques of educating teachers will be
achieved, the uncertainties and inefficiencies of present
practice reduced, and the quality of learning outcomes
dramatically improved. Within the past 25 years, such hopes
have found particular focus in the development of educational
technology (first in the form of 'teaching machines', and
today through computers), in the application of so-called
'competency based' or 'performance based' methods, and through

the impact on preparation programmes of systematic research into teaching effectiveness and the learning process. There have been gains from all these sources. None has been the basis of a major reconstitution of training, other than in a few innovative departments and institutions, and then for only a limited time.

As far as competency based teacher education (CBTE) and performance based teacher education (PBTE) are concerned, the original stimulus came from American studies rooted in behaviourist psychology, and from the developmental models, initially supported by the US Office of Education, in a number of American universities. It had originally been indended to design a variety of such models, and to test them with a view to selecting for implementation those that satisfied stringent success criteria; the full testing stage was not funded. Many of the models received wide publicity, and exerted influence beyond the programmes of the institutions from which they originated. Houston and Newman (1982) suggest there were several common elements in these models:

Teachers were viewed as clinicians (in the medical sense), applied behavioural scientists, and members of a co-operative team. The models assumed that teacher competencies and behaviours could be defined, and programmes were proposed to teach mastery of the objectives largely through modularised instruction. All relied on the use of simulation laboratories and proposed long periods of training on a pre-service/in-service continuum.

The distinctiveness of these models has been diluted by time, by staff mobility and by experience. The popularity of the methods of instruction employed 'waxed and waned' over a relatively short period in the late 1960s and 1970s. At no time did they influence practice in England and Wales to the extent that they did in the United States. In the early part of the 1970s it was estimated that 77% of teacher education programmes in the United States included a component of micro-teaching, invented ten years earlier. Competency based and performance based teacher education caught on equally quickly, and were mandated in a number of states. By 1977 only just over a quarter of all teacher preparing institutions were not involved in some way in the implementation or exploration of PBTE and/or CBTE programmes. Four years later, the percentage of non-participants had increased to 41%.

Projects were funded to develop 'protocol materials' (representing classroom situations) on tape, film, and in print, as a way of focusing student attention on actual classroom problems, and of providing opportunities for tutors and students to analyse and interpret such problems in accordance with their studies of educational foundations, curriculum and pedagogy. Many institutions made widespread use of simulation and 'critical incident' techniques, presenting open-ended problems derived from practice, in case form. More than 60% of teacher education programmes in the United States were using simulation in the early 1970s. By the middle of the decade the proportion had fallen by nearly a half.

In assessing the extent to which parallel developments are likely to occur in teacher education in this country during coming years, it is important to recognise how these models and techniques gained their rapid penetration in the United States.

First, generous funding was available (usually from Government) based on recognition of the need to upgrade teacher preparation and development in line with educational expansion, of the need to achieve greater educational equality (especially for hitherto underprivileged groups), and to achieve curriculum change.

Second, great hopes were invested in the possibilites of instructional technologies based upon behavioural psychology, free of long-standing and inhibiting disputes about values and purposes.

Third, education authorities found themselves under pressure to be more accountable to the public, and tended to respond favourably to approaches that offered 'quantifiable' results.

Fourth, the availability of cheap audio reproduction and the video camera, plus greater portability of equipment and inexpensive reprographics, permitted and encouraged the development of techniques (e.g. micro-teaching, simulation, protocol materials) hardly possible a generation earlier.

The number of institutions in the United States that consciously base their work on one or more teacher education 'models', or make regular and systematic use of particular techniques, is probably smaller today than in the mid 1970s. The number of colleges and departments in England and Wales with such explicit commitment has never been great. These developments have, nevertheless, left their mark on the teacher education scene on both sides of the Atlantic. What were formerly seen and claimed as major breakthroughs have been re-evaluated as modest, but nonetheless useful, methodological increments. Programmes have become more eclectic, but many show signs of the systematic development work that went on from the mid 1960s to mid 1970s (Wendel, 1982).

9.   Research in Teacher Education

Research and evaluation have always been recognised as the greatest problems of innovation in teacher education, and have seldom been attempted on a scale, or with thoroughness, adequate to validate one approach or method against another. In particular, the impact of much development work has been blunted by the absence of generalisable criteria of teacher effectiveness, a subject on which a great deal of research effort has been expended. The field of research in teacher education is, though, not defined by research, nor by development work on models of teaching, such as was undertaken in the United States during the early 1970s. Such research is, however, needed if a more substantial element of systematic research-based knowledge is to be available in the service of improvement. Research on teacher education, research in teacher education and research and teacher education all require attention.

The first, research on teacher education, is concerned with collecting and interpreting facts and developing theories concerning our formal efforts to educate and train teachers.

The second, research in teacher education, is concerned with how teachers can be helped to make use of research findings, to participate in research relevant to their professional practice, and to appreciate both the values and the limitations of such research.

Research and teacher education means bringing to bear all the knowledge that we can muster from scientific study and from scholarship in the social sciences and the humanities, in order to improve the organisations, processes and outcomes that characterise teacher education programmes.

The volume of research on teacher education is modest. Too little time and effort has been devoted to the systematic study of how teachers are educated and trained.

Given the size of the research literature on many other aspects of education, this is perhaps surprising. It may in part be due to the low status of work in the specialism, which is low even by the standards of educational research in general. There are few people in universities, polytechnics and colleges who are directly concerned with teacher education as such (as distinct from the curriculum subjects they prepare students to teach, or the profession or foundation disciplines for which they are responsible in the education course). High quality research usually requires early commitment, such as is made by first class honours graduates in physics, chemistry, languages or the social sciences. Research on teacher education does not readily fit into any of the existing disciplinary paradigms, and is unlikely to appeal to bright young graduates. Work in this field is frequently the product of the part-time labours of ex-schoolteachers who have acquired higher qualifications and been appointed to posts in schools and institutes of education.

Another reason for the lack of research effort on teacher education is the urgent priority that governments and research bodies attach to other matters, such as improvement in reading and mathematical skills, the education of the handicapped, and the development of positive attitudes towards industry and productive work. This, however, only partly explains why

little systematic research on teacher education has been
undertaken.

Two other factors currently inhibit research on teacher
education, and will need to change if more and better work is
to be done in the future. These are: first, the nature of our
beliefs about the possibility and limitations of teacher
education; and second, the reaction of disciplinary
specialists to the large, 'messy', multi-disciplinary problems
involving great numbers of disparate variables, which the
teacher education scene presents.

Just below the surface of the textbooks, the official
statements and the conference addresses, there is some
scepticism about the very concept of trying to 'train' a
teacher. The higher the status of the teaching activity
involved, the greater the scepticism. This does little to
encourage expenditure on research. If training outcomes are
less important than the effects of (for example) personality
and prior experience, and if the contexts in which teachers'
tasks are performed are variable and unpredictable, then why
spend a lot of money to obtain facts and findings of little
practical value and incapable of application to the real world
of schools and classrooms? Raths and Katz (1982) found such
views to be widespread, not just among the general public, or
educational professionals, but among teacher educators
themselves. They found that many such staff believe 'that
which is more useful in the repertoire of the teacher cannot
be taught by them, perhaps by anyone, and conversely, that
what can be taught is all right, but tangential and
insignificant'. They call for higher order leadership in
teacher education, of a kind that would break the cycle of
'low effort - low impact - lower effort', that low
professional morale tends to create.

The second problem, that of the complexity and
'untidyness' of the variables involved, is not likely to be
tackled by adhering to models of teacher education research of
a 'process/product' kind, or by looking for findings directly
applicable to the improvement of programmes. Models of what
constitutes research on teacher education need to be broader,
taking in work on staff and students; on curriculum, including
practical teaching; on questions of teacher demand and supply;
on the relation of in-service work to initial training; on the
assessments used in selecting and certificating students; on
the analysis of institutional cultures; on the part that
teachers play in strengthening particular orientations and
emphases within pluralist societies. The research agenda is
potentially as broad as the activity of teacher education
itself.

One aspect of that agenda to which continuing attention
will be needed is the study of teacher educators. Without full
information about the men and women engaged in the process of
preparing teachers, we are likely to act upon misconceived

'hunches' and impressions. How many years of classroom experience do lecturers in education possess? On how many occasions during the last twelve months have they taught a class under 'normal' conditions? What are their qualifications in relation to the courses for which they are responsible? Even on such obvious points we have all too little really up-to-date information.

Given the constraints and inhibitions to which I have drawn attention, it seems unlikely that the next few years will see any dramatic take-off in research on teacher education. This underlines the importance of ensuring that such work as is undertaken goes on in places where adequate disciplinary and methodological support can be provided; that it is done by people competent to handle the complex variables involved and able to make sensible and supportable interpretations of their data; and that the teacher education community shows itself willing to attend to, and where appropriate, implement the findings of, research in its own field.

LOOKING TO THE FUTURE

I have tried in preceding sections to indicate some of the considerations and conditions that will help to shape the future of teacher education. I will conclude by setting out some desiderata that teacher education programmes should satisfy if they are to represent improvements on the generality of existing practice.

First, initial teacher education programmes would be conceived and planned as only one of the elements in an eight stage sequence comprising recruitment, selection, initial personal and professional education, certification, induction, further professional study and refreshment, training for specialised roles and, finally, preparation for retirement (Taylor 1978). Each element in such a sequence would be related to those that preceded and followed it; none would be planned or executed in isolation.

Second, students recruited and selected for programmes of initial preparation would, to the fullest extent that market conditions permit, be from among the abler members of their age cohorts, comparable in ability and motivation to those planning to enter traditional high status occupations. In addition, a proportion of places would be available for older candidates, already successful in other occupations and able (for the most part) to satisfy normal entry requirements, who wished to prepare for a second career in teaching. Modes of student support and the salary reward structure of teaching would need to be such as to encourage the achievement of these desiderata.

Third, staff responsible for teaching, supervising and assessing students would need relevant and up-to-date experience in the types of schools and educational institutions for which their programmes prepare, together with a commitment to keeping such experience fresh by regular participation in the work of classroom and school. Such staff would also need to be respected in their own disciplinary fields, and be committed to their own professional development.

Fourth, departments and schools of education in universities (or in other institutions in which teachers are prepared) would have close and positive relationships with other academic and professional departments, and with the schools in which their students undertake practical training and, subsequently, obtain employment.

Fifth, the content and organisation of programmes of initial preparation would reflect the most recent and well-founded knowledge in the disciplines of educational study, be based upon carefully considered principles of coherence relevant to the success of neophyte teachers, and be likely to encourage a permanent commitment to personal learning and professional development.

Sixth, the work of initial preparation should be resourced by high quality print and non-print material and learning facilities e.g. libraries, computer information retrieval systems, micro-teaching and mini-course laboratories, observation rooms, audio-visual methods, skill development packages, and portable video equipment. The application of these technologies would not be seen as the sole province of specialised staff (although some such would be found within each institution) but as everyday means of presenting and acquiring appropriate knowledge and skills.

Seventh, schools in which students undertake practical teaching, and in which beginning teachers serve out their induction period, would be chosen for their genuine commitment to the improvement of teacher preparation consistent with the objectives of the university based elements in the course, and be directed by staff with appropriate training and sufficient release time to undertake supervisory responsibilities.

These desiderata relate mainly to initial programmes. Much more could be said about other stages in the eight-fold process. Even so, there are few existing programmes that satisfy all such desiderata, and there is plenty of room for progress to be made that does not necessarily require substantial additional resources, although these are important in relation to sustained long term gains. It is impossible to advance on every front simultaneously. It would, nevertheless, be a pity to miss such opportunities as now present themselves for securing improvement in a process that, whatever its limitations and difficulties, can and does make a difference to the quality of performance and occupational satisfaction of teachers and, through their work, to the overall success of primary and secondary education.

REFERENCES

Bruce M.G. (1981) Letter to Times Educational Supplement, 3rd April.

Cane B. (1969) In-Service Training, Windsor: National Foundation for Educational Research.

DES (1972) Teacher Education and Training (The James Report), London: Her Majesty's Stationery Office.

DES (1977) Education in Schools: A Consultative Document, Cmnd 6869, London: Her Majesty's Stationery Office.

DES (1982) HMI Series: Matters for Discussion 15, The New Teacher in School, Report by Her Majesty's Inspectors, London: Her Majesty's Stationery Office.

DES (1983) Speech by Sir Keith Joseph to mark the Sixtieth Anniversary of the University of Durham School of Education, 15 October 1982, London: Department of Education and Science.

Houston W.R. and Newman K.K. (1982) 'Teacher Education Programs', Encyclopaedia of Educational Research, New York: Free Press.

Patrick H., Bernbaum G., and Reid K. (1982) The Structures and Process of Initial Teacher Education within universities in England and Wales, Leicester: University of Leicester School of Education.

Raths J.D. and Katz L.G. (1982) 'The Best of Intentions for the Education of Teachers', Journal of Education for Teaching, 8 (3).

Taylor W. (1978) Research and Reform in Teacher Education, Windsor: National Foundation for Educational Research.

Taylor W. (1981) 'Educational Research and Development in the United Kingdom: Framework, Impact and Future Prospects', International Review of Education, XXVII.

Vance V.S. and Schlecty P.C (1982) 'The Distribution of Academic Ability in the Teaching Force: Policy implications', Phi Delta Kappan, September.

Weindling D., Reid M., and Davis P. (1983) Teachers' Centres: A Focus for In-service Education?, London: Methuen.

Wendel E.O. (1982) 'Competency-based Teacher Education: What has survived in New York', Journal of Teacher Education, XXXIII (5).

GERALD BERNBAUM graduated at the London School of Economics and, after completing his postgraduate certificate of education, taught in a grammar school and a comprehensive school in London. In 1964 he joined the staff of the University of Leicester School of Education where he was appointed Senior Lecturer in 1970 and Professor of Education in 1974. He has been a consultant to the Organization for Economic Co-operation and Development, was Chairman of the Education Research Board of the Social Sciences Research Council and is currently Vice-Chairman of the Education and Human Development Committee of the Economic and Social Research Council. His books include Social Change and the Schools 1918-44, Knowledge and Ideology in the Sociology of Education and Schooling in Decline. He has published in a variety of academic journals, mainly in fields relating to the study of the teaching profession and the sociology of education.

JIM EGGLESTON taught for twelve years at Hinckley Grammar School during which time his Problems in Quantitative Biology was published and he joined the Nuffield Science Project. He was later appointed Research Fellow at the University of Leicester School of Education, where he researched national and international assessment procedures and worked as a methods tutor on the postgraduate certificate of education course. His early work, in collaboration with Professor Maurice Galton and Dr Margaret Jones, was published in Processes and Products of Science Teaching. He was appointed to a Chair of Education at the University of Nottingham in 1973 from which he retired last year. He is presently engaged by UNESCO to undertake an evaluation of science teacher (in-service) training methods.

MICHAEL FULLAN is Assistant Director and Professor of Sociology in Education (academic) at the Ontario Institute for Studies in Education, Toronto, Canada. His publications, particularly those on curriculum implementation and educational change, have received international recognition and he has been consulted widely on these topics. His recent book, The Meaning of Educational Change, has been widely acclaimed as a landmark in educational change theory.

DAVID HOPKINS is a Senior Lecturer in educational research at the West Glamorgan Institute of Higher Education, Swansea. He has lectured at Simon Fraser University, Canada where he received his Ph.D. and collaborated with Michael Fullan and Marvin Wideen on the research project 'Management of Change in Teacher Education' funded by the Social Science and Humanities Research Council of Canada. His recent books include Doing Classroom Research, School Based Review for School Improvement, Alternative Perspectives on School Improvement (with Marvin Wideen), Problems of Access to Knowledge and Research as a Basis for Teaching (both with Jean Rudduck). He divides his time between teacher education, writing and climbing mountains.

SHEILA JACKSON was a mature student at Nene College where she graduated with a B.A. after raising her family. She then took an M.A. in the Sociology of Education and Mass Communications at the University of Leicester School of Education after which she worked as a research assistant on the National Scholarships for Priority Teachers Scheme funded by the Department of Education and Science. She then took her postgraduate certificate of education in the same department. She is currently a lecturer at Nene College.

HELEN PATRICK is a graduate of Aberdeen University where she obtained her M.Ed. in 1976. After teaching in a comprehensive school in Scotland, she worked at the University of Leicester School of Education on the research project 'The Structure and Process of Initial Teacher Education in Universities within England and Wales' funded by the Department of Education and Science. She is currently a Research Associate at the University of Leicester School of Education working on curriculum provision in small primary schools. Her publications include a number of articles on teacher education.

KEN REID is currently Reader in Education at the West Glamorgan Institute of Higher Education, Swansea. He has worked on research projects in the University of Wales Department of Education, Cardiff and the University of Leicester School of Education. He has held promoted posts in schools in Berkshire and Oxfordshire and worked in personnel and quality control departments at St. Asaph and St. Helens. He is the author of Truancy and School Absenteeism and numerous articles on teacher education, persistent school absenteeism, handicapped families, sixth form education, education in Wales and educational research. He is currently directing research projects on in-service provision in Wales, 16+ examinations and management in schools.

JEAN RUDDUCK is Professor of Education at the University of Sheffield. She was a Senior Lecturer at the Centre of Applied Research in Education at the University of East Anglia and a member of the Humanities Curriculum Project team. She has directed various research projects, including the Small Group Teaching Project, Pupils amd Innovation, Making the Most of the Short In-Service Course, Teachers in Partnership, Sex Stereotyping in the Early Years of Schooling. Her books include: Dissemination of Innovation: The Humanities Curriculum Project, Teaching Through Small Group Discussion, Making the Most of the Short In-Service Course, Problems of Access to Knowledge and Research as a Basis for Teaching (both with David Hopkins).

ALAN SIGSWORTH is a Senior Lecturer in the University of East Anglia School of Education. He was Principal Lecturer at Keswick Hall College and has taught in primary schools. His major research interests are student/teacher relationships, and the curriculum in rural schools. His publications include Innovation and Rural Education.

WILLIAM TAYLOR, CBE is Principal of the University of London. He was Director of the University of London Institute of Education and Professor of Education at the University of Bristol, a post he combined between 1968 and 1973 with that of Research Advisor to the Department of Education and Science. He has worked in the University of Oxford, in colleges of education, and as Deputy Head of a secondary modern school. He is currently Chairman of the National Foundation for Educational Research and of the Committee on the Training of University Teachers. His books include The Secondary Modern School, Heading for Change, Planning in Post-Secondary Education, Research and Reform in Teacher Education and (forthcoming) Metaphors of Education (ed.).

DAVID THOMAS is Head of the Sub-Department of Special Education, University of Liverpool. His publications include A Guide to the Literature of Special Education, The Social Psychology of Childhood Disability and The Experience of Handicap. His current interests include communication and organisational interaction between special education and mainstream schools.

MARVIN WIDEEN is an Associate Professor of Education at Simon Fraser University, Canada. He has held posts at the Universities of Regina and Boulder, has been a consultant to the International Movement Toward Educational Change, and worked as a high school Principal. He recently co-directed (with Michael Fullan) a large scale research project on the management of change in teacher education in Canada, and is conducting a continuing programme of research into the professional development of teachers. His most recent book is Alternative Perspectives on School Improvement (with David Hopkins).

I N D E X